SUFFERING WITNESS

SUNY series in Aesthetics and the Philosophy of Art
Mary C. Rawlinson, editor

SUFFERING WITNESS

*The Quandary of Responsibility
after the Irreparable*

James Hatley

STATE UNIVERSITY OF NEW YORK PRESS

The Hebrew and German pictured on the cover give the text of Isaiah 58: 5–9. The German comes from Martin Luther's translation of the Bible. "Wilt thou call this a fast, and an acceptable day to the Lord? Is not this the fast that I have chosen: to loose the bands of wickedness, to undo the heavy burdens, and to let the oppressed go free, and that ye break every yoke? Is it not to deal thy bread to the hungry and that thou bring the poor that are cast out to thy house? When thou seest the naked, that thou cover him; and that thou hide not thyself from thine own flesh? Then shall thy light break forth as the morning, and thine health shall spring forth speedily, and thy righteousness shall go before thee; the glory of the Lord shall be thy reward. Then shalt thou call, and the Lord shall answer; thou shalt cry, and He shall say, Here I am." (King James Version)

Published by
State University of New York Press, Albany

© 2000 State University of New York

For information, address State University of New York Press,
90 State Street, Suite 700, Albany, N.Y., 12207

Production by Cathleen Collins
Marketing by Fran Keneston

Library of Congress Cataloging in Publication Data
Hatley, James, 1949–
    Suffering witness : the quandary of responsibility after the irreparable / James Hatley.
       p. cm. — (SUNY series in aesthetics and the philosophy of art)
    Includes bibliographical references and index.
    ISBN 0-7914-4705-7 (alk. paper) — ISBN 0-7914-4706-5 (pbk. : alk. paper)
      1. Holocaust, Jewish (1939–1945)—Moral and ethical aspects. 2. Holocaust, Jewish (1939–1945)—Influence. 3. Holocaust survivors—Psychology. 4. Lévinas, Emmanuel.
5. Borowski, Tadeusz, 1922–1951. 6. Levi, Primo. I. Title. II. Series.
    D804.3 .H376 2000
    940.53′18—dc21

                                         99-087496

10 9 8 7 6 5 4 3 2 1

To Jennifer and Ian.
That you might carve their words into your hearts . . .

Contents

Acknowledgments

I would like to thank a variety of people and organizations who in various manners aided me during the writing of this book. Leah Fridman was particularly helpful in directing me to consider how the memory of the *Shoah* (often referred to as the Holocaust) was inevitably repressed, how witnessing it called for a discourse sensitive to the indirections of trauma and delusion. She generously shared her time and expertise during the early phases of this project when I was most in need of guidance. Sandor Goodhart, who more than any other person has influenced my reading of Levinas, was particularly helpful in his explanations of the inevitability of witness, of how we continue to be addressed by the suffering of others whether we choose to acknowledge that address or not. I am indebted to Stephen David Ross for several suggestions concerning the use of terms in the finished manuscript, as well as his earlier interest in this project. Alan Udoff also provided encouragement and many editorial comments, as well as an orientation to the manner in which the *Shoah* subverts philosophical significance and puts it in crisis. I am thankful to George Kunz for his explanations of the face to face encounter in the therapeutic situation, as well as reminding me how important the virtue of humility is for a Levinasian understanding of the ethical situation. Antje Kapust aided in my understanding of how the perpetrator sunders his or her contact with the other who is to be victimized. At the very beginning of this project, Otto Pöggler generously offered his insights into the significance of Celan's poetry and made me explicitly aware of the depth of Celan's own personal suffering in regard to his poetic vocation.

I am specially indebted to my students in several courses directly treating the *Shoah* with whom I shared conversations and moments of silence as we found ourselves claimed by the address of *the Nameless*. In these classes I first become aware of how important Levi's prologue to *Survival in Auschwitz* might be in laying out the ethical dimensions of witnessing the *Shoah*. Hugh Silverman, Fred McGlynn, Edward Casey, Robert Goldberg, and Peter Manchester provided many helpful critical comments on an earlier version of this project. Claire Katz's generous support in a variety of manners is also appreciated, particularly for our discussions on Levinas and Judaism. Michael Smith and Ernest Sherman provided important insights into the intersection of Judaism, philosophy, and ethical responsibility. Carolla Sauter, my original editor, was especially supportive at a moment when the project was in danger of faltering. Gabriela Vlahovici's generous editing of the manuscript saved me much time and embarrassment. She also provided important insights into the Romanian context of Celan's poetry.

I am also appreciative of Salisbury State University, especially the Fulton School of Liberal Arts, for its support of my research, which included stipends and money to travel to conferences. One of these conferences, the International Philosophic Symposium, a yearly meeting of a small group of scholars directed by Hugh Silverman and Wilhem Wurzer, was singularly helpful in the refocusing of my project so that it could reach completion. I am also indebted to the Philosophy Department of the State University of New York at Stony Brook, as well as to the Fulbright Commission, for making it possible to do research in Germany during the early phases of my writing.

I am particularly grateful to Mary Rawlinson for her innumerable comments and ready support during the decade it took to bring this project to completion. Her defense of literature as a mode of philosophical discourse continues to inspire my work.

Acknowledgment is extended to the following publishers and individuals who have generously given their permission to present passages from the following works:

Paul Celan's *Gedichte*, copyright Suhrkamp Verlag, Frankfurt am Main, 1975, by permission of publisher.

Paul Celan's "Welchen des Steine du Hebst" and "Vor einer Kerze" from *Vom Schwelle zu Schwelle*, copyright Deutsche Verlags-Anstalt GmbH Stuttgart, 1955, by permission of publisher.

Paul Celan's "STEHEN, im Schatten" from *Atemwende*, copyright Suhrkamp Verlag Frankfurt am Main, 1967, by permission of publisher.

Paul Celan's "Radix Matrix," "Hinausgekrönt," "Chymisch," and "Huhediblu" from *Die Niemandsrose*, copyright S. Fischer Verlag, Frankfurt am Main, 1963, by permission of publisher.

Excerpts from "Radix, Matrix," "Crowned Out," "To Stand," and "Alchemical" taken from *Poems of Paul Celan*, translated by Michael Hamburger, published by Anvil Press Poetry in 1995, also by Persea Books in 1988, by permission of Anvil Press Poetry and Persea Books.

Excerpts from Amy Colin's translation of "Huhediblu" by Paul Celan, from Colin's *Paul Celan: Holograms of Darkness*, copyright 1991 by Amy Colin, by permission of Indiana University Press.

Excerpts from John Felstiner's translations of Paul Celan's "Whichever Stone You Lift," and "In Front of a Candle," copyright 1993 by Yale University Press, by permission of the translator and publisher.

Excerpts from Tadeusz Borowski's *This Way for the Gas, Ladies and Gentlemen*, translated by Barbara Vedder, translation copyright 1967 by Penguin Books Ltd, original text copyright 1959 by Maria Borowski, by permission of Viking Penguin, a division of Penguin Putnam Inc.

Abbreviations

BC   Emmanuel Levinas, "Bad Conscience and the Inexorable," in *Face to Face with Levinas*, ed. Richard Cohen (Albany: State University of New York Press, 1986)

CP   Emmanuel Levinas, *Collected Philosophical Papers*, trans. Alphonso Lingis (Dordrecht: Martinus Nijhoff, 1987)

CPr   Paul Celan, *Collected Prose*, trans. Rosmarie Waldrop (Riverdale-on-Hudson, N.Y.: Sheep Meadow Press, 1986)

DF   Emmanuel Levinas, "Damages Due to Fire," in *Nine Talmudic Readings*, trans. Annette Aronowicz (Bloomington: Indiana University Press, 1990)

EI   Emmanuel Levinas, *Ethics and Infinity: Conversations with Philippe Nemo*, trans. Richard Cohen (Pittsburgh: Duquesne University Press, 1985)

FC   Emmanuel Levinas, "Freedom and Command," in *Collected Philosophical Papers*, trans. Alphonso Lingis (Dordrecht: Martinus Nijhoff, 1987)

HD   Amy Colin, *Paul Celan: Holograms of Darkness* (Bloomington: Indiana University Press, 1991)

LR   Seán Hand, ed., *The Levinas Reader* (Oxford: Basil Blackwell, 1989)

N   Elie Wiesel, *Night* (New York: Bantam Books, 1982)

OB   Emmanuel Levinas, *Otherwise than Being or Beyond Essence*, trans. Alphonso Lingis (The Hague: Martinus Nijhoff, 1981)

PC   John Felstiner, *Paul Celan: Poet, Survivor, Jew* (New Haven: Yale University Press, 1995)

PN   Emmanuel Levinas, *Proper Names*, trans. Michael Smith (Stanford: Stanford University Press, 1996)

PPC   Paul Celan, *Poems of Paul Celan*, trans. Michael Hamburger (New
           York: Persea Books, 1988)

RM   Raoul Mortley, ed. *French Philosophers in Conversation* (New York:
           Routledge, 1991)

SA   Primo Levi, *Survival in Auschwitz*, trans. Stuart Woolf (New York:
           Collier Books, 1961)

TB   Tadeusz Borowski, *This Way for the Gas, Ladies and Gentleman*,
           trans. Barbara Vedder (New York: Penguin Books, 1976)

TI   Emmanuel Levinas, *Totality and Infinity*, trans. Alphonso Lingis
           (Pittsburgh: Duquesne University Press, 1969)

Introduction

When an act of violence or an offense has been committed it is forever irreparable: it is quite probable that public opinion will cry out for a sanction, a punishment, a "price" for pain; it is also possible that the price paid be useful inasmuch as it makes amends or discourages a fresh offense, but the initial offense remains and the "price" is always (even if it is "just") a new offense and a new source of pain.

—Primo Levi

In his comments addressing the issue of whether there can be forgiveness for acts of violence, Primo Levi also implicitly raises the more general question of exactly how one ought to respond to that destructive impact upon another that can never be undone. History is full of such moments of violence, moments in which the perpetrator's attack upon her or his victim proves so overwhelming that the very idea of a restorative restitution becomes ludicrous. Particularly endemic to our own time in this regard is the violence of genocide, of a devastating assault upon the very existence of a people that often includes the mass extermination of its particular members. Even as these words are being written, such violence is breaking out yet again in Kosovo, just as it has occurred in the Americas, Turkey, Germany and Eastern Europe, Cambodia, Tibet, Ruwanda, Bosnia, and a variety of other sites during the progress of the twentieth century.

Within this context Levi's remarks direct our attention to that particular instance of violence that is called the *Shoah*. In doing so, he is not to my mind implying that it alone serves as the primordial instance of violence to which one must singularly attend in order to understand what violence has now become. Levi's remarks make clear that each instance of violence is already singular and commands a singular response. Even if one lists the Armenian or Cambodian genocide in the same sentence as the *Shoah*, one should not make

1

the mistake of thinking one's first responsibility is either the comparison or contrast of these events, *as if* what is most important about them is their structure and shape. What first commands one is not our power to describe a particular moment of violence but our responsibility in regard to those who suffer within that moment. How have we been addressed by those who suffer? In what manner might we be in complicity with he or she who perpetrates this violence? Only in the aftermath of these questions can we responsibly take up with any determination of the particular features of a historical moment of violence.

Thus we are called upon to determine the extent of violence only in the aftermath of having felt its irremediableness. To list diverse instances of violence is to find each of them commanding a unique responsibility. Each of them makes a particular claim for our attention that is incomparable with all other claims. One should not become obsessed with the uniquely destructive or evil character of a single instance of violence, *as if* the suffering of one moment could count more than the suffering of another. All moments of violence transcend our accounting for them. And in confronting them, our first duty is not to classify and compare but simply to respond. First it must simply matter that irremediable harm has occurred.

With this thought in mind, the following essay turns to the *Shoah*, that particular historical moment of irremediable violence that Levi himself endured and survived to recount. And even if suffering universally transcends our description of it, we must also admit that the *Shoah* in its own particular fashion has posed the question of how we might react to and take on the real impact of the violence occurring when not only one human is victimizing another, but also a people is conspiring to annihilate another. The violence of the perpetrators of the *Shoah*, as well as of the suffering caused by them, has given the generations coming after the dissolution of the Third Reich and its death camps much pause for consideration. In turning to this particular suffering, we have found ourselves called upon to regard a time in which the extremity of violence undergone by the victim revealed only too clearly the transcendence of the victim's suffering, which is to say, its irremediableness. In turning to this violence, we find we are asked not only to affirm that the other has suffered but also that this suffering continues to trouble any possible account of it. In particular we are called upon to pose the issue of how our very affirmation of the other's suffering might yet again betray the extremity of that suffering.

Burdened by the other's suffering, we are called upon not only to understand or, at the very least, to give a historical record of a particular act of violence, but also and in the first instance to witness it. By witness is meant a mode of responding to the other's plight that exceeds an epistemological determination and becomes an ethical involvement.[1] One must not only utter a truth *about* the victim but also remain true *to* her or him. In this latter mode of response, one is summoned to attentiveness, which is to say, to a heartfelt concern for and acknowledgment of the gravity of violence directed toward particular others. In this attentiveness, the wounding of the other is registered in the first place not as an objective fact but as a subjective blow, a persecution, a trauma. The witness refuses to forget the weight of this blow, or the depth of the wound it inflicts.

But what becomes of one's witness, when the wound that obsesses it is, in Levi's words, "irreparable"? In this situation, one confronts a suffering that once undergone can no longer be taken back, no matter what one does. For this reason, one's very attentiveness to the victim is incapable of being discharged. Here attentiveness only begets yet more attentiveness; the witness is called to insomnia. Part and parcel of the twisted logic of victimization is the denial of this insomnia; indeed, it can be argued that the perpetrator's aggression is in fact a manic flight from the gravity of insomnia, of its incessant call to righteousness.

The attempt to turn away from the other's suffering, *as if* its resolution were simply a manner of reversing the outcome of an event through later actions or insights, or *as if* the victim's suffering, once it is in the past, need no longer be treated as an occurrence having an actual significance, are equally abhorrent to a witnessing of the irreparable. Precisely the expectation that one can treat the victim in one of these two manners is the very gesture that comprises the original act of victimization. The victim is that person whose suffering will not have mattered, whose violation will have already been forgotten. Whether this forgetfulness is brought about by callous indifference or by the more subtle means of a rationalized justification, by the sublimation of a particular victim's suffering into the so-called "larger picture," makes no ultimate difference. In either instance the singularity of the particular victim's suffering is ignored—the outrage of an injustice and the compassion that is called for by that outrage are lost either in a pose of feigned indifference or in a rush to explanation.

The victim, and in this case the victim of the *Shoah*, does not allow life to return to normal. Indeed, the succumbing of persons to violence reveals that the notion of a normal temporality—in which possibility always stands by to supplement and ameliorate the vicissitudes of actuality—was always a delusion at worst and a temporary compromise at best. What the victim's suffering continually tells us is that our own time is already irreparably ruptured, that no resource stands at our call whereby this rupture might be repaired, that whatever else our witness might hope to accomplish, it cannot undo that which it seeks to witness.

In what manner then should a witness's response to a suffering that is transcendent or irreparable occur? And what should be the particular response of those who now in this later moment, in the very moment of this reading of this text, witness the witnessing of the witness, that is, those who inherit the legacy of Auschwitz through the words of those who were there? And if this latter response also involves attentiveness to the victim, what precisely is meant here by it? These are questions to be posed with increasing urgency and quandary in the following chapters. In posing them, the discussion turns in the main to a small number of what could be termed exemplary testimonies concerning the suffering of the *Shoah*'s victims and the violence of their victimizers: Levi's *Survival in Auschwitz*, Borowski's *This Way for the Gas, Ladies and Gentlemen*, and the poetry of Paul Celan, particularly those poems found in the volume *The No-One's Rose*.

In treating these texts, the emphasis is not, as it would be in a more literary analysis, upon a thoroughgoing reading that would consider the full range of metaphors, literary tropes, and semantic structures of which each text is comprised. Nor has one turned to these works in order to provide a series of variations on how a theme or question might be given a literary form. This text is not meant to be an introduction to the study of Holocaust literature as a genre of literary *poiēsis*. Nor is this study meant to offer literature as a mode of accounting for the historical dimensions of the *Shoah* (if by historical is meant either a chronological or hermeneutic account of its facts, its empirical events). Rather, the intent of this essay is to consider the initial stance of witnessing that each of these texts and inevitably all the texts of the *Shoah* (whether they be historical or literary) in one manner or another require of those who read them. What exactly is commanded of the reader so that she or he might step *responsibly* through the portal of any of these texts, so that she or he might read them in attentiveness to those who have suffered? One could characterize the book that follows as an uneasy meditation upon Levi's prologue to his *Survival in Auschwitz*, a prologue in which the author demands his reader consider the command to witness the suffering of the victim to be addressed within the text *before* any reading of the text itself is to occur.

Attendant on the question of how one is called upon to witness the suffering of the *Shoah* is the growing realization that one is already caught up in this act of witnessing whether one wills it or not. Thus, the purpose of this work is not one of elucidating a structure of reading that a particular genre happens to require of its readers, a structure they may or may not assent to, but of making sense of the *factum* that the very genre exists only because its readers have already been submitted to suffering, *regardless of what is to be written and regardless of whether the reader reads or ignores this writing*. From this perspective, Levi's commandment is not simply given to those who continue to read his text but to all those as well who neglect or refuse to read it.

We, the generations who come after the death camps, are already reading the *Shoah* whether we will it or not. As we pick up the texts of Levi, Borowski, Celan, and a multitude of other witnesses, we find we too have already been submitted to a witnessing of the other's suffering that we are not free to dismiss. We find that our witness of the other who suffers is itself suffered. But this suffering is not one of empathy, which is to say, a suffering that would find in its own discomfort a comparison to what the victim has suffered. The suffering of the victim, particularly the victim of the *Shoah*, is revealed in one's witness to be incomparable to one's own. We suffer, so to speak, the impossibility of suffering the other's suffering. Our account of that victim comes to know itself as always having arrived too late and having said both too much and too little.

Even the naming of the *Shoah* is fraught with the ambiguity and impossibility of a witness that is suffered for the sake of the other.[2] What terms should one use to indicate, to name, to witness this incomparable event? For example, some have chosen to refer to the *Shoah* as the "Final Solution." But as Fackenheim suggests, to employ this term would leave one's own witness indebted to a name coined by the very perpetrators of the victim's suffering. This very phrasing of the event implies the ethically outrageous assumption that the extinction of a human type can be regarded in some twisted manner as a positive accomplishment. Ultimately, this name could be invoked only in a tone of macabre irony. But irony seems a questionable effect when one considers it would be had only at the expense of distancing oneself from the inability of the victim to be distant from her or his suffering. For the victim in extremity, no time was given to be ironic, to mount a defense against the victimizer that would gain the victim some dignity, that would preserve some notion of autonomy in spite of the onslaught of the victimizer. To name the *Shoah* the Final Solution smacks too much of an avoidance of suffering by those who would use the name.

Holocaust, a Greek term denoting "burnt sacrifice," has been used by many survivors and most of the media in an attempt to acknowledge the religious implications held in the destruction of so many innocent lives. Yet

Fackenheim rejects this term too, since it glosses over the inhumane and blasphemous nature of the Nazi atrocities and assumes that murdered Jewish children functioned as a sort of sacrificial victim:

> It is true that, like ancient Moloch-worshipers, German Nazis and their non-German henchman at Auschwitz threw children into the flames alive. It was not, however, their own children, in acts of sacrifice, but those of Jews, in acts of murder. (TH, 236)

Although in a manner different from the *Final Solution*, the term *Holocaust* also distances the witness who names the suffering from the suffering that is named. To use either name as the principle mode of referring to the *Shoah* is already to be involved in a denial of the irremediableness of the other's suffering. Whether one chooses to name in irony or in a straightforward attempt to affirm the suffering of those involved, the name one authors seems destined to betray what it names.

In an attempt to resolve this dilemma, Fackenheim turns to the Hebraic term *Shoah*, which can be translated as "total destruction." This term would purportedly name the suffering of the other without irony or glorification. But does not the reference to a total destruction in turn entail that what occurred in the death camps was itself the annihilation of a mass of individuals in such a manner that their particular deaths could no longer be witnessed as an "event"? Thus, *Shoah* names an event that is itself the canceling out of the event; it also names a name that is the erasure of the name. To name an event that annihilates both names and events doubly burdens those who would witness that "event" with that "name." One finds that the suffering of one's witness is so extreme that even she or he for whom one is to witness, as well as their suffering, lies beyond the scope of being named. Levinas in an article referring to the victims of the *Shoah* simply cites them as "the Nameless." And this occurs in a text titled *Proper Names*, a text dedicated to one's election to the uniqueness of the other's address, to his or her particular angle of existence. Thus, the name of the *Shoah* names one's incapability to witness as one's act of witness. One names it because even in one's incapability to provide a witness, one is still called upon to witness gratuitously. Only in the tone of a humility that has already been deprived to its very core of an active capacity to grasp the other, to set out his or her place under the sun, can the *Shoah* find its witness.

What follows traces out a witness of witnessing, at times a description, at times an interpretation, at times an argument, and in all cases a registering of a burden in thought exceeding that for which an argument or description or interpretation might adequately be given. Methodologically, one begins in a phenomenological analysis of one's already having undergone a command to witness him or her whom Levi names as the *Häftling*. In working out this analysis, the issue of the twofold nature of the attack upon autonomy in the death camps is also to be treated. In Auschwitz not only the *Häftling*'s personal autonomy was to be crushed but also her or his capacity to offer her or his own life to a succeeding generation. In its shame for the other's humiliation, one's witness of the *Häftling* finds itself in a double bind, in quandary.

In the middle chapters one turns to Levinas's account of the face-to-face relationship in order to argue for the transcendence of the victim's address. No matter how radically the autonomy of the *Häftling* is rendered servile in the death camp, her or his plight continues to command its witnesses to resistance. But as the argument progresses, one understands one must also witness the victim's address within a historical context by a filiation of witnessing. One inherits one's witness of *the Nameless* through texts written by other persons. How then is one to understand the truth of this witness? And how is one to place the writing of history in relationship to the writing of witnesses like Levi, Celan, and Borowski? These chapters argue for a Levinasian notion of prophetic witness and prophetic writing, in which the indexicality of historical witness is superseded and troubled by a witnessing under the aegis of an address toward and by the other that is "exposed like a bleeding wound."

By the end of this text, one is engaged in a rereading of one's own witness that finds itself under accusation, involved in incessant correction. The poetry of Paul Celan in particular provokes this mode of discourse. To witness the other's persecution is to find one's words already ringing in tones that implicate one in a history permeated with shame and violence. No scene elaborated in a poem or philosophical text is without the resonance of those tones. To take responsibility for one's words, one must take responsibility for the history of their address. Not the argument per se but its address of the other becomes the most pressing issue in this moment of rereading.[3] One's language suffers a turn toward the victim that leaves it in a state of cellular irritability, in a discourse of ambivalence that addresses and is addressed by many voices and many times.

But Levi raises the issue not only of witness but also of forgiveness. In moving from witness to forgiveness, one poses the issue of what tone one's witness will adopt in regard to those who perpetrate violence, of whether outrage over the victimizer's actions can also become compassion for her or him. In raising this issue, Levi responds to that particular moment of Simon Wiesenthal's internment in a concentration camp when he was brought to the bed of a mortally wounded Nazi soldier who had been involved in atrocities against Jews. Asked by the youth for a word of forgiveness, Wiesenthal refused to offer him any explicit pardon. Yet Wiesenthal also continued to listen, continued to suffer the dying man's address. And after this other man's death, Wiesenthal himself remains burdened by the question of whether he acted justly or compassionately.

What many respondents to the question of Wiesenthal's silence have pointed out is that more important than any words he might have facilely offered the other was his attentive silence. In his thoughts on Wiesenthal's story, Matthew Fox argues that this already is compassion—"to stay and listen and even to remain silent and refuse to offer cheap forgiveness to so heinous a crime" (*S*, 144). For Levinas as well, this silence would be that moment of the victim's persecution in which the very suffering of the other's hatefulness and its effect upon the persecuted is rendered back to the persecutor's face as an address that reveals for the persecutor the extent of his pitifulness, the impotence of his hate.

Wiesenthal himself remarks that his original desire "to get away" from the youth's grasp is miraculously transformed: in his desperate gesture the boy is revealed to be "so pathetically helpless that all of sudden I felt sorry for him" (*S*, 35). Could not one argue that in this particular context Wiesenthal's silence transcended violence, which is to say, a play of force against force, by means of an election, a vocation, that seized him before he himself could have accounted for it, let alone resisted it? Wiesenthal is helpless before the perpetrator's suffering at precisely the moment when he might have reasonably been tempted to cruelty, to cold revenge, or at the very least, to a lasting indifference. From Levinas's viewpoint this turn in Wiesenthal's address of the youth provides not a full-blown act of forgiveness but an "expiation," a making possible of conversion and forgiveness in a world where it had reasonably seemed impossible.[4]

Yet Levi's own thoughts on the matter disturb any facile resolution of this moment of transcendence. He points out that the youth's actions can also be seen as "impudent," as "using the Jew as a tool, unaware of the danger and the shock his request must have constituted for the prisoner" (*S*, 183). And Wiesenthal's response to this other, this Nazi youth, must also give witness to all the other others, to the slaughtered youths of the Jewish ghettos and death camps for whom no sunflower would be planted, for whom no public memory of their individual deaths remains possible. Forgiveness, no matter how transcendent remains infected with the burden of atrocity, with an irreparable harm. Compassion cannot leave outrage behind but must somehow honor its urgency even as it is seized by the perpetrator in his or her impotence and pitifulness. Forgiveness in the aftermath of the *Shoah* is as impossible and yet as necessary as its witness.

CHAPTER ONE

The Imperative to Witness the *Häftling*

I commend these words to you
Carve them in your hearts
At home, in the street,
Going to bed, rising;
Repeat them to your children,
    Or may you house fall apart
    May illness impede you
    May your children turn their faces from you.
                 —Primo Levi

The Phenomenology of a Command

Carve these words into your heart. But first carve into your heart that these words must be carved into your heart. The prologue from which the passage above was taken stands at the portal of the reader's entry into Primo Levi's *Survival in Auschwitz* (*SA*, 8). Before Levi begins his story, before any fact is imparted by him concerning Auschwitz, the reader must be addressed. The reader Levi has in mind is he or she who lives "safe" in her or his "warm house," who comes home at night to "hot food and friendly faces." These readers, Levi's words charge, live outside the confines of Auschwitz. But they do not live beyond its implications, nor dare they live in ignorance of its legacy. For this reason Levi begins his account with a twofold command, as well as a curse: Listen to me. Meditate upon what I say. If you do not, may you lose your home, your health, your children.[1]

My students and I, when confronted with this prologue, find ourselves immediately disturbed at its implications. "What right does the author have to curse me?" is our question. "What have I done personally to have deserved these harsh words?" "Why can't I read this simply for my own personal edification or to learn about the historical truth of what occurred?" "What difference does it make what I do?" These questions come at times from persons who often have only a minimal, vague knowledge of what occurred during the *Shoah*. Not only were they not alive during that time, but their parents often were not as well. Further, in most instances, the members of the class are not even remotely related by family to the perpetrators or the victims of the *Shoah*. How then can one be so involved in, so commanded by an event for which one is not even remotely guilty?

These objections to Levi's tone presume that one has responsibility for the *Shoah* only if one is guilty of having perpetrated it. But Levi's address to his readers implies that one's personal guilt in regard to the suffering that occurred in Auschwitz is not what is at issue in reading his text. Beyond the *guilt* of those involved in victimizing millions of human beings is the *responsibility* to respond to that victimization *regardless of one's guilt*. Being guiltless does not excuse one here. Further, responsibility is not reducible to or attendant upon guilt. Whether one was a perpetrator or not, one ought to be aware of and concerned about what happened to human beings in Auschwitz.

The prologue already implicates one in carrying out a phenomenological reading of its command. Because one is commanded from beyond guilt, from beyond what might seem a reasonable notion of one's personal involvement in a morally questionable matter, one finds oneself struggling with the very significance of what it means to be commanded. As in Kafka's *Trial*, one is brought before a tribunal in which not the explicit charges against one but the very structure of one's responsibility is at issue. One is commanded *before* the issue of the truth or falsity of the commandment can be raised, as well as *before* one's personal involvement can be determined from a consideration of what actually occurred. Thus, the ethical as it is commanded in Levi's command already involves an *epoche*, a shearing away of the determination of a matter's truth from one's responsibility for whatever that truth may turn out to be or to have been. Before there is knowledge, before the exact shape of the world and its entities can be fixed, *one must already have considered that one is obliged to consider*. Before one can determine exactly for whom one is responsible, one is already responsible. No longer able to justify one's actions by an appeal to normally accepted truths, one is cast out of the naive attitude, out of the edenic assumption that the world must be and has been placed before one before any other consideration can begin. Levi's command reverses the normal relationship between ontology and ethics: before the world could have existed, one was already responsible.

In this phenomenology of a command, one's heart is found to be carved upon twice. In the first instance, one takes the words of the text Levi has written, the words lying beyond the prologue that one has yet to read, and inscribes them in one's flesh. In the second instance, the very words, "carve them in your heart," are to be carved into one's heart as well. But the second instance is in fact the first. Before one's heart attends to Levi's description of his life in Auschwitz, one must already have attended to the command to attend. One's responsibility here is doubled—one must hear Levi precisely by hearing *how* one must hear him. It is not enough to simply let his words be said. One must ask if in their saying one has *really let* them be said. And in asking this question one is brought to acknowledge that one never had the choice *to let* these words be said but that the words to which one attends have claimed one even *before* one could let them be said. Put more concretely, Levi's words will not find his reader, unless that reader realizes these words have already found him or her before she or he had the chance to decide to be found or to listen.

 Carve into your heart that you are to carve these words into your heart. The disturbing fact is that no one who comes after the *Shoah* can justifiably protest a lack of responsibility concerning it. One is born into the world already involved, already claimed, already addressed by Levi's prologue. Whether or not one *knows about* the events at Auschwitz or any of the events that occurred in what Antelme has called *l'univers concentrationaire*, one is *already responsible* for them. The "you" of Levi's prologue picks out each and every reader uniquely. Not just any reader but I who now read this text am in particular enjoined to meditate upon and to repeat the words I am about to encounter. I am to do so for the sake of those whose annihilation or survival is recorded in what follows. Who exactly these others are is itself expressed ambivalently: "if this be a man . . . if this be a woman . . .". I am not sure for whom I am responsible, but I am responsible nonetheless. I must eventually admit that my indifference to the *Shoah* was only an illusion, that I was already involved regardless of my intentions in the matter.

 Thus, Levi's prologue claims its reader *before* he or she could have had any conscious or self-critical interest in the historical event of the *Shoah*. This claim does not occur simply because in the normal course of events I have ferreted out a series of historical details concerning National Socialism and the Final Solution and am now prepared to entertain its pertinence to my own existence. Paradoxically, I ought to search out these details, from the perspective of Levi's voice, precisely because I have been always commanded to be faithful to those who have been annihilated, even if I was not aware of them, even if they have ceased in the aftermath of this event to be immediately recognizable as a man or woman. For this reason, the reading of *Survival in Auschwitz* does not revolve around encountering a text for the sake of that text. As one enters its domain, an obligation ensues that claims one from beyond art and artistry, as well as beyond a mere knowing for the sake of knowing.

Faithfulness to the victim precedes any determination of the historical truth about the victim. This does not imply that Levi is indifferent to such historical truths. Indeed, the whole point of his writing corpus was to give an orientation to the very fact that the *Shoah* had occurred and that its occurrence had a particularly disturbing shape. But the fact of that occurrence was inevitably secondary. What was primary was the victim. In the words of Philip Hallie: "The victim is the authority."[2]

The Phenomenology of a Curse

The discussion so far has concentrated upon the command, but there remains a curse. What makes Levi's prologue particularly provocative to its addressee is its menace, its threat, its malediction. The prologue promises an unbearably violent outcome for he or she who reads it, unless the prologue's command to remember the victim is heeded. Even more than the command, the curse prohibits the reader from assuming a pose of naiveté, of an unquestioning good-will toward the author of what is to be read. I hear the curse and ask myself: What could I possibly do in the reading of this book that would make me so inimical to its author? Why am I the possible target of such hatred?

The very comfort in which I live, my assumption that friends and food are a normal course of my existence is held up as evidence against me. I am, so it would seem, incapable of listening, already disposed to indifference, precisely because I read this document in a modicum of comfort. The very normality of my life makes me irresponsible. For how can he or she who comes home to warmth and friends understand the man "who fights for a scrap of bread," or the woman whose eyes are "empty," whose womb is "cold like a frog in winter"? But the issue transcends simply my ability to understand. Implied in the command, as well as in the curse, is the possibility not only that I will not understand but also that I will avoid the attempt to understand.[3]

The pose of innocence referred to above—acting *as if* the memory of the *Shoah* merely involved the question of one's own personal guilt or innocence— is revealed to be the real object of Levi's curse. To act *as if* all that is involved in responsibility is one's guilt or innocence is already a *pose* of innocence! For in the assumption that one need no longer be responsible if one is not personally guilty, one has already assumed a pose of indifference in regard to the other's suffering. This indifference can be arrogant and self-justifying, or simply preoccupied with other pressing matters, or perhaps bored at the thought of attending so minutely to sorrows so distant from one's own time and place. In all of these cases, this indifference actually sustains the perpetrator's original betrayal of her or his victim. Like the Nazi, one prefers to forget the reality of the other's suffering. One is so ashamed of the *Häftling's* shame that one prefers not to consider it.[4] The Nazi depended upon exactly this troubled indifference to the past, and, in particular, to the victim, the powerless, and the marginal, to ensure the success of their so-called *Endlösung*, their final solution. For those indifferently aiding this betrayal, for those furthering an indifference to the memory of those who were annihilated, Levi commands a repetition of the *Shoah*, in which the indifferent will now be submitted to annihilation.

For the Sake of the *Häftling*

But by whose authority does Levi command? This issue cannot be resolved by a merely phenomenological approach to Levi's text. Simply to describe how one is commanded, to work out the manner in which Levi would call each reader to a particular responsibility for those who suffered at Auschwitz,[5] does not resolve the issue of why this command obligates. In fact, to remain in a mode of declarative discourse, *as if* one could simply talk about the structure of this command *as command*, *as if* one had the time and leisure to engage in a phenomenological reduction of the command in order to uncover its *eidos*, utterly misses the commanding aspect of the command. The command is not given in order to be appreciated and questioned but to be listened to and followed.

In giving the command as he does, Levi throws the very issue of its authority into crisis. By making the command prior to providing the truth for the sake of which the command is given, Levi risks allowing his command to become absurd. In play, children give absolute commands for which no reason can be given. So too did the camp guard who commanded Levi to remain silent rather than asking questions about the rules by which he and the other inmates were to be governed (*SA*, 25). If the reader is put under a command whose reason she or he cannot question, why is the reader not already in Auschwitz with Levi, already submitted to an authority that would undermine the dignity and integrity to be had in the fact that one is a reasoning being?

But above a hint was given to how one might answer this question about the irrelevance of the question in the face of the command. Levi claims that he does not command for the sake of himself, or by the measure of some arbitrary passion or anger, or even by the measure of his reason, but for the sake of the victim her or himself: the victim is the authority. Levi's very command would bring the reader before this victim in a mode of obsession for his or her torment, dehumanization, demolition. We are commanded later in the text to "imagine" that human "deprived of everyone he loves and at the same time of his house, his habits, his clothes, in short, of everything he possesses." This man (or woman!) is "hollow . . . reduced to suffering and needs, forgetful of dignity and restraint, for he who loses all often easily loses himself" (*SA*, 23). Levi terms this human the *Häftling*, the "prisoner," a German term actually used in the camp to denote all its inmates.[6]

On the one hand, Levi's command commands a phenomenological reduction, but on the other hand, the very same command cuts off, implodes, interrupts this reduction. On the one hand, one is commanded to consider the command *as command*, shorn of its reasons and prior assumptions. In this consideration of the command one discovers that because the command leaves no time for asking why, one is to be submitted in the command to the command itself. One discovers that the command remains before one without one's having recourse to one's reasons, to one's notions of how the world might be. One discovers that even to discuss these issues one must already have been commanded to be faithful to the victim, the *Häftling*. One comes to these conclusions about the command, *as if* the very precipitousness of the command were something one could reflect upon in leisure. But on the other hand, the command is not given in a discourse *about the command* but in an imperative *to oneself.* The command *already* places one, as Emmanuel Levinas would put it, "in the accusative." One finds oneself *already* under a responsibility to act that interrupts even that gesture of considering the structure of one's being commanded.

The very urgency of the command is what the command articulates. This urgency has no time except for the *Häftling* by and for whom one is commanded. Given this urgency, the very gesture of the phenomenological reduction is reoriented away from knowing the other and toward responsibility for her or him. In the wake of this responsibility, the very structure of the reduction, in which one forgets for the moment or *neutralizes* the assumptions that the phenomena before one signify the presence of a real entity, of another being, is revealed as a form of murder.[7] If one forgets the actual existence of the *Häftling* to whom one is obligated, one forgets the very resistance to one's spontaneous and self-serving inclinations that is given in being obliged. The command has *already* commanded that one not forget the

Häftling for whom one is responsible. Yet the command also precedes any determination on the part of oneself concerning exactly who is this *Häftling* to whom one is obligated.

In the interruption of the command's phenomenological structure, the reader is brought before the *Häftling*. But one is not brought before the *Häftling* in order to determine for oneself who she or he might be, or to make clear to oneself what is the explicit structure of one's own intentional consciousness of the *Häftling*. Rather, one is brought before the *Häftling* in order to attend to her or his suffering. The *Häftling* commands insofar as she or he suffers. Levi's command to reflect upon the *Häftling*, to imagine the human deprived of everyone he loves and of everything that nurtures him, is directed not to the identity of the *Häftling*, not to the determination for one's own satisfaction of the qualities by which the *Häftling* is a person. Instead, one is directed to imagine about the *Häftling* what cannot be imagined positively, namely, the submission of the *Häftling* to that undoing, that undergoing without remission, that constitutes her or his suffering *in extremis*. Further, in bringing one before this suffering, Levi's command already assumes one has forgotten that suffering.[8] As the last section pointed out, one is called by the command to question the very sincerity of one's sincerity, to ask whether one might already have found a manner of forgetting that suffering to which one was always already submitted. One comes to admit that one's approach to the *Häftling* is haunted by a pose of innocence.

For Levi, the *Häftling*, more than any other victim, resists my approach of her or him. This resistance to my approach is precisely what Levi would have the reader approach in her or his imagination of the *Häftling*. In her or his suffering, the *Häftling* is shorn of every possible capacity, of every possible grace, of every possible resistance to his or her fate. Perhaps the most disturbing instance of this reduction of human being to consuming pathos comes from an observation made in the very last entry of Levi's account: *"January 27th*. Dawn. On the floor, the shameful wreck of skin and bones, the Sómogyi thing" (*SA*, 156). Levi's insistence that we confront what has become of human beings at Auschwitz does not console, would not offer the reader a false sense of security, of hope, of confidence in the world's goodness. Indeed, Levi is intent upon confronting the reader with the realization that the human personality is "fragile" and far more in danger of being destroyed than one could ever imagine. His command to imagine the *Häftling* in actuality commands one to imagine beyond the limitations of one's imagination.

Thus, in the prologue, the command for reflection upon the *Häftling* is doubled. One is to consider not only *that* the *Häftling* has suffered, but also and more disturbingly *whether* she or he remains human: *Consider if this be a man. . . .* Who or what could be possibly left in "the Sómogyi thing," Levi asks his reader, that would command one's respect, one's attention, one's responsibility? It is as if the very dehumanization of the victim might end up cheating one of any possibility for empathy with her or his fate. One can feel empathy with those who both suffer and resist that suffering with some small shred of dignity intact, but what compels respect before the face of one who suffers to the point of abnegation? Elie Wiesel, in his account of his internment at Auschwitz, recounts the story of a father being choked to death by his son, just so the son might take a piece of bread from the father's mouth to satiate his own hunger. Even as the son grasps for the bread, other prisoners fall upon him and murder him in turn (*N*, 105–6).[9] Even more than in the case of Sómogyi, who in his last cogent moments a week before his death *took bread from his very mouth* in order to share it with his comrades, the moment recounted by Wiesel seems utterly shorn of moral or ontological dignity.

The Reader in Crisis

Confronting the Servile Soul

How then can the victim, precisely in his or her victimization, command one's attention to him or her? Levi's insistence on emphasizing the dehumanization of the *Häftling* does not allow the reader an easy out, which is to say, does not allow the reader to rely on that sort of rationalization coming from the world of safe houses and warm food in which one would argue some intrinsic power of autonomy still resides in the victim. No matter how deeply one is dehumanized, goes the wisdom of a normal world, one can still resist with one's will, with the smallest gesture of one's body, with the thought in one's mind. To allow this sort of interpretation of the *Häftling*'s plight, from Levi's viewpoint, would be to encourage the reader to forget the reality of Auschwitz, its shamefulness, its attack not only upon human life but also upon the human personality. One must not romanticize the condition of the victim, particularly the victim of what Levi calls extermination. For extermination has a doubled sense for Levi—it involves not only the eradication of lives but also of any sense that those lives have an intrinsic worth.

"That one can create a servile soul is not only the most painful experience of modern man, but perhaps the very refutation of human freedom" (FC, 16).

Emmanuel Levinas, like Primo Levi, is eminently aware of the ability of tyrants and torturers to undo that knot of human dignity founded upon a capability of resisting force with force. The torturer has become all too adept at claiming the body and mind of her or his victim, of dominating the victim's consciousness, of reducing it to a pure delirium of need: "Fear fills the soul to such an extent that one no longer sees it, but sees from its perspective" (FC, 16). In a similar vein, Wiesel remembers a time when

> Bread, soup—these were my whole life. I was a body. Perhaps less than that even: a starved stomach. The stomach alone was aware of the passage of time. (*N*, 50)

Levi too remembers that moment when he continued to share his hospital bed with the deceased Sómogyi in order to continue receiving an extra portion of bread. Of that experience, Levi reports: "It is a man who kills, man who creates or suffers injustice; it is no longer a man who, having lost all restraint shares his bed with a corpse" (*SA*, 156). In all these instances, the victim had become so possessed by his victimization that he no longer was capable of even seeing it as victimization. One did not see one's victimization because one saw so thoroughly with the eyes of a victim.

If this be a man . . .

Levi's command—not only to look upon the victim but to consider whether he or she is human—torments the reader. One would rather look away than admit the degradation of a human being. But even if one manages to turn toward the victim, one still experiences the tendency to reduce her or him to a mere spectacle, a mania of appearance in which no focal point resides, for which no meaning can be given. One looks away, even as one looks. But this too Levi not only forbids but also curses.

At this juncture the reader begins to sense an infectious quality in Levi's discourse. Not only is one commanded to confront the torment of the victim, but one finds that torment somehow communicated to one. One is infected by these victims, one is wounded by them. One's confidence in the meaning of one's own existence is not only put into question but mysteriously sapped. One feels at times as if one's very affect has been emptied out, as if one no longer could feel, or as if all of one's normal feelings had been disrupted by an overwhelming sense of shame.

In classes where Levi's witness and others like it have been encountered, one comes to a moment where the very notion of discussing or analyzing that witness seems offensive. For the ultimate significance of these testimonies is not to be found in their ability to provide a structure or a collection of categories for what they would address. The testimony exists in the first place in order to bring one into an immediate and compelling contact with those who have been degraded, suffocated, victimized. The text is the voice of one who would witness for the sake of an other who remains voiceless even as he or she is witnessed.

Discussing Levi's text, or writing about it as is occurring here, ultimately fails to carry the actual significance of what Levi himself has been commanded to do and in turn commands us to do: to attend to the inmates of Auschwitz, and most specifically to the *Häftlinge*, to those inmates who did not survive, who died unmourned and in utter degradation. At moments, the urgency of the claim these others makes upon one becomes overwhelming—my classes sometimes react against any discussion whatsoever of Levi's text and descend into a troubled yet committed silence. As the book *Testimony* by Shoshana Felman and Dori Laub itself gives testimony to, following Levi's command to reflect upon the victims of the *Shoah* leaves one and one's students in crisis.[10]

Ethical and Ontological Silences

The reader's silence before Levi's testimony in this matter is not ontological in its structure. One is not drawn in wonder by the poetic spirit of a literary work toward a humble and renewed attentiveness to a particular being. In ontological silence, a being fulgurates, suddenly comes near, as it emerges against a background of uncanny depths. The overall mood of such an encounter involves the fecundity of a mystery that continually withdraws from any ultimate revelation. One becomes silent in respect for the very actuality of what one confronts. Shakespeare's sonnets continually make use of this sort of attentive silence as the metaphor of the beloved's beauty:

> And more, much more, than in my verse can sit
> Your own glass shows you when you look in it. (103)

Or again:

> There lives more life in one of your fair eyes
> Than both your poets can in praise devise (83)

In these poems the poet's silence before the beloved is itself the chief metaphor and proof of the beloved's beauty and worthiness, as well as of the poet's faithfulness and veracity. For centuries, readers have taken up with these poems in order to cultivate this silence as a type of humility before the ineffable dignity and beauty of other persons. In reading these poems, no matter how dark their irony, how poisoned their suffering, one finds life is essentially worth living, and that no matter how deep one's suffering might be, the very fact that the beloved exists justifies all.

But the silence of Levi's reader is ethical: one is silenced in shame for the other, a shame that makes one all the more uncomfortable if one thinks of it as having enriched one's own existence. Thus, to react to "the Sómogyi thing" in wonder would utterly betray what has occurred. One would have transformed the degradation of this man into some sort of significance showing the goodness, the beauty, the worth of one's own existence and of existence in general. "True, he suffered," one might muse, "but we are saved because he did so." This very transformation of the other's degradation into one's own affirmation is utterly unfaithful to the actual conditions of the other's demise. One clothes the humiliation of the other in garments of wonder, and in doing so represses the torment of the other's suffering. One ends up degrading the other's degradation.

In ethical silence the reader finds her or himself in crisis. One confronts the treatment of another human being that is so outrageous, so indefensible that one must intervene. But the very capability to intervene is taken away from one, because the person one confronts has already been crushed. No recourse is possible that would undo the other's suffering. One finds oneself in an impossible situation—one ought to care for this other, one ought to be outraged, but the very care and outrage one feels are utterly useless. For this reason, one's energy is sapped, one's feelings are muted, one's consciousness is traumatized.

Quandary in Post-Shoah Existence

This crisis is redoubled when the reader comes to consider the inevitability of the first of a series of unresolvable dilemmas, which are to be termed quandaries, that characterize post-*Shoah* existence: In considering the victim, particularly victims of the *Shoah*, one must remain true to the victim's degradation. One must not turn away. *But this loyalty leaves the victim victimized.*

Yet to transform this degradation, to somehow interpret it, *as if*, at a "deeper" level, degradation actually constituted a sort of blessing, would be to utterly ignore the victim's plight, to become untrue to it. *This too would leave the victim victimized.* One is left in an impossible situation: No matter how one approaches the *Häftling*, she or he cannot be rescued. Yet the more one realizes this victim cannot be restored to a full existence, the more one becomes impatient with exactly this state of affairs. One experiences one's consciousness of the *Häftling* as a sort of explosion, a mania of intentions for the other that end up having no effective significance whatsoever for the inexcusable state to which the other was subjected.[11]

In quandary one finds that the very attempt to work through in reason the dilemma presented by Levi's command, *as if* it were nothing more than a creative paradox, leaves one outraged. One is outraged, because the attempt to reason out the paradox is in actuality a repressing of what is at issue. One cannot overcome this contradiction—that to be loyal to the victim is to leave the victim victimized. This is what reason attempts to forget. But the contradiction is itself to be submitted to: one is to live in the torment, in the unrest, that lies in the impossibility of Levi's command.

This quandary emerges particularly in relation to the victims of the *Shoah* because of the extremity and finality of the violence to which they were subjected. Levi speaks of that moment in which he finds himself transformed into the very phantoms he had encountered only a day before as he entered into the Monowitz Work Camp[12]:

> In a moment, with almost prophetic intuition, the reality was revealed to us: we had reached the bottom. It is not possible to sink lower than this; no human condition is more miserable than this, nor could it conceivably be so. Nothing belongs to us . . . if we speak, they will not listen to us, and if they listen they will not understand. They will even take away our name. (22)

In experience after experience within this camp, the extremity of degradation becomes clear—one is victimized in a manner that is so thoroughgoing, so carefully designed to undermine human dignity, that the very nature of the camp makes Hell itself seem positive by comparison.

In Dante's Hell, the damned are submitted to unending suffering because G-d resists the very attempt of the damned to undo their own existence. In Hell, wonder is still possible, wonder at a love that persists in spite of the delusions and hatreds obsessing those who insist on dwelling there. To meditate upon the punishment of the damned is to meditate upon a degradation that was induced by the those who are being punished.[13] As a result, Dante's visit to hell leaves him chastened yet capable of affirming its vision of justice. For ultimately the damned can be given a reason for their state of suffering.

But the "damned" of Auschwitz find themselves in a world where there is *Kein Warum*, no why. They are not even persecuted for their beliefs, since that manner of persecution implies one's clinging to an alleged fault or untruth for which one is held responsible. In the normal logic of persecution, one could give up one's commitment, one could cross over to the other side, and so no longer be subjected to degradation. And insofar as one might remain committed to one's alleged truth, one dies a hero or martyr—one dies for a cause, a purpose.[14] But in Auschwitz one is simply annihilated. One is not even allowed the status of being innocent or guilty. One is classified as submoral, as vermin, as racially defective, as garbage to be disposed of.

Alan Udoff writes of the Nazi death camp as that locality "where the totalization of person as victim became, at last, possible":

> Nothing was intended to survive this loss, the retreat in stages of de-generacy: the death of the "juridical person in man," then the "moral person," and finally, "the one thing that still prevents men from being made into living corpses . . . the differentiation of the individual, his unique identity." (PD, 332)[15]

But Udoff also argues that to call the *Häftlinge* of Auschwitz "living corpses" already assumes too much—namely, that the *Häftlinge* were given the possibility of death, that corpses could actually be a part of the landscape of dehabitation established within the camps (PD, 341f.). For the camps marked the collapse not only of the *Häftling*'s individual autonomy but also of her or his succeeding generations. Those who entered into Auschwitz found that not only were they marked to disappear but also all those who would have followed them in time were also to disappear. When no surviving generation is left to honor the dead, to bury their corpses and to mourn their memory, one cannot say the annihilated have even died.

The Death World

At this point in the phenomenological analysis, one must consider yet another dimension of Levi's witnessing of Auschwitz that has yet to be given adequate attention: Auschwitz was a place not only where human beings were emptied of their autonomy but also in which entire generations of a people were annihilated. Auschwitz, as an extermination camp, involved more than the crushing of an individual's autonomy. This "activity" was itself attendant upon a project of even more malevolent intent—one that might be termed for the time being as aggressive genocide.[16] What burdens the inmates of Auschwitz and what undermines their autonomy even more than their incessant hunger and fatigue is the background against which their degradation occurred.

"We traveled here in the sealed wagons; *we saw our women and men leave into nothingness*; we, transformed into slaves, have marched a hundred times backwards and forward to our silent labors, killed in our spirit *long before our anonymous death*" (*SA*, 49; italics mine). So far our analysis has concentrated upon the *Häftling*, the prisoner who was allowed a brief moment of existence before he or she also disappeared into the gas chambers and crematoria whose work was the actual reason for Auschwitz's existence. But what Edith Wyschograd has termed the death world also looms everywhere in Levi's account and yet receives little direct treatment. In the passage above, Levi refers to "anonymous death," to all the others who "leave into nothingness." But for the most part his narrative is about those at the portals of this final act of annihilation and not the annihilation itself.

Early in his account, Levi, asks some of the older prisoners, "*Wo sind die Andere?*", which is to say, where are all those who came with you and me but are nowhere in evidence. Levi himself suggests, "Perhaps transferred to other camps." One of his companions remarks to the other, "*Er will nix verstehen*," he does not want to understand anything (*SA*, 49). At this moment in his experience of the death camp, Levi records his own utter incredulity at the scope of the annihilation to which he too has been delivered. Not only is his autonomy to be undermined, but he is also to be consigned to a faceless death, a death without name, which is to say, a massing of death in which any particular death loses its significance.

As both Edith Wyschograd and Alan Udoff make clear in their descriptions of the death world instituted in camps like Auschwitz, the very notion of death is paradoxically under attack. To die, Udoff argues, is to be in a situation where one's demise is mourned, in which one's death finds a future beyond one's own dying. In being remembered, in having the palpable sense of one's own existence passed on to those who have been intimately involved in one's own life, one's death binds one into a historical community transcending one's own time. The rites of mourning respond to the dignity of one's having existed by giving a public and cultural expression to the fact that one's passing on belongs to other human beings as well.[17] Or as Wyschograd argues, "the temporal mode of our having been, of having ever existed,"[18] is something one normally believes cannot be eradicated. One dies with the unquestioned expectation that beyond one's individual death lies a future for whom that death matters. But in mass death the very future of one's death collapses.

Wyschograd argues, "the phenomenon of mass death makes vividly present the possibility of the foreclosure of all experience by destroying countless living beings together with the structures that make human existence possible" (*SpA*, 13). In the death world, one can no longer count upon the future of one's death. For not only will one be dead, but also all the generations following upon one, those future descendants who would have mourned one, who would have carried on the rich network of significances constituting one's own existence, are themselves to be eradicated. As Hannah Arendt puts it:

> The concentration camps, by making death itself anonymous . . . robbed death of its meaning as the end of a fulfilled life. In a sense they took away the individual's own death, proving that henceforth nothing belonged to him and he belonged to no one. His death merely set a seal on the fact that he had never really existed.[19]

In the future that was to have been opened up by Auschwitz, the very existence of Levi's text, *Survival in Auschwitz*, would have been impossible, since Levi too would have ceased to have existed: "Surviving Auschwitz" would have been an absolute oxymoron. But because of Levi's miraculous survival, along with his commitment to witnessing the annihilation that wiped out millions, we who live in the future of that event are allowed after all some access, no matter how tortured and contradictory, to what occurred there. The very command at the beginning of Levi's text to remember the degradation of the *Häftling* would itself have been lost, if Levi and all the others like him had died too.[20]

One moment in *Survival* when the effect of the death world upon its inmates is made more fully apparent occurs during a "selection," in which Levi and the other *Häftlinge* of his barracks run naked in a line before an SS Officer, who in the scope of a few seconds decides who will continue to exist and who will be consigned to, in what could be termed an euphemism by understatement, the "*schlechte Seite.*" Two moods are striking in this description. The first is the lack of affect, the overall resignation with which most prisoners accept their fate. Levi and his friend Alberto decide that only through a mixup of cards has Levi been mistakenly consigned to those who continue to live. Over this fact, Levi "feel[s] no distinct emotion." What does preoccupy the men is their stomachs and their other bodily needs. "Must I go and tell [Sattler] that his shirt will be of no more use?," Levi wonders. Ziegler's only recorded reaction to his selection is to insist on his extra bowl of soup, his "right" on having been selected. After receiving it, "he goes quietly to his bunk to eat."

But the second mood involves a sharply articulated affect on the part of Levi as he watches Kuhn, who "is thanking God because he has not been chosen." In spite of his numbness, Levi becomes outraged at Kuhn's assumption that simply being saved from dying at this time in this place is an inherent good. Levi writes:

> Kuhn is out of his senses. Does he not see Beppo the Greek in the bunk next to him, Beppo who is twenty years old and is going to the gas chamber the day after tomorrow and knows it and lies there looking fixedly at the light without saying anything and without even thinking anymore? Does Kuhn fail to realize that next time it will be his turn? Does Kuhn not understand that what has happened today is an abomination, which no propitiatory prayer, no pardon, no expiation by the guilty, which nothing at all in the power of man can ever clean again. (*SA*, 118)

Explicitly Levi finds fault with the address of Kuhn's prayer, as well as its tone. Kuhn *addresses* G-d precisely by *ignoring* the suffering of his fellow *Häftlinge*. This indifference to the fate of others who are suffering mirrors the narcissism of the camp guards, the SS officers, and the National Socialists in general. In the terms of Levinas's discourse, one goes about the daily struggle for one's place in the sun without much regard to the effects of that struggle upon the others surrounding oneself. One is thankful for one's own daily bread but fails to ask the effect of having procured this bread upon the life of the one who might be starving. Kuhn acts *as if* sheer existence itself were the greatest good one could affirm. But from Levi's viewpoint, Kuhn's response lacks the goodness of having been addressed by the suffering of others regardless of one's own interests, regardless of whether one will continue to exist.

In remarks delivered during a conference in the 1980s, Levinas contends that National Socialism was defined through an "obstinacy to be" so utterly taken up with its own survival, its own needs, that it became "contumacious and unpitying," resistant to "all kindness or mercy," and disdainful of any "sacrifice that would yield to the irreducible alterity of the other (*autrui*), who being irreducible, would be the singular (*unique*)."[21] For Levinas, what is particularly telling about the politics of National Socialism was the refusal of its practitioners to be addressed and questioned by the effects that their victimization of the other had upon that particular and unique other. Indeed, the whole point of such victimization was to render the victim incapable of making any appeal to the victimizer whatsoever.

Certainly, one would be hard pressed, at least from the viewpoint of the normal world, to condemn Kuhn too harshly for his lapse in compassion. This man, as well as the other inmates, suffers under the weight of an immense coercion to forget his humanity. In the scene above, even the men condemned to burn react numbly, indifferently to their impending demise. Further Kuhn is not the one who initiates this annihilation but who attempts in his own way to survive its onslaught.

Nevertheless, Levi is quite harsh with Kuhn's attempt to find a meaning for what has occurred. Paradoxically, Kuhn is out of his senses precisely because he insists that his situation makes sense. Making sense of one's survival at the expense of one's indifference to those who suffer is a pyrrhic victory—one resists one's victimizer only to become the underwriter of her or his very indifference toward oneself and one's fellow humans.

But beyond his indifference to Beppo and Sattler, Kuhn's prayer also implicitly ignores that his moment of grace is at best a temporary reprieve from an institution whose very "justice" consists in a fanatical and obsessively universal attack upon the Jewish people's existence. In undergoing the selection, Kuhn confronts not only the cruelty of one human being to another but an orchestrated attempt to do away with his fellow Jews altogether. Cruelty here is instantiated within a death world. Fackenheim has pointed out that one facet of this structure of a universal submission to death involved how it rendered sacrifice on the part of individuals irrelevant.[22] For instance, one might suppose that Beppo and the others selected for the "bad side" have paid for Kuhn's survival by the forfeiture of their lives. In a more normal world one would consider this sacrifice heroic—they give their lives up so that another, in this case Kuhn, might live. But here their "gift" is paradoxically due to nothing more than the indifferent working of the machinery of the death camp. The inmates did not offer themselves in the place of Kuhn but were chosen, in many cases randomly or mistakenly, by an SS subaltern.[23]

The very question of whom Kuhn is to thank for his continued existence, to whom he might direct his address, ends in a quandary. To thank the SS subaltern or the men to be sacrificed seems to be just as insensitive a gesture as to thank G-d. There is no one to thank! Kuhn's stay of execution is revealed to be dependent upon the maintenance of a structure whose final intent is Kuhn's eradication, as well as the eradication of every human being surrounding him. In his prayer of thanksgiving, Kuhn has not confronted the fact that his survival occurs only in order to aid the camps to function in their ultimate work of mass extermination. In effect, Kuhn is thanking G-d for letting him continue to exist so that the work of Auschwitz not only could continue but also be manned by himself. Given this implicit context Levi's own negative reaction becomes more comprehensible: "If I were God, I would spit at Kuhn's prayer."

Yet another moment in which the death world is given a more explicit thematization, one discussed at length by Langer,[24] occurs when Levi engages in a conversation with a few other inmates concerning Odysseus's speech to Dante in the *Inferno* of the *Divine Comedy* (*SA*, 102ff.).[25] Much of the story Levi tells is absorbed in his struggle to remember the actual words Dante wrote, a struggle that is made all the more daunting by Levi's fatigue, as well as how differently the words of Dante's text now resonate within the death world where Levi and his fellow interlocutors find themselves. Near the end of his discourse, Levi strives to connect the clause "I had never seen the like on any day," with what comes after it in Dante's text. But his attempt to reconstruct the canto at this point falls into a silence he cannot undo. In this silence Dante's words now find themselves stranded within the death world.

The phrase Levi cites from Dante's text refers to the moment in Odysseus's story when his own striving brings him to the very shores of the mountain of Purgatory that serves as the gateway between earth and heaven. Immediately upon this moment, Odysseus's ship is overcome by a tempest, founders, and sinks into the oceanic depths. Odysseus finds himself stranded in hell. His pagan attempt to reach toward heaven through a purely human striving for excellence and knowledge is revealed as the outcome of an arrogance deluded by its own frail and derivative powers. Coming just before his wreck, Odysseus's remark that he had never seen the like of the purgatorial mount with its sheer heights indicates his dawning awareness of an order of reality he had consistently spurned during his entire life. The mountain in its tempestuous interruption of the ordinary world of human beings becomes the sign of the transcendent power of a creator G-d.

But Levi now considers these lines within the confines of the death world. This world also introduces those who are brought into it to a landscape that is unparalleled in human existence, which disrupts one's connection with an ordinary world. But this world, unlike the world in which Dante places Odysseus, does not lead to a vision of metaphysical grandeur mediated by a Virgil and a Beatrice, the incarnations of reason and theology, but ends up before a pot of soup that "inspires" an obsessive craving for *Kraut und Rüben*, cabbages and turnips.

The struggle for mere survival in the death world ironically betrays the "flash of intuition, perhaps the reason for our fate, for our being here today" that Levi feels he was close to articulating to his fellow interlocutors. The line ending Dante's telling of Odysseus's story, which also ends Levi's own account of retelling that story, rings all the more ominously in this context:

And over our heads the hollow seas closed up. (SA, 105)

Like Odysseus, Levi has confronted a reality disrupting the ordinary world and has foundered on its abrupt shores. In what manner do these words in Levi's mouth now signify a rupturing of human purpose, a submission to one's own failure, as well as an exposure to a greater power transcending human dimensions? Beyond the craving for one's immediate survival induced by the cruel treatment of the *Häftlinge*, lies the infernal promise on the part of the Nazis and their *Führer* that all Jews will cease to exist upon the face of the earth. Not only hunger but annihilation is threatened, not only a suffering that leaves a particular person obsessed with turnips but also one that leaves every Jewish person reduced to a body to be disposed of *as if* it were nothing more than refuse.

Auschwitz as Betrayal

Thus, an unmitigated annihilation became the background against which each *Häftling* was inevitably forced to measure the significance of her or his own individual torment. Even to pretend, as Kuhn does, that one's chief responsibility is simply to preserve one's own life is already to measure one's actions and sentiments against one's eventual annihilation, although in a mode that represses rather than acknowledges this ultimate threat. In fact, the trauma of the very realization of annihilation was so overwhelming that it often became the deciding blow in the collapse of an inmate's autonomy. The universality of annihilation canceled the very meaning of one's death. Who could even begin to imagine this, let alone *live* in a world where one's very life served nothing more than to wipe out life?

But to characterize this wiping out of death as well as life, this annihilation, in terms of a death world is also problematic. For the very logic of Arendt and Wyschograd's argument, at least as it is reproduced above, could be applied to any natural disaster involving a massive loss of life. For instance, a comet hitting the earth and eradicating the entire sum of the earth's human population would involve a dying without humans left to mourn it. There too the future as a mode of one's temporality would be annihilated. What makes the issue of Auschwitz most disturbing, as Levi's own anger at Kuhn shows, is not that mass death occurred but that it was intended and carried out by one's fellow human beings as a matter of so-called social wisdom and political policy. Auschwitz is not only an *attack upon* but also a *betrayal of* every human's right to a death that is mourned, to a future in which the significance of one's having existed is acknowledged. This betrayal gains an even more malevolent dimension when one remembers that it was directed not only at individuals but also at a *genos*, an entire human type.

For this reason, the *Shoah* is often characterized as an attempted act of genocide, which is to say, the killing off of an entire category or culture of people. The events at Auschwitz were earlier termed an aggressive genocide because they involved not only an attack upon Jewish culture but also upon each and every body even marginally tied to that culture by birth to the third generation. Another term, which will be developed in more detail in the next chapter, could also be used for this form of genocide: *aenocide*, a murdering of the generations. In aggressive genocide, one not only murders a type of human being, but also one deprives a people, a *Geschlecht*, of their generations.

Levi's *Survival in Auschwitz* is in turn the resistance of the attempted genocide or aenocide of the *Shoah*. Levi's prologue calls his readers to an uncanny and disturbing responsibility for those very generations that Hitler and his Nazi followers had condemned to disappear. In this way one is given a filiation, is initiated into a *genos*, and so remains in contact with an articulation of time that would again be *diachronic*, that would again allow difference and so open up into the generosity of one generation succeeding another. Levi's prologue gives all of its readers the occasion to become that generation who inherits Auschwitz, who are the children of the *Shoah*.

But this very resistance is burdened by a curse and commands one's recognition that Hitler's aenocide was largely successful. Saul Friedlander remarks:

> When the final solution was implemented, metaphorically speaking, an apocalyptic dimension entered history, took place within history. In some remote areas of eastern Europe, the total annihilation of millions of human beings was being systematically implemented. But for those who were not the victims, life went on, during the events and after them: the apocalypse had passed by unnoticed. We are confronted with an "end" that happened, that was entirely consummated for millions of human beings, but which surrounding society hardly perceived, possibly did not want to perceive at all. Life continued—and continues—its normal flow. (*MHE*, 51)

Friedlander's remarks allude exactly to how aenocide is accomplished—generations disappear, time as an articulation of a responsibility collapses, and no one remains who can carry on that specific line of responsibility. One finds here a time that cannot be mourned, that cannot be structured as mourning. Mourning is impossible because not only was one generation done away with but also all the remaining generations who would have mourned that death have also been annihilated.

And so one finds Levi's text has brought one to yet another quandary: to mourn the dead of Auschwitz is an impossibility. For if what is meant by mourning is the carrying on of life from generation to generation, from *aeon* to *aeon*, then mourning was already made impossible by the slaughter of the generations at Auschwitz. The very conditions for mourning, that one's life be carried over into a future beyond one's own, that the generation one has mothered and fathered treat one's death as the opening into its own birth, are undone in Auschwitz. One is annihilated precisely because the very possibility for mourning has been annihilated. To mourn the annihilated of Auschwitz involves remembering them *as if they had not been annihilated.* This act would dishonor the *Nameless* precisely by forgetting the dishonor to which they were incessantly subjected.

But to fail to mourn the dead of Auschwitz is to find oneself in complicity with the Nazi attack upon the future. By failing to mourn one accepts aenocide as an accomplished fact. One encounters the Nazi project to eradicate the generations and one does nothing about it whatsoever. Thus, one finds an obligation to remember, "to carve these words upon your heart," *even if all that one can remember is one's inability to remember, even if all that one can mourn is one's inability to mourn.* One has nothing left to do but to mourn the loss of mourning. One is enmeshed in an impossible mourning from which there is no extrication. One's very responsibility to mourn the preceding generation is burdened by a curse.

Witness in Crisis

"Carve these words into your heart." But the very committing of these words to one's heart involves one in quandary, in unresolvable torment, in impossible mourning. One has been asked in this first chapter to consider a phenomenological reading of that command with which Levi begins his own testimony concerning Auschwitz. In doing so, one has stepped back from the immediacy of the command in order to illuminate the structures of meaning and involvement that it articulates. One forgot, for a moment, that a command does not leave one time to appreciate its significance, that its very syntax is meant to interrupt the rational impulse, as well as the impertinence, motivating a question. The very doubling of the command—not only to carve the words into one's heart but also to carve that one must carve these words into one's heart—makes exactly this point. To speak phenomenologically about a command is to be involved in a paradox.

In normal times this paradox could perhaps be sustained: one could balance an appreciation of the *logos*, of the pattern or rationality of a command, over and against its urgency. Kant, in his insistence on deriving the categorical imperative from the structure of a rational being, which is to say, a being who must inevitably give reasons for what she or he does, cultivates exactly this sort of paradox. One acts out of an obligation that is unconditional, and yet one also finds in the structure of reason itself that one can only make sense of what one does insofar as one acts without contradiction. To act without contradiction illuminates the very significance of obligation. The very urgency of urgency is rational. The very rationality of reason requires urgency.

But at crucial moments in the phenomenology of Levi's command, one finds the tension between the rational and the ethical either explodes or implodes. One *feels* as if the very point of Levi's command is to undo reason, to subvert freedom, to submit his reader unconditionally to what has been termed a quandary. Unlike the life world in which phenomenology finds its place, Levi's "death world," which is in reality a "world betrayed," is mired in a past that is incapable of being carried over into the next generation. The crushed autonomy of the *Häftling*, as well as the annihilation of her or his *genos*, leaves those in the present, those who inherit Levi's testimony, in utter helplessness. One confronts the shift in time—from past to present—as the articulation of asymmetric and transcendent loss. What happened to those who entered into Auschwitz cannot be undone, cannot be remedied. These others were not only victimized but also annihilated. The very attempt to act *as if* one could undo these moments, or reinterpret them in a better light, *as if* in one manner or another one could go back and right what was wronged, would only cover over exactly how powerful the Nazi attack upon the life world actually was. For this reason, as the introduction above suggests, the entire array of events of which Auschwitz was one instance is to be termed the "*Shoah*," a "total destruction." In an uncanny twist, the very goodness of one's response to the victimization that occurred in the *Shoah* demands that one admit one can do nothing about it. But this admission is anything but consoling.

One finds that one has already been commanded both to mourn and not to mourn the annihilated, both to resist and not resist the victimization of the *Häftling*. In being brought into these quandaries, philosophy's confidence in the capability of reason to illuminate the significance of the world finds itself in crisis. The crisis revolves in particular around the status of negation. From the beginning of the philosophical tradition, one has struggled to articulate how negation is a temporary perturbation in the project to affirm reality. Eventually, the believer in reason argues, negation plays a positive role in experience. Philosophy might even be defined as that confidence in the world that assumes negation is reasonable, which is to say, that all events appearing destructive, appearing without reason, *ohne Warum*, ultimately are revealed to be explicable, part of a grander scheme. No matter how profoundly negation may be at play in reality, its gesture somehow sparks a creative possibility.

But Levi's testimony concerning Auschwitz suggests that reason fails when confronted with a *Verneinung*, a negation, that is in fact a *Verderben* and *Vernichtung*, a corruption and annihilation of the world. The very struggle to make sense of the world, to render it in a manner that allows it to be illuminated, to show forth in a *logos*, a pattern that is self-consistent and reasonable, perversely aids rather than resists the Nazi project to transform the life world into a death world, a world betrayal. Insofar as one makes sense of the crushed autonomy of the *Häftling*, insofar as one argues that genocide has its reason, one betrays yet again the victim already betrayed.

For example, the Hegelian confidence that history is ultimately a theodicy[26] in which "the negative is reduced to a subordinate position and transcended altogether" is vulnerable to exactly the criticism just outlined. Because of his notion of determinate negation, Hegel feels justified in arguing that the suffering of those who are "immolated upon its [history's] altar" is secondary to the larger work of Spirit in history. The immolation, as regrettable as it may be, is ultimately the articulation of a larger affirmation, of the growth and development of Spirit in its historical odyssey. For Hegel "particular ends are submerged in the universal end."[27] Thus, what stands out in the historical process is not the suffering of particular individuals but the "larger" ends toward which that suffering leads. For this reason, Emmanuel Levinas charges that for Hegel: "the will of each [particular human being] . . . from the start consists in willing the universal or the rational, that is, in negating its very particularity" (*TI*, 217). The particular human is not only to be negated through her or his suffering but also is expected by Hegel to will this negation! In this manner the particularity of the individual who suffers in history is absorbed into a political society thought merely as a system of achievements. Hegel's account of negation remains blind to the outrage, as well as the shame, in the particular instance of human victimization.

Hegelians would address the *Shoah* not by turning to the particular individuals who were done away with, to the victims of history, but to the institutions and ways of life emerging from that annihilation. In these larger, more inclusive configurations of Spirit, one would encounter a world evolving toward an even broader and more exhaustive articulation of reality in reason, as well as of reason in reality. Thus the Hegelian might argue: *because* of the *Shoah*, we now have Israel, a functioning United Nations, the Nato alliance, and so on. As a statement articulating a certain causal connection between one series of historical events and another, one might agree to this claim. But to argue that one lives in a world where the suffering of individuals is a *necessary* condition for the improvement of institutions is itself outrageous. For in that case, the whole plot of being, of the articulation of Spirit in history, is tainted to the very core. Hegel's understanding of negation addresses the justice of what succeeds in evolving, in what continues to exist, of how beings are articulated in an ongoing historical evolution, but what he fails to consider is Levinas's rather startling question: "Is it just to exist?"[28]

But the crisis provoked by the *Vernichtung* and *Verderben* of Auschwitz is not simply a matter of the immolation of victims upon the altar of history, *as if* history were to remain intact after this immolation. What also must be addressed is the loss of historical existence altogether. By practicing aenocide, an aggressive and universal form of annihilation, the Nazis showed that the very force of reason in history can be undone simply by murdering the historical future. The historical future is not simply an indefinite and ultimately inexhaustible openness upon possibility. As Wyschograd points out in her analysis of Zeno's paradox in *Spirit and Ashes*, history survives by means of a finite collection of bodies, institutions, and resources. If one attacks any of these in an overwhelming manner, the very historicity of its existence will collapse (*SpA*, 37–38). If the very generations who populate and articulate historical institutions disappear, then the institutions comprising that larger notion of subjectivity that Hegel ultimately terms Spirit will also disappear. Reason does not find itself in a world of infinite possibilities, although it is commanded to infinite responsibility within the context of a finite, historical world.[29] In the Nazi elaboration of *force majeure* human beings confront their newfound technological capability to wield a power so extensive and so destructive that the very temporality of human experience is in danger of collapsing. This is what Wyschograd would term the "death world" and what has been reinterpreted in this chapter as "world betrayal."

Philosophy then is put doubly in crisis:

1. Within history, philosophy is called on to witness that the voice of the victim transcends history. To speak of the actual victim as secondary to what history makes of that victim is to conceive of the historical arena as a mode of bad faith. One condemns those who would explicitly victimize others, yet one justifies this victimization retrospectively. Reason, insofar as it is a *logos*, an ordering into a pattern or scheme, actually aids those who would forget the victim, who would dismiss his or her loss as irrelevant or subsidiary. Philosophy must resist that notion of reason whereby the victimization of the victim comes to be explicable and justified.

2. But philosophy is also called upon to witness that history itself is in danger of imploding. As explored in the discussion above, the crisis of *Vernichtung*, of annihilation, involves not only the crushing of individual autonomy in individual cases but also the eradication of the future of a line of generations, a *genos*. In this second mode of victimization, the victim is so victimized that even the memory of victimization is eradicated. One would not even remember this eradication as secondary or irrelevant. It would be forgotten altogether.

This second mode of crisis (annihilation *of* history through annihilation of *genos*) is far more difficult to isolate or articulate than the first (annihilation *within* history of the individual's autonomy). For instance, one could object that insofar as humans in general have survived the *Shoah*, that the *Shoah* is itself hardly an example of the annihilation of history. Indeed, the very fact that the *Shoah* is being discussed here already demonstrates that history has survived the *Shoah* and that *within history* one can confront the crisis posed for history by the *Häftling*, the victim of history. And one could imagine the possibility for such a discussion, even if Hitler had succeeded in rooting out every Jewish person who lived upon the earth. Hitler's attack upon Jews, as morally vicious as it may be, should not be confused with the utter implosion of history.

According to this line of thought, the notion of the annihilation of history would be more appropriately applied to the use of nuclear weapons to function as a deterrent through a policy of mutually assured destruction. In that scenario, one threatens to use a weapon (although purportedly for the purpose of not using it) whose effect could very well be the extinction of the human race in its entirety. In confronting that situation one could then ask the question Jonathan Shell poses in his *Fate of the Earth*: "How are we, who are a part of human life, to step back from life and see it whole, in order to assess the meaning of its disappearance?"[30] In that situation, one could truly ask the meaning of the collapse of historical existence.

But one could also argue that aenocide, insofar as it roots out an entire culture has also wiped out an entire voice that would have made up the history of history. *In this fashion, history has become lost to itself.* To recall Friedlander's words: "We are confronted with an 'end' that happened, that was entirely consummated for millions of human beings, but which surrounding society hardly perceived, possibly did not want to perceive at all. Life continued—and continues—its normal flow" (*MHE*, 51). In considering Friedlander's point, one cannot ignore the fallacy Wyschograd points to in her analysis of Zeno's paradox. One cannot treat history *as if* it were a field of infinite possibilities. One does not murder six million European Jews only to find six million more immediately rising up in their place to be murdered in turn. When one murders a *genos*, as opposed to an individual, no one is left to speak in its place. As a result, the history that one writes after the collapse of a *genos* is without the voice of that *genos*. In order to appreciate this implosion of history, one must give up the Hegelian notion that only a larger subjectivity is the author of history and that great historians only arise in order to fulfill the opening for a significance that history as the odyssey of reason in its own self-discovery has already prepared for them. One must also remember that at the root of the "death world" is in actuality "world betrayal." The death world comes about because humans comport themselves in a certain manner—they betray the generations around them in order to wipe out the very memory of human experiences that would have otherwise been translated into historical awareness. In the Nazi policy of aenocide, history is revealed to be as vulnerable to betrayal as are the individuals populating it.

How then is philosophy to respond to the *Vernichtung* and *Verderben* that is the hallmark of Auschwitz and with which Levi's own testimony is so obsessed? Put in other words, how might philosophy become a testimony to the victim for the sake of the victim? And how might philosophy responsibly articulate the vulnerability of history to annihilation? Further, how might philosophy do this without becoming immediately lost in its own capacity to generalize, without speaking in abstractions of what must always remain a singular instance in a singluar being's life? If one takes this last question seriously, one finds that the very phrasing of the questions immediately preceding it have already failed in their witness. For one already speaks of the singular victim in a manner that makes her or him part and parcel of a more general philosophical issue.

This observation leads one to a more explicit expression of the quandary in which philosophy finds itself in the aftermath of the *Shoah*: on the one hand, one finds that reason, insofar as it takes up with the singular victim, must articulate her or him in terms of a category or concept. Even to term her or him a "victim" is already to have translated her or him into a conceptual formulation. In order to speak *about* someone, one must translate that someone into a defined quality or set of qualities. In doing philosophy, one ceases to be addressed by the victim but instead speaks *about* her or him. The very act of reasoning is continually in danger of betraying the situation of the victim, of transforming the particularity of his or her suffering into a category that can be given an explicit significance for all who reason. The victim enters into a *logos* in which he or she becomes one of many examples of the same type.

On the other hand, not to reason about the victim is also indefensible. In this case, one would aid those who already were intent on constructing in Auschwitz a mode of history with "*Kein Warum*," with no why. In Auschwitz, the *Kommandanten* and *Kapos* could murder or not murder based simply upon a whim. While being rebuked by a guard for sucking on an icicle during his first day in camp, Levi asks him, "why?" But for this too he is rebuked and shoved back inside the window, as he is told, "There is no why here" (*SA*, 25).

To demand "*why*" in the face of those who carried out the annihilative work of Auschwitz, to call out for the reasons that these so-called actions "ought" to have occurred, is perhaps the most obligatory mode of resistance to a heartless violence. It would call those who murder, who act with impunity, into giving an accounting for what they do. It would shame the victimizers into articulating some principle according to which their actions might make sense both to themselves *and to others*. It would as well demand a confrontation with the possibility that one has betrayed these others. In the following chapters the return to asking *why* in the aftermath of the *Shoah* hinges upon a reinterpretation of reason in the first instance as an address, as a speaking *toward* the other rather than simply *about* her or him. To give reason its "*why*" is not to find the foolproof explanation for the manner in which one chooses to act but to find oneself before the other who suffers one's actions and who reveals both the possibility of and the command against murder. It will be argued via the philosophy of Emmanuel Levinas that the very vulnerability of the other to one's actions already interrupts one's explanations and calls one to self-accusation and conscience.

The philosopher is commanded by Levi's prologue to bear witness in reason to the incapacity of reason, to bring one's "why" to the other who transcends one's own reasons, to begin the interminable effort of an exposure to the other that can never be finished. *Carve these words in your heart.*

CHAPTER TWO

The Scene of Annihilation

Testimony's Ethical Resistance

The Quandary of Imagination in the Act of Testimony

Carve these words into your heart. In response to Levi's command *to consider* and *to imagine* the crushed autonomy of the individual *Häftling*, as well as the annihilation of her or his entire *genos*, one turns again to Levi's text, to those words following the prologue. In order to supplement Levi's characterization of the death camp in which he was interned, attention will also be given to a series of passages drawn from the writings of Taduesz Borowski, Elie Wiesel, and Frieda Aaron. Levi's testimony, it was discovered in the first chapter, curses the reader who would encounter Levi's own witness *as if* it were merely the objective portrayal of a series of events, *as if* one could simply consider it from the warmth and security of one's own environs. The gravity and shame of what occurred within the confines of the death camps demands one already be partial to their victims. Yet one also has been warned that one's capability to imagine the victim, to respond to the command of Levi, is itself an impossible task. One is submitted to unresolvable dilemmas, to quandary.

The act of an imaginative response to the events of the *Shoah*, an act that has been in progress from the very first words of this book, is an inescapable duty. But one should be wary of interpreting that duty in terms of an aesthetic or ontological imagination. As the distinction between ontological and ethical silence made clear, the purpose of imagining the *Häftling* is not to illuminate his or her situation, *as if* the *Häftling* were the occasion for *my* increased appreciation of the world, or *as if* the *Häftling* existed precisely in order to be praised for having existed. The *Häftling* ought not leave me in wonder. Existence itself is put into question if it involves one in a primordial injustice to others. Neither should the confrontation of the *Häftling* provide an inspiration for my feat of aesthetic imagination. The *Häftling* did not exist so that one might write compelling works of literature about her or him.

For Levi what should command the reader's imagination is attentiveness to the victim her or himself. This attentiveness listens for a suffering, an undergoing of compulsion, that is utterly inexplicable in one's own terms. One does not suffer *as* the *Häftling* suffers. One does not even think as the *Häftling* thinks. Levi emphasizes this fact by incessantly pointing out the disjunction between the reader who is nested safely in his home and the *Häftling* who is utterly exposed to a cruelty that puts her or him beyond the bounds of categorization. One is no longer even sure if this other remains a person: *"Consider if this be man."*

Thus, the act of imagination required by Levi would put one at the very limit of imagination. One becomes involved in what Arendt has termed an act of "fearful imagination." One is "aroused" precisely because one has "not actually been smitten in [one's] own flesh" and so remains free "to keep thinking about such horrors."[1] Yet, in contrast to Arendt's own characterization, this imagination does not leave one the time to think of such thoughts as "useful," or in terms of how they might precipitate "a change of personality." As the phenomenological reading of Levi's command in the last chapter demonstrated, one is inspired by the *Häftling* to imagine how one fails to imagine the suffering, the collapse of both affect and reason, that the *Häftling* undergoes. One imagines how one cannot imagine. In this negative or passive "act" of imagination, one becomes vulnerable to a silence inspired by the other that leaves one in anarchic disarray, in what Levinas might call "a cellular irritability" (*OB*, 143). The free play of imagination that one often praises in literary works is undermined by an infectious imagination, an imagination running amuck to the point of utter collapse, to contradiction and quandary. One might call this imagination masochistic if one cultivated it for one's own purposes. But precisely that gesture, the taking of pleasure in the quandary, in the frustration of imagination's failure, in the impotence that one undergoes in the failure, is prohibited by Levi's command.

Put more positively, the command already has interrupted the movement to one's own enjoyment by a claim placing one in attentiveness to the other, to the *Häftling*. Before one's own pleasure could even become an issue, one was already called elsewhere. This decentering of the human psyche, one that will receive more attention in the next two chapters, allows no time for suffering to become masochism. One suffers beyond one's own intentions and personality. Further, what above has been called infectious imagination, the draining of affect, should not be interpreted as a sharing of felt experiences. One does not become united to the other by whose memory one is traumatized. Indeed, the very issue of traumatic impact, of the passing on of an experience before one is conscious of its content, needs nuanced discussion.

Before taking up explicitly with Levinas's philosophical response to the *Shoah*, a response that gives decisive insights into the trauma and quandary of the witness, several issues deserve a provisional discussion. These include:

1. How testimony as a genre of writing not only articulates an ethical relation to those who have suffered but also becomes the last possible gesture of ethical resistance to that suffering.
2. How imagination is drawn beyond its limits in giving witness to these victims.
3. How testimony concerning the victim has both an affective and rational dimension.
4. How the Kantian emphasis upon an absolute ethical responsibility to others, *insofar as it is founded solely upon reason,* collapses within the death world.

In the midst of this analysis, it will also be necessary to fill out the "schema" of aggressive genocide that was begun in the previous chapter. Particular emphasis will be given to how this sort of genocide is in fact aenocide, an attack upon the very structure of human, as well as ethical, temporality through a wiping out of the generations.

The ultimate question to be posed is whether any resistance to the victimization of the *Häftling* can remain absolute. Seemingly aenocide so radically undermines human temporality that the very possibility of ethical resistance is rendered impossible or at least impotent. If the future can be wiped out in the annihilation of generations, if past victimizations are incapable of any true remedy, if harm done to the other is truly transcendent, then nothing one can do here and now makes any difference to what happened there and then. What goodness can be expressed in a witness that must continually affirm its inability to affirm, that must continually find itself in quandary, and whose most articulate response to the victimization of the other must simply leave the other victimized? Only in confronting the philosophical crisis precipitated by this question, can any relevant response to the *Shoah* be articulated.

In moving into the analysis of the issues listed above, one should also consider how the situation of the reader in Levi's prologue, in which one must struggle to inherit the testimony of Levi concerning the *Shoah*, is also paradoxically the situation of Levi. For Levi and the others who give testimony concerning the *Shoah* also inherit the *Shoah*. Insofar as Levi survives and steps beyond the boundaries of Auschwitz, he returns from the death world, the world betrayed, in defiance of its attack upon human autonomy and a human *genos*. Although victimized by the *Shoah*, Levi does not count himself among its ultimate victims: when Levi states "the personages in these pages are not men," he also adds that his friendship with Lorenzo kept him from forgetting "that I myself was a man" (*SA*, 111). He has been to some degree saved from the "uniform internal desolation" (*SA*, 111) characterizing the lives of those who were suffocated by annihilation. Levi's responsibility to witness the *Häftling* arises not from his own anguish but on behalf of those others who were utterly overwhelmed, whose anguish became so extreme that all sensitivity to life vanished.

The struggle to remember the death of other humans *in spite of their annihilation* remains the last possible human act of ethical resistance against their desolation. The witness of the survivor, of the one who resisted annihilation by continuing to live, serves as a fragile and tenuous link with that *genos*, those millions of human beings who simply disappeared, first in the collapse of their autonomy, secondly in the collapse of the generations coming after them. The witness inscribes the written page with the memories of one who survives and whose voice now carries the ephemeral weight of *the Nameless*. This voice is burdened by the shamefulness of the other's extermination, as well as of the failure of all other human beings to prevent this extreme violation. That this witness remains commendable in spite of the crisis it induces is nothing less than miraculous.[2]

Regardless of its miracle, the imagining of annihilation instantiated in this witness should not be confused with traditional genres of commemoration in which the death of single individuals or groups of individuals are recorded and recited for the preservation of their glory and the praise of their sacrifice. The *Häftling* makes the notions of glory and sacrifice themselves irrelevant and troubles any notion of commemoration which celebrates the heroism of dying one's death.[3] The pagan values of the Iliad, in which a fearless confrontation with death becomes the crowning characteristic of an extraordinary life, are no longer applicable in a time of *Shoah*, of unmitigated destruction.[4]

Setting the Scene for Annihilation

Consider the Häftling. In doing so, let us turn to the following passage from Tadeusz Borowski's short story stemming from his own experiences in

Auschwitz, "This Way for the Gas, Ladies and Gentlemen." In it the narrator recounts an incident that occurred as he helped to unload a "transport," in which all women and children were destined for immediate death and in which only the strongest of men were to be picked out for slave labor in the maintenance of the very institution that would eventually exterminate them as well. The narrator, as Borowski also was in actuality, is a non-Jewish political prisoner who is more or less assured of his survival, even as he is confronted by the genocide of Jewish persons during his internment at Auschwitz:

> Here is a woman—she walks quickly, but tries to appear calm. A small child with a pink cherub's face runs after her and, unable to keep up, stretches out his little arms and cries: "Mama! Mama!"
>
> "Pick up your child, woman!"
>
> "It's not mine, sir, not mine!" she shouts hysterically and runs on, covering her face with her hands. She wants to hide, she wants to reach those who will not ride the trucks, those who will go on foot, those who will stay alive. She is young, healthy, good-looking, she wants to live.
>
> But the child runs after her, wailing loudly: "Mama, Mama, don't leave me!"
>
> "It's not mine, not mine, no!"
>
> Andrei, a sailor from Sevastopol, grabs hold of her. His eyes are glassy from vodka and the heat. With one powerful blow he knocks her off her feet, then, as she falls, takes her by the hair and pulls her up again. His face twitches with rage.
>
> "Ah, you bloody Jewess! So you're running from your own child! I'll show you, you whore!" His huge hand chokes her, he lifts her in the air and heaves her on to the truck like a heavy sack of grain.
>
> "Here! And take this with you, bitch!" and he throws the child at her feet.
>
> "Gut gemacht, good work. That's the way to deal with degenerate mothers," says the S.S. man standing at the foot of the truck. "Gut, gut, Russki."
>
> "Shut your mouth," growls Andrei though clenched teeth, and walks away. From under a pile of rags he pulls out a canteen, unscrews the cork, takes a few deep swallows, passes it to me. The strong vodka burns the throat. My head swims, my legs are shaky, again I feel like throwing up. (*TB*, 47)

In this passage, the reader begins to sense the "uniform internal desolation" that characterized Auschwitz, a desolation that in Levi's words included "the evil and insane SS men, the Kapos, the politicals, the criminals, the prominents, great and small, down to the indifferent slave *Häftlinge*" (*SA*, 111). In this scene all levels of the hierarchy appear. One also senses both affective and rational dimensions to this desolation.

Particularly striking in the scene is a tone, *Stimmung*, mood, affect of what has been termed *Rausch*, an infectious and uncanny elation that Friedlander reports was "created by the staggering dimension of the killing, the endless rows of victims."[5] *Rausch* seemingly provides the background, which is to say, the basic orientation of world against which the events figured within the scene transpire. This *Rausch* is in turn "heightened" within the scene by the effects of heat, of drunkenness, of hunger, of pressing work. In the development of the scene bodily impulses play a predominate role—the impulses to be protected, to flee, to murder, to drink, to vomit. The actions portrayed in the scene do not grow out of thoughtful judgments, or even spontaneous decisions, but are driven by overwhelming urges—the rage to annihilate, the fear of being killed, the fear of being abandoned. One acts incessantly without pausing for any question, for any reaction, for any assessment. For this "reason," Andrei angrily dismisses the "*Gut Gemacht*" of the SS officer, who obviously still lives in the delusion that the actions occurring before him make sense, that somewhere in Auschwitz one might ask "Why?" and receive a reasonable answer. In fact, the very supposition that one's question will even be heard as an addressing of one's auditor, that one would simply be listened to, is itself not at all assured.

The dialogue at the center of the scene, in which Andrei challenges the comportment of the woman, presents a brutal but direct confrontation between two worlds described in Levi's command—the world nurturing life beyond Auschwitz and the world betrayed of Auschwitz. In this confrontation one senses a collision both in thought and in feeling. Caught between these two worlds, the narrator, Borowski, functions as a witness who is helpless to save the woman or the child, but whose capability to observe and so to remember them leaves him in a state of nausea and vertigo. This feeling counters and resists the overwhelming sense of *Rausch* otherwise at play in the scene. One finds in Borowski's bodily, affective response, the only overt ethical sentiment left in the entire world surrounding him.

But the *Rausch* also haunts the reader at another level, for it is not only presented as the determining attunement of the death world but supplies at least one aspect of the tone for the narrator recounting the scene. Borowski who vomits, who becomes sickened at the sight of child and mother being summarily consigned to death, also recounts the scene in a narrative voice suffused with elation, with carnivalesque bacchanalia. The scene in effect has a doubled narration. There is the "I" who speaks directly of his experiences. He is overwhelmed, barely able to function, dizzy with nausea. But there is also another narrator, one whose rhythms and vocabulary are caught up subversively in the very *Rausch* he would resist by his testimony. This second narrator, one who has the time to construct a narrative, to order and to interpret his experiences, could only be introduced after the event.

In being so constructed, the scene brings the reader into an affinity with two conflicting modes of feeling. One may be horrified by the feelings of all the participants, especially those of Andrei, the mother, and the SS officer, but when one turns to the narrator for the assurance of another perspective, a safer viewpoint, the narrator is for the most part caught up in a species of sarcasm, a sort of mimetic *Mitmachung*, collaboration, in which the elation of annihilation spills over into an elation of description. The proliferation of exclamation points in the dialogue is but one indication of this slippage.

As a result, one is sickened by a certain playfulness, a "devil-may-care" attitude that must be adopted if the very quality of *Rausch*, as it was played out in Auschwitz is to register in one's own imagining. But at the very same moment that this affect is registered, one is also given the counterweight of nausea, of a collapsed moral outrage. The scene would both outrage the reader and contaminate her or him with that very feeling against which the outrage is expressed. Thus, the narrator mimics the *Rausch* in order to speak against it. He adopts the tone of *Rausch* in order to bring it into *Widerruf*, a repudiation. This trope will be discussed in more detail in chapter 6 in regard to the witness of Paul Celan.

One is obligated to return to the events themselves and the people they concern. In this passage, the reader confronts the memory of an event in which human beings become servile and disappear. The woman and the child struggle for their futures, their existence. Such a struggle in the situation of everyday life, that is, of life outside of the *Shoah*, offers the possibility for heroism, precisely because a future remains even for those who die. But that is not the case in this selection: the Jews of an entire village, "Sosnowiec-Bedzin," will go up in "great columns of smoke." Again one senses in these words the problematic conjunction of nausea and elation. This doubled affect revolves around the realization that after this event, after the unloading of this "transport," not only will people be done away with, but also no one will be left to remember the dead, to accept the gift of their memory, to mourn their loss. In Primo

Levi's words: "We saw our women and children leave into nothingness" (*SA*, 49). Borowski's sketch gives the instance of one such passage into nothingness.

One must open up one's imagination to the uncanny, *unheimlich* dimensions of this nothingness, if the situation of Andrei, the nameless woman and the narrator loosely identified with Borowski are to be appreciated. The horror of this nothingness is not simply that this particular woman and the child who follows her are to be loaded into a truck, gassed, and then burned until they are nothing but powdery ash. This transformation of flesh into waste, as powerfully unsettling as it is and demanding of further attention, does not address the full extent of the violence at play in Auschwitz. One must also consider that this woman and child are to be given over to oblivion, to utter, implacable forgetfulness. An entire village is to be destroyed. No one remains to mourn, to repeat the life's story of those who have died, to make some sense, some use of who the dead had been and what they had done. The woman and child, as they move into the nothingness of Auschwitz, are utterly without temporal weight. Their future has collapsed and they walk into its disappearance.[6]

The Collapse of Ends in the Collapse of the Future

So far the analysis has concentrated upon the affective dimensions of the scene's construction. The implications of these dimensions will be worked out in fuller detail in the following chapters. In turning to Levinas's thought, one will consider how the command to respond to the victimization of the other is already at work in the heart of one's affect, one's sensitivity to the other's sensitivity. The present chapter will concentrate, on the other hand, on the collapse of reason as it is played out within this scene. For the very attempt of the woman to act in Auschwitz in terms of a rationally determined outcome only implicates her more deeply in quandary. Even as the woman senses danger, she fails to recognize the extremity of her situation. She wagers that there is yet the chance of survival, if only she can rid herself of this child. Further, the reader, safely situated outside the gates of Auschwitz, is tempted to condemn her wager, to judge her as cowardly and immoral. From a reasonable point of view, the reader would suggest that the woman embodies the failure to respond heroically or ethically. But what if one were to give up one's normal presumptions, as Levi commands in his prologue, in order to imagine the situation of this woman within this death world not only in its emotional but also rational significance?

The judgment of Andrei reinforces the tendency to see the tone of Borowski's exposition as one of moral condemnation of the woman—she ignores a child's plea for help (whether he is actually her child is never established) and suffers punishment for her lapse in responsibility. Certainly a semblance of reason is at work in Andrei's reaction to her behavior. He disapproves of the woman's disloyalty to a child and then judges it before others to be morally outrageous. Certainly the fleeing of another who is threatened with death in order to save one's own life at least raises the question of one's acting in a self-contradictory fashion. Subversively infected with the *Rausch* at play in this scene, the reader may at first even feel some hint of a disturbed sympathy for Andrei's judgment. But the obscene irony of Andrei's response to the woman is that it is meted out by one whose very work involves her moral and empirical annihilation and whose judgment, along with its brutal punishment, is itself outrageous. The very activity of judgment can only appear within the scene in the trope of *widerruf*, of repudiation. Judgment judges in order to be judged an inversion of judgment.

Caught in this narrative trap, the reader is forced to turn back on the line of narration in order to reason out more carefully for her or himself the actual situation of the woman as she abandons the child. In doing so, the reader is already implicitly admonished from assuming too quickly that the actions of the woman are so obviously to be condemned. Like Levi, Borowski demands that the reader overcome her or his aversion to imagining in its full implications the plight of the *Häftling*. The very construction of the scene becomes a command to attentiveness, to looking again, to considering the situation of those to be annihilated in a manner that no longer assumes a confidence in normal truths, in the warmth and safety of a life world. One must reason yet again in order to find whether reason itself can make sense of this situation.

Consider this woman, this newly arrived Häftling. She attempts, although inconsistently, selfishly and perhaps immorally, to willfully assert the worth of her own life. In doing so, she imagines a possibility left upon which to build a future—the mere fact of her survival. Perhaps this is not praiseworthy rational behavior. Perhaps her actions may even end up in undermining her own rationality, as a Kantian would indeed argue, but her attempt to avoid the child is nevertheless done for a reason. She acts *as if* she can make decisions about how she will act based on the outcomes of those actions. But the utter unwillingness of the camp structure to see this woman as the embodiment of a set of distinct and differing possibilities renders futile all her actions, even her attempt to act immorally. Her only remaining possibility is a submission to annihilation—either she will be disposed of or she will dispose of others until she is incapable of fulfilling her quota of work. She has become for the time being a mere commodity, a unit of possibility that is entirely at the disposal of those who are in control of the camp. Ultimately, she is even less than a commodity, since the very work of the camp is to process her *as if* she and her child were refuse.

Normally, immoral, as well as moral judgments are made in situations in which a future remains to be lived—decisions have a meaning because what is decided *will affect* some entity *in the future* who survives at least long enough to bear the effects of that decision. Those who live beyond one's own choice, who benefit or are harmed by what is chosen, are an essential element in the *moral* significance of one's decision. For if one decides to harm someone who one knows will already have been dead by the time that harm could be registered, then one would be hard put to argue this is an immoral decision. In the case of an impossible harm, the decision to harm functions as the fantasy of a decision—one considers doing something, one wishes one could have done something, but one never really will have accomplished this something. One finds one's actions are without any temporal weight, without real, empirical possibility.

Within the confines of Auschwitz the possibility of the inmates' harming one another wavered before the more encompassing harm of annihilation that was intended for them universally. Entering the death world as a prisoner entailed entering an entire society bent on depriving one not only of one's own future but also of all the futures of all the other persons with whom one shared that society. Of course, even the notion that one was to share a society with others was belied by the incessant attack upon one's own and one's fellow prisoners' autonomy. Thus, what might have been morally outrageous in other situations became merely morally pathetic here. The woman "wanted to live." But wanting to live in Auschwitz, when one was a Jewish *Häftling*, was rendered a delusion—the only possibility provided for within the society of that camp was annihilation. It was planned to be only a matter of how and when. Andrei corrected the woman's delusion brutally and efficiently. He, even more than the S.S. officer who praised his actions, understood the essential work of Auschwitz. Here, there was to be no possibility of heroism, or even of a reasonable response—ultimately there was to be no possibility whatsoever.

One is tempted to argue that no matter what the woman decides, both the child and his mother have already been in effect annihilated. Borowski, in the guise of the Kapo bystander, witnesses a collapse of the possibility to act morally that occurred the moment the inmate stepped into the camps. In the wake of this collapse, the bystander feels the urge to vomit, overwhelmed by the obscenity of what he too, as another "unwilling" participant in the machinery of destruction, helps to accomplish.

A Kantian Objection

Yet the desire to affirm a principled albeit tragic heroism persists. What if the woman had turned to face the child, comforted him, and accompanied him into his death? Would this not have been a gesture of faith in and love of this particular being, a recognition of his innate worth, an action that would in itself be sufficiently moral? What need does one have of a future, of "temporal weight," in order to justify such moral decisions? Moral actions ought to be in themselves good. In Kantian language, although another may seek to deny my autonomy, this does not require my own self-capitulation. I can still act according to an imperative demanding that one act out of *respect* for my own autonomy and the autonomy of others, rather than submit to the impulse of a cause external to the principle of my autonomy. In Kantian terms the heteronomous forces and drives of the sensual world cannot be used to justify the denial of human autonomy. To the contrary, respect invokes the *transcendence* of human freedom—the claim to human autonomy remains, whether the forces of nature and culture recognize it or not. Human action remains to be praised or blamed in regard to a standard exceeding the immediate and merely personal needs and inclinations of human beings.

Kant's claim for the inviolability of human autonomy announces an absolute resistance on the part of the individual to any action that would use another person as a means rather than as an end in her or himself. The node of this resistance is found in the claim that each human being possesses a will that is free, which is to say, is a law unto itself. Being a law unto itself, the will is incapable of belonging to another, its very structure transcending the attempt to subjugate it to external forces. But this quality of being a law unto itself does not mean that the free will assigns itself whichever action might strike it as preferable in a given situation. To act in such a manner would make the will a victim of whatever impulse or need happened to be the strongest at that particular moment. Instead, a free will is autonomous (giving itself its own law) only insofar as it gives *reasons* for the way in which it acts. In such reasons resides the resistance of the will to the sway of immediate and merely arbitrary impulses.

The freedom of the will lies in the obligation of the will to its own reasons for acting. If reason were to decide one thing and the will were to do another, then the will would not be acting freely but only arbitrarily or under external compulsion. Further, the will could not be its own law, if reason itself were without internal consistency. Thus, the principle of noncontradiction, of logical compatibility, underlies human freedom's imperative to act as a law unto itself, that is, to act "according to no other maxim than that which can at the same time have itself as a universal law for its object."[7] It is precisely the rationality of the law which demands its universality, that is, that none of its applications be self-contradictory. *For Kant, the principle of autonomy is precisely the experience of one's own freedom as being the demand for its own logical self-consistency.* Such a demand for self-consistency prohibits the will from treating another will as if it were not free. The autonomy of the will utterly transcends the drives and inclinations of individuals or groups and allows human freedom a resistance against all attempts to control it from without or to use it against itself. This resistance announces itself in the feeling of moral obligation.

Given this line of analysis and given the moral intuition that the autonomy of another human being should be implicitly respected, one is tempted to conclude that the woman who abandons the young child to her Nazi tormentors acted immorally. But if this is so, what then would be the maxim under which the woman should have acted? If her action is to be judged blameworthy, then seemingly there must have been a praiseworthy alternative.

The child, insofar as he is not yet able to act with sufficient freedom, is incapable of fulfilling all those duties toward his own being which that being's dignity requires. Thus, being without a guardian puts the child in danger of acting in a way that would destroy his own autonomy (or the autonomy of others). His desire for protection is morally justifiable. The woman is obligated to respond to the child's need for protection (even if the child did not request it!), since to deny it would posit a universal law that would have denied the woman her own right to the same protection when she was a child.

Such would be the analysis of the child's situation, if the child had been found alone on a city street or in a "normal" civilian internment camp. But the child of this story has been brought into Auschwitz, where he is scheduled to be annihilated. He has been delivered into the hands of adult powers, whose "guardianship" consists in the complete destruction of the child's autonomy, as well as of his entire *genos*, including his mother. In this situation is given that perversion of normal human values, that overturning of the world of safety and warm food, that Saul Friedlander has termed the deepest perversion, the most radical form of evil constituted within the camps (*MHE*, 105).

As a result, it could be argued that the woman's real responsibility to the child is not to save his life, but to help him to die with as much dignity as can be salvaged. Since the cruelty of murder, not to mention mass murder, would be so overwhelming to the mind of a child, the respect of his autonomy would obligate his guardian to protect him, as much as possible, from succumbing to the uncanny violence of the death world in which he finds himself. Unfortunately, the issue here is not *whether* the child will die but *how* he will die. The maxim by which the woman is obligated demands that she act in such a manner that the integrity of the child's death is preserved. Such a maxim motivated many Jewish parents to enter into the camps hovering over their children, protecting them at every turn, praying with them as they were led away to die. In her own testimony, Frieda Aaron records how her mother and sister traded places with two other women in order to accompany Frieda on a train that seemed destined for a gas chamber rather than another camp.[8] Here certainly is an exemplar of Kantian altruism.

While one ought to praise this decision, one must also consider the fate of those two other women. One chose to be with one's own children, and, precisely because of one's good intentions, others who were *also* innocent were annihilated. As this example demonstrates, the goodness of any ethical choice within the confines of Auschwitz was undermined by the very form of life that the camp imposed upon all its inmates, whether they were *Häftlinge* or *Kommandanten*. No matter what one chose, indefensible outcomes ensued. Hannah Arendt has observed:

> Totalitarian terror achieved its most terrible triumph when it succeeded in cutting the moral person off from the individualist escape and in making the decisions of conscience absolutely questionable and equivocal. . . . Through the creation of conditions under which conscience ceases to be adequate and to do good becomes utterly impossible, the consciously organized complicity of all men in the crimes of totalitarian regimes is extended to the victims and thus made really total. The SS implicated concentration camp inmates—criminals, politicals, Jews—in their crimes by making them responsible for a large part of the administration, thus confronting them with the hopeless dilemma whether to send their friends to their death, or to help murder other men who happened to be strangers, and forcing them, in any event to behave like murderers . . . the distinguishing line between persecutor and persecuted, between the murderer and his victim, is constantly blurred.[9]

Exactly this sort of blurring is evident in the situation where Borowski's narrator must serve both as witness and perpetrator. He has the urge to vomit in reaction to the violence inflicted on the incoming *Häftlinge*, even as he has enlisted himself in helping out their victimizers in order to secure a pair of boots for his own survival. In Levi's account of Kuhn who gives thanks for his own survival, even as Beppo is sent to his annihilation, is found yet another example.

To survive Auschwitz one must become indifferent to the victimization of all the others. Or as Levi put it, "The Law of the Lager said: "eat your own bread, and if you can, that of your neighbor" (*SA*, 145). To discuss the ethical situation of the camp as if it consisted in various individuals struggling to act in a praiseworthy manner ignores the most critical ethical dimension of annihilation as a human praxis. Auschwitz itself was an assault upon the very fabric of human autonomy and its integrity. The machinery of death often left no possibility for a moral decision in which the autonomy of someone else was not also destroyed. In this context, Langer has spoken of how "maternity infected by atrocity" becomes one of the most telling paradigms of oral testimony concerning the camps.[10]

Further, in the death world of Auschwitz the strength of compulsion, of "external influence" was so magnified that individual human beings lost the possibility to act with the presence of mind that an appeal to the categorical imperative requires. Thus, not only was one denied the possibility of a moral outcome to one's decisions, but also the very capability for decision itself was attacked. Also ambiguous in Borowski's story is whether the young woman who refuses to care for the child had not already been rendered incapable of ethical decisions during her long transport to the gas chambers and crematoria.

Genocide

The Collapse of Kantian Rationality

One could still argue that this scenario only shows the shortcomings of any consequentialist notion of ethics. Langer in his discussion of this issue refers in turn to Zygmut Bauman, who argues that "the lesson of the Holocaust is the facility with which most people, put into a situation that does not contain a good choice . . . argue themselves away from the issue of moral duty . . . adopting instead the precepts of rational interest and self-preservation."[11] Because Frieda Aaron's mother was committed to the goodness of an action regardless of its outcome, she becomes morally praiseworthy in a manner that the mother in Borowski's story was not. One cannot abandon one's responsibilities to one's family simply because one faces extreme consequences.

But the woman in Borowski's text is also under the obligation to protect her own life—a life that is in as much mortal danger as that of the boy's. One could argue that the woman judges the situation of the boy to be hopeless but that her own survival, as well as the survival of yet other persons, is still a possibility to be fought for. (Of course, this assessment turns out to be wrong, since all the women and children of this transport are evidently to be gassed.) In this case, would not her duty be to fight for the survival of those who truly might survive, to resist extermination in her insistence that at least one person of the two would not be transformed into ashes?

The answer to this question is not clear. It may be, in fact, impossible to answer. For even if one cannot justify abandoning one's children by considering it as a universal maxim of nature, neither can one justify a commitment to die with one's children, if this too were to become universally necessary. *If all beings chose to die simultaneously with all other beings, then none would be left to populate the very nature whose laws must be universal.* One has a moral duty to survive in order to mother and father the succeeding generations.[12] Yet one also has a duty to die in defense of the autonomy of the generation one has already fathered and mothered.[13]

The dilemma is terrible and impossible: if one survives, one aids the machinery of annihilation; if one dies, one succumbs to it. In both cases, the maxim under which one acts defies the universalization Kant would demand of it. What must be given broader consideration at this moment in the analysis of Borowski's testimony is the nature of what has been termed aggressive genocide in the previous chapter. For beyond the attack upon individual autonomy in the camps was an assault upon an entire *genos*. This second assault provided the context whereby the first found its ultimate significance. The death camps were not simply instituted to torture individual beings, to render them servile, and, in so doing, to become a sort of demonstration of how quickly one could undermine the humanity of other persons. The camps were instituted in the first place in order to do away with a people altogether.[14] Not only would they disappear, but all those who might mourn them, who might respond to their death by inheriting it, would also disappear. Without a more detailed consideration of this second level of victimization, the level of what has been provisionally termed aggressive genocide, one has difficulty in determining the significance of what is occurring at the first level, the level of individual autonomy.

Genocide as the Denial of the Other's Face

One should begin this larger analysis by pointing out that the designation of the attempted annihilation by the Nazis of the Jewish people (as well as other peoples including the Roma and Sinta) as "genocide" is already suspicious and in need of much clarification. The problem lies in the manner in which the notion of a *genos* comes to be interpreted in this term as a "race" or genre of human beings. The very notion that a people can be definitively characterized as a *genos*, insofar as this term denotes generic types or categories of human beings, is already too deeply allied with the Nazi cultivation of biologism and racism in a pseudoscience of genetic inheritance.

The Nazi notion of *genos* picks out groups of humans as races or lines who possess allegedly discrete and predictable qualities that are allegedly passed down from generation to generation. This project renders all those who belong to a *genos* as synchronous with all other members. The Nazi then concludes that insofar as one is part of a line of "good" qualities, one deserves to continue to live. If one has "bad" qualities, or is even associated through birth with that line possessing so-called bad qualities, one would become a threat to the next generation and should be eradicated. Thus, Hitler could sermonize: "The discovery of the Jewish virus is one of the greatest revolutions which has been undertaken in the world. The struggle we are waging is of the same kind as in the past century, that of Pasteur and Koch. How many diseases can be traced back to the Jewish virus? We shall regain our health only when we exterminate the Jews."[15]

Given these grounds for the determination of a *genos*, the Nazi claimed to offer the argument that one was under a moral obligation to exterminate Jews in order to protect the viability of the human species, as well as of its surviving members. But the fact that this argument can be made to look even remotely logical demonstrates all too clearly how profoundly askew are the argument's premises. The Kantian response to the Nazi's preoccupation with genres of human beings argues that the humanity of every human being precedes and transcends any particular *genos* to which human beings might belong. *Genoi* provide a particular human being his or her concrete, historical, or biological identity only in the aftermath of an intrinsic and universal human identity. In the Kantian view, the Nazi is guilty of a category error—he or she mistakes those concrete qualities that give the particular or cultural or national identity of human beings with that universal quality that sustains the moral identity of the human.

Put in other words, the Nazi forgets that the other human's capacity to reason makes her or him an example of the law by which reason assigns to itself the burden of giving reasons for its own claims. One cannot mistreat this other without mistreating the very manner in which one's own reason must *address itself*, which is to say, must take seriously the call of its own reason to the giving of its reasons in a reasonable manner. This reduplication of reason—that is, that to reason is to do so reasonably—is not redundant but the very practice of reason. Reason is commanded by its very nature to be reasonable, a quality that it has already been argued Kant then interprets as a call to self-consistency and so to autonomy, freedom, and universality. This call does not involve a truth claim about reason, but involves the very structure whereby reason finds itself reasonable. Without this structure of reduplication, in which reason listens to itself and takes its own giving of a reason in utmost sincerity, the very practice of reason would be arbitrary and a nonarbitrary truth claim could never be made.

Given this analysis, one is brought to conclude that not only the *cidere* of genocide, the murdering of others, but also the *genos* of genocide, at least insofar as this term involves the reduction of humans to a set of objective qualities or categories, is morally objectionable. *Genocide* in actuality denotes a doubled action: one murders in the flesh what one has already rendered in one's thought as morally inconsiderable. Our moral relationships to other human beings should not in the first instance be based upon how they fit into various categories that provide the qualities by which human moral considerability can in turn be measured. The very raising of the issue of a kind of human, it would seem, is incompatible with attending to the moral considerability of the human.

Yet the Kantian reading of this Nazi surreptitiousness before the other ends up claiming that human beings in their moral considerability are after all a sort of *genos*, although one that exceeds the normal boundaries of a genre defined through a quality or substrate that one might actually perceive or measure. Kant concludes a human cannot know "himself" definitively as a reasoning creature but is obligated to treat "himself" and "his" fellow humans *as if "he" was and they were reasoning creatures.*[16] The soul of the human transcends determination within a world of spatial and temporal objects known through the mediation of the senses. One cannot truly know the human being as a kind, but one is called upon by the very use of one's reason to treat the other *as if* one knew her or him as another sort of kind, as the kind that reasons: "And when he thinks of himself as intelligence endowed with a will and consequently with causality, he puts himself into relation with determining grounds *of a kind* altogether different from *the kind* when he perceives himself as a phenomenon in the world of sense (as he really is also) and subjects his causality to external determination according to laws of nature" (57, italics mine). This claim is true for the other as much as it is for me.

In his own criticism of the Nazi "moralist," Berel Lang points out that the utilitarian argument of the Nazi is in actuality a pose underneath of which one finds an enduring intention on the part of the Nazi to deny "any semblance of humanity or personhood to members of the group singled out."[17] Lang implies that what needs attention is not the substance of the Nazi's claim, not his or her argument that the other is a *genos* that is defective, but the Nazi's "pose" that this argument is given in a sincere tone of address. The Nazi addresses the other surreptitiously, which is to say, he or she addresses the other without acknowledging the true nature of her or his address. Hearkening to Kant's emphasis upon rational autonomy, Lang's assessment of the Nazi tone of nonaddress, of this denial of the other, focuses on how it ultimately attacks the other by undoing her or his "agency and self-determination," as well his or her capacities for "continuing identity and character" and "intersubjective rationality or power of discourse."

But in confronting the victim, one must consider that the acuity of one's attentiveness to the other already exceeds that acuity found in an attentiveness to his or her autonomy. For autonomy itself is expressed by a human face enmeshed in its flesh and so vulnerable to my attack upon it. As Levi insists, one is called upon to witness not the moment of the *Häftling's* resistance of force with force, in which his or her autonomy is matched against the torturer's resolve to undermine it, but the very moment of the crumbling of the *Häftling's* autonomy, of his or her submission to a suffering that exceeds the parameters of ordinary existence. In this scene of dehumanized suffering, the issue of *genos* is given an even more radical formulation than in Kant: the claim of the other human upon me transcends its *genos* beyond any determination that is rational. Autonomy is not enough to save human dignity—in fact the very vulnerability of the other's autonomy to the attack of the torturer is revealed as a scandal or embarrassment to reason.[18]

Might one not add in the tone of Levinas that in addition to the Nazi attack upon the autonomy of the other human being, an autonomy founded upon the presumed (although in a presumption that is commanded by the very force of one's being a moral being) *capacity* of the other to reason, lies the very face of the other and the *vulnerability* to suffering that this face expresses? And in facing that face who suffers does it not come to one's mind that the very gesture of insisting that one respect the other as an *example* of the autonomy of reason ignores the very urgency of obligation expressed in the other's face? For in that face, one confronts a singularity, a specificity beyond a genre or type or kind, even beyond that other kind of kind whom Kant would specify as a reasoning entity. In facing the other, one is not only called upon by one's *own* reason to give reasons to which one must then listen but also is called into an unavoidable responsibility for *another*'s suffering for which no reason, no justification, could ever be given. *In being called to this responsibility, the very urgency of moral obligation is rendered as more than rational and as exceeding any measure or call to self-consistency.*

In analyzing what goes wrong with the Nazi notion of *genos*, one should not fall into the trap of attempting to come up with a better definition, a better category, by which the human *genos* or its diverse *genoi* might be determined. Rather, one should pay attention to how the very squabble over "correct" categories diverts one's attention from the transcendent dimensions of the other's claim upon the Nazi. What is crucial about the Nazi argument for a good *genos* is that it covers over a hard-heartedness, a refusal to be addressed by the other, that is at the core of the Nazi attitude toward the other. Not the substance of the argument that is given by the Nazi *but rather its tone* demands the most discerning critique! The Nazi's very argument surreptitiously covers over what is actually at issue, namely, that the other is to be accorded respect according to a command the Nazi in fact has no means of avoiding. What the Nazi attack upon the other in genocide reveals is a virulence of tone that would ignore the other not simply as an example of one's own rational autonomy but more importantly as a node of suffering before whom one is, in Levinasian terms, utterly incapable of being capable. In the tone of the Nazi's indifference to the other's suffering, one hears the resonance of a struggle with the other that is not explicable simply in terms of rationally constructed moral obligations. The ferocity of the Nazi attack upon the other stems from a transcendent claim that interrupts even the giving of one's reasons. Kant's ear, insofar as it is preoccupied with a tone that is universal and imbued with a reason that provides its own measure, cannot attend to the exact nuance, the toning of this other tone, in which the very measure of measure is disrupted.[19]

But one needs perhaps to go further in criticizing Kant's moral rationalism. A careful attending to the tone of the Nazi should utterly disrupt one's expectation that one approaches the other morally *only after* one was called upon to demonstrate for one's own satisfaction the other's moral considerability by means of an argument. This lapse in urgency is what makes the very issue of a human *genos*, as it is constructed by the Nazi, so disturbing in the moral context. The very fact that the Nazi would consider that there might be any argument allowing her or him to disregard the address of other human kinds already shows the Nazi to be utterly at odds with any acuity of attentiveness to that human other. As the phenomenological account of Levi's prologue has already suggested in the previous chapter, one does not have the leisure in which to demonstrate whether one is morally obligated to another. One must begin instead with the premise that simply to be addressed by the other already demands a respect that no derivation of responsibility, no leisurely consideration of the reasonableness of the moral imperative, could ever provide. Put in more positive terms, the command to respect the other transcends any ground that can be given for that command by means of a *capacity* that would involve being human, even if that capacity be a transcendental or transcendent notion of reason. The modes by which we might define categories of human beings or even the category of humanity itself comes only in the wake of an ethical responsibility to have already been addressed by the face of the other.

Thus, beyond Lang's list of the powers and capacities of the individual human to be denied by the Nazi lies the vulnerability of the other's face, a passivity that nonetheless disarms my very gesture of murder, of attack, of appropriation toward the other. As Levinas puts it: "What characterizes violent action, what characterizes tyranny, is that one does not face what the action is being applied to. To put it more precisely: it is that *one does not see the face in the other, one sees the other's freedom as a force, savage; one identifies the absolute character of the other with his force*" (FC, 19 [italics mine]). In the argument being developed here, the other is approached as a victim the moment his or her freedom is even treated as a power or capability arrayed against one's own power. In the scene of power arrayed against power, one then does one's best to manipulate the other's freedom, to dominate it and take it for one's own. But this willful interpretation denies the transcendent dimension of the other's freedom—that the other's freedom is always already an expression, which is to say, an address of one's own freedom and that this address already requires that one has listened attentively to the other even in order to counter his or her ideas or to respond to her or his initiatives. Before any play of power would have been possible, the other had already called one to an interminable reign of peace, to an attentiveness that cannot be undone. Intent upon countering what in principle cannot be countered, the victimizer wilfully creates a delusional scene in which the other's discourse loses its face, and in losing its face, the vulnerability of the other's reason to my own violence is no longer attended to.

One can argue that the victimizer attacks not only the capabilities of the victim but also the victim's very suffering. This phrasing may sound odd, since the victim can only be said to be suffering after he or she has already been attacked by the perpetrator. What sense does it make then to say that the victim's suffering is also attacked? But as Lyotard makes clear in his reflections on victimization in his *The Differend*, what makes the victim a victim is not only that she or he has sustained a damage but that the suffering of this damage renders her or him incapable of registering its harm.[20] The victim's suffering is used doubly by the perpetrator—once to harm the victim and then to overwhelm his or her capacity to register upon the perpetrator or anyone else that this harm actually matters. In the genocidal attitude, one looks upon the other *as if* he or she were without a face, which is to say, *as if* one had never even been called before or called out or called to by her or him.[21] Through discounting the *address* of this other, his or her *suffering* can then be systematically denied and ignored. Or even worse, the other's *suffering* can become a source of ridicule and self-justification for the perpetrator. For in the victim's *suffering* he or she is betrayed by his or her very body. In being tortured, the victim becomes so obsessed by her or his own needs that rationality and its power for discourse collapses. After having rendered the human being a *Häftling*, the Nazi can point to her or him, as Andrei does in the passage from Borowski, for the confirmation that this is what the other deserved to become. In this manner, the dehumanization of the other provides its own delusional justification for its attack upon the other.

The question of moral considerability lies not merely in whether the other is rational or capable of discourse. One must admit that one *is also addressed* by this discourse—that the other's expression breaks open my own attempt to elaborate a series of premises that would lead to a conclusion that justifies the other's position regardless of what the other has to say. The anonymity of a universal discourse operating entirely within the third person is forever broken up and open by the mere fact that this reason both addresses and is addressed by an other who is vulnerable. One must also consider that one will still be addressed even when the power or capability of rational discourse collapses in the suffering of the tortured subject. As the discussion in the next chapter details, the suffering of the other addresses one regardless of how rational or self-consciously insightful that other is about her or his suffering. Underlying consciousness is a prior passivity or sensitivity that the torturer seeks to exploit. As Levinas puts it: "War is ambush" (FC, 19). But this very vulnerability of the other to my torture, as Levinas argues again and again, reveals a resistance rather than a succumbing to my violence. The address initiated in the other's suffering is not exclusively dependent upon a *capability* for discourse, since the very collapse of that capability is what torture would effect. Not rationality as a force *but as a vulnerability* is revealed to be that modality by which the other is most fundamentally revealed to me as commanding my responsibility.

While the discussion here agrees with Lang's assessment of duplicity in the manner in which the Nazi approached the *Häftling*, one must go on to argue that attending to the rationality of the victim as a *capability or power* for discourse does not fully appreciate what is at stake in the victim's becoming a victim. In assigning Jews to a *genos*, the Nazis treated their victims in such a manner that they no longer would matter, *not only in regard to their rationality but also in regard to their suffering*. No matter what his or her victims might say, the Nazi had already conspired not to have heard that saying. The Nazi conspired both with himself and his fellows to forget that the opposition of the other's face to my potential violence "is prior to my freedom" (FC, 19). One must admit that one has already been called to turn toward the other precisely in order to hear her or his discourse, or to appreciate his or her rationality. Precisely this conversion, this turning toward the other to whom one was already called to turn, is repeatedly and covertly undermined by the Nazi notion of "racial cleansing," as well as its notion of *genos*.

Genos as the Generations

But *genos* can be given an entirely different meaning. For *genos* also suggests an ongoing series of ethical relationships that come about through *inheriting* one's type or culture, either through being born into it or through acculturation, through education or through conversion. Here, diachrony rather than synchrony is more fundamental to the characterization of the notion of *genos*. To be in a *genos* is to be responsible to a people, a *Geschlecht*, which is to say, to be a member of that group in which relationships are articulated by means of an engendering and nurturing through time, the mothering and fathering of succeeding generations. Because each generation dies, the next generation takes up with the lives of the preceding generation in a spirit of commemoration and reverence, as well as criticism and shame. One passes on one's wisdom, memory and traditions, even as one passes away. Further, the very existence of wisdom, memory and tradition in oneself is itself an inheritance one has received from those who have lived before one's own life.

A human *genos* can be seen as a wave of memory, insight, and expectation coursing through time, a wave that lifts up and sustains the individuals of each succeeding generation, even as those individuals make their own particular contributions to or modifications of that wave. In some cases, individuals even strike out into the desert and leave a particular line of birth and death behind. Abraham's departure from Haran, a sundering of roots that began the Jewish tradition, is a perfect example of this possibility. Further, one can and does belong to multiple *genoi*. One can be born and enculturated within a line of farmers, yet also be a Jew, as well as a German, and perhaps be educated as a scientist or poet. In the Bukovina of the poet Paul Celan, for instance, one found a rich intermixing of German, Hebrew, Russian, and Rumanian cultures. Not only intermarriage but also "intereducation" and "interlingualism" were outstanding features of this cultural locality. One's body carried and responded to multiple waves of time, of generations begetting generations.

This sense of *genos* is diachronic even as it is polyvocative. One is involved in several *genoi* at once, yet each *genos* is itself articulated as a crossing-over, a transgressing transitively, a *diachronos*, moving from one time to another.[22] One's forebearers, whether they be can characterized in bodily or figurative terms, address one from across a temporal differentiation in which is articulated the forebearers' deaths, as well as one's own birth. Situated in the difference between death and birth, one is addressed by the lives one inherits. These lives inspire one, literally, breathe into one one's own possibility for existence. Yet the existence one receives in this inspiration does not belong to one's forebearers, precisely because the very terms of its inspiration is a transitive crossing-over that generates a new existence characterized in terms of a new responsibility.

When thinking of temporal succession in terms of a difference between generations, one no longer can characterize time as the simple lining up of one moment after another. Nor can one think of time à la Neo-Platonism as the integration of several different temporal dimensions (e.g., past, present, and future) into a unified field. In the elaboration of *Geschlecht*, time is articulated as a differentiation across which and by means of which responsibilities are born. Precisely because one is not one's forebearers, one experiences one's time as a gift, the proffering of one's own existence from out of the bodies and lives of the beings who preceded one. One in turn offers this gift to those who come after one. Time is in this offering the articulation of a generosity beyond primordiality. No longer tied to an ultimate time at the beginning of time, the very crossing-over of time both remembers and renews yet other crossing-overs, other transitivities. *Geschlecht* harkens not to a *first* time but to the renewal of time through its alteration. As a *genos*, one does not live in one's own time, as if time were a habitation, a nesting together of moments and memories for the sake of dwelling securely within one's own place. But one does live time as an address across generations, as a responsibility to carry on the voices of those who have existed by the manner in which one responds to them. And even as one responds, one also addresses those voices who come after one, voices who arise out of one's own flesh (be it bodily or figuratively) only to articulate a time utterly beyond one's own death. In this manner, one lives a time in which one's death is given a future, although a future that is to be thought of in terms of the survival of one's responsibility rather than the survival of one's discrete existence.

Aenocide

Given this second analysis of *genos*, one can begin to see how the Nazi attack upon human types was in fact an attack upon human temporality. Rather than genocide, one might term the Nazi policy of annihilation an *aenocide*.[23] For the Nazis wished nothing less than to treat time as if it were a resource, a field of possibilities standing before one over which one had utter control. As Arendt puts it, for the totalitarian *Führer* not only is everything permitted but ultimately "everything is possible" *(OT*, 440).[24] All differentiation in time, as it had been marked out by generation after generation, was to be leveled. Only the leader's will and the leader's being would remain to populate this time.[25] In this vein of thought, the emergence of a superrace that utterly conformed to the leader's vision of a healthy human species is revealed not to be for the good of those individuals constituting its generations but for the accomplishment of the *Führer's* will.

In the *Führer's* vision of time no room is left for the ongoing generation and generations of responsibility. Human temporality itself would collapse into a "final solution," an apocalyptic moment in which the ongoing bearing and birthing of differentiation and heterogeneity that so disturbed the Nazi consciousness would simply end. Hitler spoke of a "Thousand Year Reich" and meant this literally. One's empire was time itself—the next thousand years and inevitably all the thousands of years after that. Rather than finding himself submitted to the inevitable rupture of his own time, of a fathering leading to new and diverse generations, Hitler insisted that all generations coming both before and after him were his own peculiar property. He alone could guarantee their health and he alone would provide them with their significance. For this reason he was so insistent at the war's end that the entire German nation be destroyed if his own Reich could not survive intact.[26] In this treatment of his own people, Hitler becomes the exemplar of what Levinas argues is the deciding characteristic of violence: "Violent action does not consist in being in a relationship with the other; it is in fact an action where one is as though one were alone" (FC, 18).

Even worse than the extinction of the human race through a cosmological cataclysm would be the annihilation of the *aeons*, of the crossing-overs in time of the responsibility of one generation to and for another. This latter crossing-out of time occurs only through the efforts of human beings themselves. Only humans can conspire to repress, to destroy the future of a human *genos as a genos*. In doing so, humans show the reprehensible capacity to turn their history, their remembrance of time across the aeons, the generations, into a sort of narcissistic mirror. One eliminates all the strangers, all the disruptions of one's own vision, so that one's history only articulates one's own concerns, one's own needs. One writes the past and the future as a mode of colonization. All the other times are resources for one's own.

In the wake of a cosmological cataclysm, nature in its own way might remember humans, even after we have disappeared. As we remember the dinosaurs through their fossils, as well as through the very manner in which our bodies carry on the structures of their previous bodies, so too might and probably will future generations far removed from our own time remember our human species. Nothing compelling suggests that humans as a species have anything more than a finite time allotted to them on the planet earth and within the universe. One might even develop the notion that the very crossing-over of aeons is not confined a passing from one human generation to another, but can be expanded to a multidimensional crossing-over of species into species, of kingdom into kingdom, of matter into life. All these diachronies could be as well articulations of responsibility.

A human conspiracy to forget the generations is implacable. The Nazis' forgetfulness of the Jews involved not only an initial gesture of looking away, of refusing to honor the dignity of each human being as he or she stood before one. One did not merely transform a human being into Levi's *Häftling*, a being of crushed autonomy. One also sent this being to the "*schlechte Seite*," to annihilation. In the wake of this annihilation, all trace of the other's death within human memory was to disappear. Not only the other but the generations coming after her or him would have disappeared. In the future the perpetrators and their descendants would have comported themselves *as if* the *Häftling* had never existed. That this comportment is itself a delusion, that it rests on an interpretation of time that is utterly undercut by the very fecundity and diachronicity of one generation succeeding another, does not keep the perpetrator from working out a historical project in which history itself is imploded, in which generations succumb to the *force majeure* of empirical annihilation. One's descendants will already have been responsible for the disappearance of these generations,[27] but they will not know it. Nazis sought to undermine the transcendent dimension of time, of its articulation as a passing across of responsibility, by simply destroying so many lives and so many sites in which those lives were sustained that a historical accounting for that event becomes fragmentary and garbled, if not impossible.

Maternity Infected by Atrocity

In returning to Borowski's account, one now brings three axes of analysis by means of which the ethical context for the mother's betrayal of a child is to be more fully elaborated. One must consider within the confines of Auschwitz: (a) how the attack on one's physical well-being affected moral judgment; (b) how any possible good was always contaminated by morally unacceptable consequences; and (c) how aenocide, the murdering of generations, became the historical background against which any individual act of goodness within the camps articulated its significance.[28] In following out these three axes, one finds that they interact with one another in their effects. For example, the attack upon the Jewish *genos* in aenocide ultimately debilitated the vitality of those who were allowed to live in the death camps. One could not look upon the collapse of the future without finding one traumatized in every aspect of one's existence. In bringing these axes of analysis into consideration, one is submitting to Levi's command to step outside of one's everyday world, a world in which one's viability as a human being and as a member of a human *genos* is assured. One must imagine the *Häftling*, which in this case requires one imagine the situation of a mother "infected by atrocity," a mother who steps out of her everyday existence and into the world betrayed of Auschwitz.

Consider, if it is at all possible, the train ride that the woman and child in Borowski's narrative have already undergone: To call it a train ride is already to use language in a way that disregards the annihilative nature of the project of extermination. This "train ride" has already begun the inevitable destruction of the community of an entire village. Overcrowding and the lack of sanitary facilities mean that children and mothers and fathers sleep upon one another, drenching themselves in their own feces and urine, as the train brings them to the crematoria. The lack of water, hunger, and excessive heat and cold inevitably causes mental instability—hysteria, psychosis, beatings ensue.[29] As

Elie Wiesel remarks of his own experience: "The world was a cattle wagon hermetically sealed" (*N*, 33).

Consider in yet another passage Borowski's account concerning the same "transport" on which the woman and child of the above excerpt arrived:

> The train has been emptied. A thin, pock-marked S.S. man peers inside, shakes his head in disgust and motions to our group, pointing his finger at the door. "*Rein*. Clean it up."
>
> We climb inside. In the corner amid human excrement and abandoned wrist-watches lie squashed, trampled infants, naked little monsters with enormous heads and bloated bellies. We carry them out like chickens, holding several in each hand.
>
> "Don't take them to the trucks, pass them on to the women," says the S.S. man, lighting a cigarette. His cigarette lighter is not working properly; he examines it carefully.
>
> "Take them, for God's sake!" I explode as the women run from me in horror, covering their eyes.
>
> The name of God sounds strangely pointless, since the women and infants will go on the trucks, every one of them, without exception. We all know what this means, and we look at each other with hate and horror.
>
> "What, you don't want to take them?" asks the pockmarked S.S. man with a note of surprise and reproach in his voice, and reaches for his revolver.
>
> "You mustn't shoot, I'll carry them." A tall, grey-haired woman takes the little corpses out of my hands and for an instant gazes straight into my eyes.
>
> "My poor boy," she whispers and smiles at me. Then she walks away, staggering along the path. (*TB*, 40)

What is most striking in this passage is not only that the babies die under terrible conditions, most likely crushed inadvertently in the overcrowded boxcars of the transport, but also that their dead bodies are abandoned. An entire community has become so disoriented that its members fail to care for the bodies of their own children. When one considers the importance placed upon the family and especially upon the care of children within the Jewish tradition, such negligence on the part of this community is doubly astonishing. The process of dehumanization, as it was played out in this particular transport, was so effective that even before its participants arrived in Auschwitz the social bonds of responsibility by which each member found him or herself obligated to her or his fellows seemingly had been shattered.

One characteristic of the shattering of these bonds was the collapse of memory. The failure, or rather, the inability of the transport community to remember these dead bodies as the children one once tenderly held and attentively nurtured transformed them into troublesome objects to be scraped off the floor and disposed of. In the world outside of Auschwitz, memory was capable of sustaining the ethical heritage of the other beyond her or his death, so that one's life might become a gift of generosity embodied in the flesh of her or his survivors and inheritors.[30] The dimensions of memory in the "normal" world transcended the individual and enabled him or her to be responsible to others whose experiences and lives could never be one's own. In the wake of this transcendence, individuals found the means to build an ethical community, that is, a community based not only on the appropriation (i.e., the "making one's own") of the other's experiences but upon the mourning (i.e., of the "responding to loss") of the other's life. But after suffering the utterly inhuman conditions of the transport, its victims had already begun to lose the empirical, bodily means to organize their experiences in relationship to what they once had been. With this breach in memory, the community began to break into smaller and smaller groups whose individual members became increasingly preoccupied with their own survival at the very expense of attending to the other's demise. The very structure by which humans recognized one another began to dissolve. Under such conditions, one's consciousness of and commitment to the categorical imperative began to waver and disappear.

This failure of memory is tied in the case of Auschwitz to the systematic deprivation of human possibility, particularly through an attack upon the human body. One's body is driven to its limits of endurance and becomes so obsessed with its own needs that memory itself, along with the autonomy of the individual human will, gradually dissipates. A culture of possibility is replaced by a culture of sheer survival, in which isolated individuals seek to preserve the minimum level of the body's organic vitality in order to negate the onslaught of extermination. Such bodies inevitably will cease to sustain the necessary level of intrapersonal memory, let alone interpersonal, needed to insure human autonomy. How Primo Levi speaks of Auschwitz as being "walking hunger," or how Elie Wiesel spoke of his entire life reduced to "a plate of soup and my crust of stale bread" (N, 60) has already been noted above. The "possible world of ends" becomes impossible for a will that is seized by its own bodily hunger. There is only so much energy in the human psyche that can be made available for its various projects: "When one works, one suffers and there is no time to think: our homes are less than a memory" (*SA*, 49). In the netherworld of survival that persisted around the crematoria, all that remained were the smallest particles of obsessive awareness—one's consciousness was reduced to Wiesel's "starved stomach."

One needs more than the memory of one's stomach to mourn the dead. The community of survival, the one concession the administrators of Auschwitz were forced to make to the demands of life, afforded little time for the work of memory. As a result, the dead often died *as if* they were no longer persons. Surrounded by such annihilation and helpless before it, those chosen for temporary survival gradually succumbed to the annihilative betrayal of the crematoria, often long before their living bodies were disposed of. Primo Levi observes that "our personality is fragile, that it is in much more danger than our life" (*SA*, 49). The reader has already encountered in the passages from Borowski's story that "uniform internal desolation" infecting those who lived on in the work camps of Auschwitz, those "who were no longer alive, . . . who had already gone half-crazy in the dreary expectation of nothing" (*SA*, 94). The expectation that the moral autonomy of the *Häftling* could and should survive the collapse of human temporality is revealed to be naive. Autonomy can found the moral only insofar as it is already provided for within a heteronomous order, insofar as human effort and cooperation across the generations has already secured an open sphere of possibility where human expectation can flourish and human character can develop. Only then can the limiting of a person's expectation, of his or her liberty, through an ethical imperative founded upon the autonomy of the individual have its meaning. The poetics of annihilation provides the limit conditions, beyond which that moral law depending upon the autonomy of the human being seemingly disappears, beyond which the expectation that one's life will be remembered is confronted with the collapse of the future in the opaque, empirical nothing of extinction. The *Häftling* learns in Auschwitz that human dignity is far more fragile than he or she had suspected.

Survival and Impossible Witness

The *Häftling*'s plight also teaches that the last possible historical resistance to the systematic destruction of human autonomy and memory is the struggle to survive extermination Here one's ethical duty is fulfilled in bare, biological endurance.[31] But endurance alone still leaves the *Häftling* resisting force with force. Against the overwhelming force of the camps, the survivor would match her or his tenacious clinging to existence, *no matter what other costs were entailed*. But in the aftermath of Auschwitz, in the return to the so-called normal world, the question arises whether the collapse of moral values that occurred within the precincts of the death camp was so great that survival remains the only realistic moral command, that the Nazis were right to act *as if* the play of force was the major engine of history and that the very power of a *force majeure* provides its own ethical justification. A son wrenching the bread from his father's mouth might ensure the survival of at least one man. But what of the values of peace?

Levinas argues: "in crucial times, when the perishability of so many values is revealed, all human dignity consists in believing in their return" (*PN*, 121). Thus, coupled with the command to endure came an additional imperative—to be addressed by and to remember those who were being crushed, so that their annihilation might be witnessed, so that the truth of their plight might address the succeeding generations of humanity. In this witness, one honored the *Häftling* in a gesture that transcended the return of force with force. One acknowledged that even in Auschwitz, the other's face continued to be commanding no matter how perversely he or she was treated. No matter how anonymous and shameful the *Häftling's* death might become, this very anonymity and shame provokes responsibility. In this manner, the *Häftling* becomes the *Nameless*, which is to say, no longer simply the one who suffers degradation but more importantly the one who commands responsibility in spite of that degradation.

In addressing his own motivation for writing *Night*, Wiesel introduces the imperative to remember the victim as one that was first announced to him through the ties of family and friendship, ties that sought to sustain themselves amidst the darkening clouds of extermination:

> Remember, said the father to his son, and the son to his friend. Gather the names, the faces, the tears. If, by a miracle, you come out of it alive, try to reveal everything, omitting nothing, forgetting nothing. Such was the oath we had all taken: "If by some miracle, I emerge alive, I will devote my life to testifying on behalf of those whose shadow will fall on mine forever and ever."[32]

As Wiesel's remarks make clear, this community of survival was and is held together by the *address* of those who suffered and were unable to survive. But a distinction needs to be made between those whose intimate, embodied memory Wiesel can personally carry on (friends and family) and those who perished without one close to them who could testify for them. One witnesses not only for those whom one can remember but also for those of whom no one has a memory, for the *Nameless*. The engagement in a witness *beyond* human memory emerges as a particularly daunting yet commanding task of the survivor, in which the annihilation not only of individuals but also of their memory, of the residue of their life in the bodies of their fellow human beings, must be addressed. This incommensurable loss, this drifting of memory itself into sheer forgetfulness, confronts the survivor with an obligation at the very limit of obligation. To remember the loss of this or that individual to the ravages of war or to the sadistic impulses of a Nazi guard cannot suffice for the responsibility now accorded to witnessing. In his or her remembrance of Auschwitz, the survivor resists not only the wanton murder of individuals but the loss of their very deaths. Wiesel reports:

> A million children massacred: I shall never understand . . .
> All these children, these old people, I see them. I never stop
>   seeing them. I belong to them.
> But they, to whom do they belong? (WW, 203)

The situation of the survivor is to belong to those who belong to no one, whose very loss remains articulated only in the loss of its loss.

The witness of the *Shoah* cannot return to the values of peace without also having demonstrated the fragility of individual autonomy and having articulated an imperative in which one must seek to remember the sheerness of historical loss, its immemoriality. The immemorial spoken of here is different from that developed by Derrida in which every life is found to transcend its memory, in which every witness of the other's life must ultimately suffer its incapability of rendering that life in its own terms.[33] The address of the generations coming before, as well as after us address us from beyond what we know or could ever know of them. But the generations of Auschwitz, both those who came before and those who will never come after, address us with an added dimension of transcendence. For not only does this address exceed our capacity to render it in its own name, but it also has been decisively emptied of its familial, fraternal, and social efficacity. The address of those who were annihilated at Auschwitz can no longer be directed toward children and friends, toward lovers and enemies, but only toward those whose hearing is without any particular clue as to the specific person for whom that particular witness is to be given. If these others are remembered at all, they are thought of as names upon a list, as anonymous photographs by a village photographer—the *Nameless*. Their involvement in a following generation as those who would inspire a living tradition transcending their own time, whose specific actions, words, gestures, commitments, creations, and so on would be offered to those who come after them, has been forever undone. Not just murder but aenocide has occurred. Any return to the values of peace cannot restore to history what has been annihilated in it. Yet the very vulnerability of the other to historical annihilation makes even more pressing that one embrace peace, that one be true to the other's commanding address.

Gabriel Marcel has argued that to be a witness is "to act as a guarantor."[34] But in giving witness to the *Nameless*, Wiesel acts as a guarantor for those who belong to no one, at least to no one who remains among the living to mourn them. In turning to these victims, his witness commands a mourning for those for whom no mourning is possible. Thus, Wiesel acts as a guarantor for what in principle exceeds a guarantee. In this sense, Wiesel's witness involves a testimony to his failure to be a witness. Further, Wiesel's mourning is endless, without a scope, since it is directed toward a loss precisely of the capability of its being mourned.[35] The loss registered here is irremediable, incompossible, irreparable.

Only through the paradoxical memory of this loss exceeding any possible historical restitution, can humans come to recognize the profound vulnerability to the diabolical will of those cultural structures that sustain the possibility of moral action within history.[36] One confronts in this moment what Levinas in the next chapter will term "an extermination without justice." The survivor, as well as the inheritor of Auschwitz confronts the capability of human beings to will the total destruction of history and perhaps even of terrestrial nature, a capability that was given a limited but striking application in the technology of genocide practiced at Auschwitz.

The diabolical will-to-death, like Kant's free will, seeks a project with universal breadth, but now universal in its self-destruction rather than in its self-position. In doing so, this will refuses categorically that address of the other to whom it has already been submitted and for whom it has already been given responsibility. In doing so, this will wills its own delusional state—it acts *as if* it were its own creator, *as if* it might never die, *as if* the other's suffering meant nothing at all to it, *as if* everything were possible. This will conspires to act in relation to the other who suffers "*as though* one [i.e., the diabolical will] were alone." When this proves impossible, this will clings ever more obsessively to its delusion to the point of destroying anything that is vulnerable to attack including itself. The will consumes itself in its own violence rather than admitting the priority of the other's suffering.

That such a will acts in disregard to the address of the other's suffering, an address whose reality cannot be undone no matter how the will may comport itself, does not undo its implicit power to destroy the empirical existence of the "kingdom of ends," that is, the sum of wills (both present and future) *within history*. That such a will might possibly disrupt the entirety of human history places a new, heretofore unthought responsibility upon those who have survived the first attempts of such a will of annihilation to articulate itself. Ethical responsibility must now articulate a response to the phenomenon of radical evil, to that diabolical project that would lay waste to memory articulated across the generations to the point where perhaps even the entirety of humankind might disappear.[37]

For those who inherit Auschwitz, the irreversibility of loss and the vulnerability of the other to a universal will-to-death become fundamental axioms that any ethical discussion must take into account. Kant discusses the problem of radical evil, that is, of a will that "corrupts the grounds of all maxims,"[38] but fails to place its possibility within the scope of human actions. Yet, as Arendt argues, "radical evil has emerged in connection with a system in which all men have become equally superfluous" (*OT*, 459). The radical evil of such a system is witnessed in the account with which this chapter began: a child and a woman are treated *as if* they are faceless. What resists this submission to their extermination is the nausea and vertigo that the narrator, the survivor, experiences as he witnesses their erasure. This nausea occurs, the next chapter will argue, precisely because the face of the other continues to address the witness, even in the very collapse of the other's rational autonomy. To survive and to recount such nausea, this shame at the shame of the other's plight, becomes the overriding ethical responsibility of those who would resist the facelessness of such evil and who would resist the will-to-death by another means than a struggle of force with competing force.

CHAPTER THREE

The Transcendence of the Face

Testimony in Crisis

But even if a poetics of testimony manages to carry over the memory of those submitted to annihilation, the survival of that memory may itself be the final gesture of the very annihilation the writer had set out to resist. For the assault upon the humanity of the other human, as well as the attempt to follow Levi's command to imagine this assault, leaves the reader in yet another quandary. If the assault is as thorough as it has been argued, and if the assault did indeed succeed in crushing the autonomy of the *Häftling*, as well as in murdering the generations who would have mourned her or him, then why need the reader have any ethical regard whatsoever for the end product of this infernal process? The very response to the *Häftling* presented by the first two chapters has been from the start in crisis; for the very authority by which the command is given—that is, the inherent dignity of the victim—seems utterly undermined by the content of the command—to remember these persons as being dehumanized in extremity.

If human beings are utterly vulnerable to domination, as Levi suggests, if their very presence in time can be wiped out as well, why respect them at all? If reason itself is left in helpless contradiction by those quandaries into which one's witness of the *Shoah* continually brings one, then what remains that might offer an *absolute* resistance, that is, a resistance that cannot be corrupted by the very degradation it resists, to the attack made upon the *Häftling*? This question has haunted the discussion of the first two chapters without becoming explicitly developed. In those chapters, the discussion revolved around obeying a command, regardless of its consequences, to remember the *Häftling*. In this chapter, one must now turn more reflectively to that recurring question presented in the wake of this confrontation with the

73

Häftling: Why even bother to remember, if memory only succeeds in reenacting a trauma that can only convince one that humans are without any ultimate ethical standing? In a more positive manner, one could frame the question thus: In what manner, if any, can the *Nameless* be said to transcend the attack made upon them by the death world of the camps?

In posing this question, one is also asking whether ethics itself has any real significance. For as Emmanuel Levinas puts it in his preface to *Totality and Infinity*, the very issue of whether we are "duped by morality" emerges as a matter of course when one considers that the world in which one finds oneself seemingly requires "the permanent possibility of war" (*TI*, 21). For the world, insofar as it consists of a scene in which intention is arrayed against counterintention, meaning against countermeaning, is already a battlefield. Against a background dominated by the play of force and counterforce, morality emerges with reason to limit the play of each force against the other and to elaborate some larger order by which all these forces can be mollified. "But this rational peace," Levinas argues, "is calculation . . . a reciprocal limitation and determination" (*OB*, 4). Peace based upon the balancing of mutual interests lacks a patience, "an allergy toward intolerance" (*OB*, 4), that would precede and forever be uneasy with merely calculating a place for the other.

In crushing the intentionality of other humans, the death world set up by the Nazis at Auschwitz would suspend the rational limit of morality through a return to an initial *polemos*, to that "trial by force" that "is the test of the real" (*TI*, 21) and that lies at the basis of any articulation of reasonable restraint. In doing so these perpetrators of violence would fit among those who in Levinas's mind would "divest the eternal institutions and obligations of their eternity and rescind *ad interim* the unconditional imperatives" (*TI*, 21). Since the interval over which *aenocide*'s annihilation acts is without limit, or, paradoxically, the utter collapse of a limit, the *ad interim* of which Levinas speaks becomes an *ad indeterminatum*. In the wake of Auschwitz, even more than in the wake of all other wars, morality is in danger of becoming "derisory."[1]

Yet, in posing the question of whether ethics itself is ultimately a delusion, and of whether the memory of injustice can do nothing more than remind one of this, one must be careful not to betray the efficacy of the assault upon the integrity of the victim that one would argue must be transcended. One cannot resolve the crisis in testimony by clinging to a naive idealism that would simply deny the extremity of the collapse of autonomy and temporality that has occurred in Auschwitz. This would resolve the crisis only by means of denying it ever occurred. This does no honor to those who suffered in Auschwitz, as well as the other camps and campaigns of annihilation that made up the *Shoah*. One's response must take seriously the suffering of the *Häftling*, even as it would resist it.

One aspect of the phenomenology of the world-betrayed developed in the first two chapters offers an important hint as to how one might begin to respond to these disturbing questions. For no matter how radically human nature is degraded, it continues to matter to the reader that this has occurred. In fact, a relationship between command and attention emerges that is exactly the inverse of what the previous paragraphs would imply. For the more the *Häftling* is dehumanized, the more intensely felt is his or her claim for respect by the reader. Precisely because Sómogyi is so vulnerable to being rendered a "thing," Levi, as well as his reader, intensely protests against this factum, this event of reduction. Here to consider the *Häftling* only in terms of his ontology, in terms of *what* or *who* he or she has come to be, fails to respond to the crucial issue. What demands consideration is how the very vulnerability of the *Häftling* to an ontological collapse, to a suffering unto annihilation, already claims one regardless of "what" or "who" the *Häftling* comes to be because of that vulnerability. Whether "what" is eventually placed before one by the memory of Auschwitz is or is not a crushed autonomy is not the final or ultimate significance of that person and of what Auschwitz involves.

Exceeding this thematization of autonomy, this valuing of the human based upon what the human *is* positively, is one's submission to the other human being precisely in the wake of her or his vulnerability. What commands one here is not the other's ontological integrity, not the ability of this or that being to cling to his or her identity, but his or her ontological vulnerability, precisely the susceptibility of the other to an attack upon her or him. As Emmanuel Levinas might argue, placed before the *Häftling*, as well as before every other human being, one confronts a dimension to the *other as other* in which one's own power over the other becomes meaningless. Before the other, I find "I am not able to be able" (*CP*, 55). One's restlessness before this vulnerability was precisely what constituted the telling discomfort of ethical silence discussed in the first chapter.

Put in the terms of Emmanuel Levinas, what fails to be undermined by the perpetrator's attack upon the victim is an absolute disruption of one's own power over the other that is revealed in the face of the other. No matter how thoroughly one seeks to undo the victim's knot of identity, the face resists any attack upon the victim from beyond his or her identity. The face *transcends* whatever the other might turn out *to be*. In coming before the face of the other, one does not simply confront a being whose projects differ from one's own and so would resist one's intentions with counterintentions, a balancing of identity against counteridentity. One finds that before any intention might even have been expressed, before one might even have had the time to determine the identity of he or she who bears this face, one was already claimed by a responsibility to listen to the face, to the other. The face of the other addressed one before one could have even consented to its having spoken.

Borowski's Faces

As the two passages from his short story considered in the last chapter illustrate, Borowski's writing is obsessed by images involving the face. For example, what first strikes the narrator as he confronts the child abandoned by his mother is a "pink cherub's face." The mother in turn responds to the child's pleas by "covering her face with her hands." Andrei, who murders her, is first characterized in terms of his face as well—he has eyes "glassy from vodka and the heat." This face "twitches with rage" as he pulls up the mother from the ground by her hair. Even the mode of murdering this woman alludes to the face in a powerful manner—by choking her, Andrei literally squeezes the breath out of her mouth, empties her face of its empirical life, and renders her voice incapable of any further response to the situation in which she finds herself. Rendered faceless, she is no more than "a heavy sack of grain" to be heaved upon a truck and driven away for disposal. Without a face, the body becomes inert matter. The child's "pink cherub's face" is given the same treatment—no longer a face but a weight to be disposed of, he is thrown at the mother's feet. Borowski's vomiting also implies the face—where words might issue forth that would greet these strangers who had been brought before him, he retches up the vodka meant to render him oblivious.

   Underlying all these images of the face—a pink cherub's face, a face twitching with rage, a face covered over by its own hands, a face gasping for air, a face retching up its last swig of vodka—lies the issue of the face itself. For the face, particularly in Borowski's narrative, is not simply a metaphor or symbol, a mode of collecting together various meanings where they might be given a more emphatic or artistic articulation. Rather than using the face as a metaphor, as a mode of presenting some meaning that is carried across to the reader by means of an extraneous image, Borowski's narrative implies that the face is in itself the basic issue in any meeting between two persons. The face is that entity that carries itself across as itself, καθ' αὐτο. It is, so to speak, a metaphor exceeding the metaphorical, a metaphor whose own being-carried-over is the point of its carrying over. Put in other terms, the theme of the face is how the face itself announces all themes, how before one can even speak about speaking, one must speak *to someone*, that is, *to her or his face*. This face is precisely what is under attack in the world-betrayed of Auschwitz.

To illustrate this point more concretely, one need only turn to the scene just after that in which the mother and child appears, where Borowski records yet another *Häftling*'s reaction to her entrance into Auschwitz. A woman steps out of the train and "looks around inquiringly . . . gazing at the crowd, then turns and with a gliding look examines our faces, as though searching for someone" (*TB*, 44). Her gaze finally stops at the narrator who, unbeknown to himself, is staring back at the woman. To him she speaks, because only for him—among all those she encounters—does she still register *as someone who ought to be listened to, as someone whose address commands an answer, even if that answer is a refusal to answer*. "Listen, tell me, where are they taking us?" is the woman's question. Implicitly she understands that the command to listen, a command that is implicit in any statement or question addressed to the other is at issue in Auschwitz. Faces disappear in the world-betrayed, because no one listens. Standing before the *Häftlinge* and the *Kommandant*, the newly arrived inmate must struggle to command explicitly what every saying commands implicitly. She seeks to regain her face. She commands that she be listened to as someone who addresses others and in so doing obligates a reply. Borowski's narrator, even as he says "I remain silent" has listened to her and has responded. The fact that the woman then makes a reply to his silence, a reply that he remarks upon in his own heart, says as much.

The mode in which the recalcitrant mother and her child are listened to by Andrei and the S.S. Officer is quite different from Borowski's own response (within the story) to the second woman. Even though Andrei actually speaks *at* the mother, he categorically refuses to be commanded by her saying—he resists letting the speaking-*at* slip into a speaking-*to*. In keeping with this resistance, Andrei lashes out in rage at the mother not so much for *what* she has said but rather for the fact *that* she dared to say anything to him at all. The greatest threat to Andrei's position over and against the mother is held in her very address of him rather than in any particular information that this address might convey. The mother, according to the infernal *logos* of the extermination camps, lived outside any society of address. Her voice had been seemingly deprived of its capacity, so to speak, to command listening. As Levi reports it in slightly different terms, the *Häftling* suffers a look from her or his captor that "was not one between two men [or women]." This look, "which came as if across the glass window of an aquarium between two beings who live in two different worlds" held according to Levi the key to understanding "the essence of the great insanity of the third Germany" (*SA*, 96).

In a manner similar to Andrei, the mother disregards the plea of the child. Like Andrei, she too is obsessed by a mood that renders the child invisible, although not so much one of rage as of desperation. The mother flees the very voice of that child and the face which articulates that voice as a command of the mother to listen to the child as someone *other* than herself. The mother's *no* responds not to the question of the child, but to the very authority of the child even to utter a statement worthy of her consideration. In both Andrei's and the mother's responses to the face, one finds not only an attack upon another human being, but also a rendering faceless of the other human. Whatever she or he might say in her or his defense is already unheard.

But Borowski's own response to this denial of the face suggests a further and decisive twist in the face-to-face encounter that he has in turn passed on in his witness to the reader. *For the very denial of the face by Andrei and the mother only emphasizes the resistance of the other's face to an attack upon her or him.* Borowski vomits. Struck to his very quick, he reacts in revulsion against the disregard the various figures within Auschwitz show for the face of the other. As was suggested above, an inverse relationship between autonomy and command occurs where the other suffers even unto her or his humiliation.

Borowski's response suggests that the face of the other undermines one's own hold upon one's intention to ignore the other. Borowski himself had set out to exploit the incoming "shipments," to help unload the transport in order to provide himself a new pair of shoes. In doing so, he was holding himself to that ethical mode of comportment Levi described as "The Law of the Lager"—to eat one's own bread *and* the bread of one's neighbor. But in spite of his own intention to ignore the other, he finds himself commanded by what occurs to all the others before his eyes. Borowski finds he cannot escape the face of the other.

Precisely because the face's hold upon one is so uncanny, so incapable of being evaded, the Nazis were adamant about rendering faceless the faces of *the Nameless.* Like the attack upon the inmate's autonomy explored in the previous chapters, this attack upon the face was twofold, as the scene Borowski has presented for the reader illustrates. At one level, one simply murders someone who has a face—Andrei addresses the mother as an individual and chokes the life out of her. But at a second level, one murders not only the person carrying the face but also the face itself. One acts *as if* this entity—this *Scheiß*, these *Schmattes, Figuren, Stücke*[2]—was always nothing more from the very beginning than waste to be disposed of. As the S.S. officer states, the woman is nothing more than a "degenerate mother," which is to say, a defective piece of human merchandise whose fate is to be recycled as waste. So one throws her on the cart like a bag of spoiled grain, and one murders the very child whom just a few seconds earlier the mother had been accused of so callously abandoning. One murders the other but does not leave behind even a corpse because *"what"* one has murdered is systematically denied to have ever been a person. One murders in such a manner that the murder itself disappears. From this position over and against the other comes the macabre work of disposing of millions of corpses *as if* they were simply waste material, the so-called function for which the death camps were designed.

Vulnerability as Nonintentional Resistance

It could be objected that what Borowski pictures above shows exactly the opposite of what was just claimed, namely, that the camps did not set the scene for the resistance of the face to its murder but actually gave an empirical demonstration of how the face can indeed be rendered faceless, of how any ethical response to the other is ultimately derisory. Would not Andrei's very response to the mother's plea for continued life, his categorical rejection of the implied command to listen to her, demonstrate precisely how vulnerable the face is to betrayal? Would not the very vulnerability of the face to a violence worked upon it be a compelling argument for a collapse of the ethical that already has haunted a discourse emphasizing autonomy? For with autonomy, one still could speak of a rational will, and of an inner necessity energizing that will, by which one could offer an effective resistance to the harm inflicted upon one. One could choose to think in opposition to what the victimizer intended. One could resist the victimizer's intentions with one's own. But not even this recourse is given in the notion of a face. For the other's face commands not by means of an intention countering its interlocutor's intention but by means of its very fragility to the intentions of its interlocutor. One listens to the other, because the other can be wounded.

But what could possibly give the claim associated with the face an authority that commands one's attention regardless of how deeply one defaces the face? What is it that distinguishes Borowski's response, his vomiting in the face of the other's being rendered faceless, as *ethical* rather than simply psychological? And what is to be made of the fact that neither the mother nor Andrei, not to mention the S.S. officer, seems to show a similar response?

For Emmanuel Levinas, the vulnerability of the face to an attack upon it does not suggest a weaker form of resistance to the intentions of the perpetrator but one of an entirely different order. In responding to the questions of the preceding paragraph, as well as in determining whether ethics becomes derisory in the aftermath of Auschwitz, Levinas's account of the face as the very paradigm of ethical significance deserves careful consideration. In turning to Levinas's account of the face, one finds a witnessing of the *Häftling*, of *the Nameless*, by a philosopher who lost most of his family in Lithuania to the *Shoah*. Levinas only survived because, being an officer in the French army, he was interned during World War II in a military prisoners' camp in France. Peperzak reports that Levinas himself characterized his thought as being dominated by "the forebodings, the memory and the reality of the Holocaust."[3]

But unlike either Levi or Borowski, as well as many of the other survivors of the *Shoah*, Levinas's own witness remains oblique in regard to the picturing of the empirical conditions of the camps along with their psychological impact, or at least in regard to those conditions in which force was brought to bear upon individuals in order to destroy their autonomy.[4] In approaching what he terms *the Nameless*, Levinas is not as concerned to show the rendering faceless of the face that characterized the *Häftling*'s world, as he is to show how the face *as commandment* transcends all plots to overwhelm its authority. In an interview Levinas argues that the truly difficult and essential thing to explain in the aftermath of Auschwitz is not that persons acted unethically but that in spite of everything, "there is a moment where someone plays without winning," where, in other words, someone acts gratuitously, "with grace." This moment occurs "when one can hear and understand this commandment [which comes from the face]."[5] For Levinas the most crucial moment to witness in Auschwitz is precisely the one in which one resists the ongoing devolution of the other's significance in spite of everything.

In turning to the face, Levinas would draw attention to a mode of resistance to violence on the part of others that does not resort to a countering of one's own intentions by means of the other's intentions. The very scene in which two *beings* struggle with one another, each for his or her respective understanding of what the scene in which they find themselves should come to mean, is itself the mode in which philosophy, as well as most of the world's history, occurs. From out of this initial *polemos*, this initial plurality of conflicting perspectives and opinions, the various participants are drawn by their commitment to reason into a dialectical discourse that moves with an ineluctable logic toward a summary view, a totality. In the most subtle and fairminded accounts of this movement, such as Hegel's, the intention is not to dominate any given perspective by means of another but only to give each moment in the articulation of a whole its proper place in relation to that whole.

The understanding oriented within the initial *polemos* finds this ultimate, totalizing view as the very expression of peace, *eirēnē*. Above and beyond individual intentions and distinct perspectives is an anonymous movement toward order. By following this movement, or better put, by letting one be taken up in this movement, one allies oneself with the construction or organic development of a comprehensive harmony in which all dissonance, all heterality, is soothed and rendered docile. Kant's argument, considered in the last chapter, for an ethics based upon the willing of a universal law in which no contradiction arises fits exactly this sort of structure. So does Hegel's argument for an explanation of historical catastrophe that emphasizes the achievements of history at a universal level in spite of the suffering undergone by particular individuals.

For Levinas, this incessant movement toward totality, toward a masterly ordering of all perspectives, is itself the culmination of war rather than the onset of peace. Totality cannot stand alterity, in which the very otherness of the other interrupts any rational discourse infinitely. Such an interruption is classified in the logic of totalization as irrational and nonsensical. In its very confidence that all perspectives can be ordered into a universal account, reason institutes a narrative in the third person, an accounting for the world in which speaking *about* others rather than *to* them becomes the guiding characteristic of its *logos*. Confident in the implicit fairness of its approach, reason constructs a world in which one need only respond to the other in the measure of one's own notion of how the world itself provides a place for this other. The other is given a place only insofar as he or she can make an argument for it and that argument can fit into an overall context that provides for all the other arguments reasoning entities might make. One has the time to consider the other's claim, to debate with the other about his or her status, and to reach a decision in relation to the other based upon the measure of reason rather than the exigency of the other's need. The other comes after reason and is articulated only through the patterns instituted in reason.[6]

But in a truly peaceful scene between two beings, one must accede to the other in a way that does not involve insisting on one's intentions, that does not assume *a priori* that in hearing the other one has already entered into a contest between two countering wills. One might say that in peace one encounters the other rather than countering her or him. But this encounter would not be characterized in the manner of Martin Buber as a reciprocity of exchange. For in reciprocity the very issue of the translation of one being into the terms of another would inevitably begin the *polemos* all over again. For Levinas, the only way in which the scene between two persons can be resolved irenically is to find oneself already under an asymmetrical obligation to the other. One is already responsible for the other without having the time to demand whether the other is responsible for oneself in turn. Only in this way can the dilemma between conflict and cooperation be resolved without introducing a mode of depersonalization into the process. The dilemma is resolved by introducing a movement toward the other prior to either conflict or cooperation, the movement of responsibility.

Because it precedes either conflict or cooperation, the articulation of asymmetrical responsibility is not coercive—one is not driven to accede to the other because of a force at work generally within being. One finds one is already responsible for the other in the very articulation of one's own affectivity, one's own incarnation, one's own subjectivity. To be a subject is to be *sub-jectum*, always-already-thrown-under the other. Thus, to come intimately into contact with oneself one must first turn to the other who commands one to be responsible. Rather than depersonalizing the subject, this command of the other brings the subject into a singular responsibility *for which no other can take one's place*. All of this occurs in the wake of a vulnerability, a passivity revealed by the face of the other that interrupts forever the movement toward an accommodation between competing intentionalities.

The Nudity of the Face

In *Otherwise than Being*, Levinas argues that the face "is the very collapse of phenomenality" (*OB*, 88). From the beginning of one's confrontation with Levi's command to remember the *Häftling*, one has been ensnared in this collapse. One discovered that the phenomena instantiated by Levi's prescription could be described until that moment when one asked about the authority by which they were given. This authority, the victim *kath' auto*, in her or himself, turned out to be resistant to appearance or description. Further, this resistance did not leave one in wonder but in shame. One did not come before the victim in awe of his or her being but was reduced to a discomforting silence, a *dis*-ease, a being-put-*ill*-at-ease, in which the very difference between the suffering of the other and one's own well-being plagued any attempt to make sense of the other's suffering for oneself. One was called into a responsibility for the sake of the victim that exceeded any possibility of its being as well for the sake of oneself. The victim's suffering transcended a phenomenological description, in which a series of profiles or perspectives emerging within the field of consciousness might be given. Instead, the very attempt to imagine the victim, to render the *Häftling* in phenomenological terms, was itself brought into unresolvable quandary. Phenomenality itself began to collapse. In the wake of this impending collapse, one was called upon to imagine negatively, against the grain of imagination, the unimaginable dimensions of the other's suffering *in extremis*.

For Levinas, the source of this collapse resides not inherently in the humiliation or degradation of another human being but in the face's revelation through its nudity, its vulnerability to violence. By "nudity" Levinas would suggest a "non-form, abandon of self, ageing, dying . . . poverty, skin with wrinkles" (*OB*, 88). All of these "traits" do not depend upon the actual violation of the other for their instantiation but are from the very beginning already a feature of the other's revelation *as other*. For Levinas, the issue is not the subjection of the other's face to violence but its initial susceptibility to this subjection. Regardless of the violence one does to the face, the face and only the face has already opened up the issue of its violation by means of its own vulnerability.

By speaking of the face as a revelation, Levinas suggests a mode of approaching the other that is otherwise than that of phenomenality. In the face's revelation, one is claimed by the inability of the face to emerge into an appearing that can become significant for an intentional consciousness. One cannot make sense of the face *as face* so long as one expects this sense to be articulated in categories constituted by and making sense of one's own experience of the world. In fact, the very mode by which the face appears before one is in those traits that utterly resist being experienced by one or being adopted as one's own—for example, wrinkles. At one level, wrinkles do support phenomenality. For in their appearance, wrinkles can suggest a durability through time, the accumulation of experiences, the weakening of powers. All of these categories hold significances that are implicitly shared by all biological entities possessing a consciousness. Like the other before me, I too can age, can accumulate experiences, can find myself slowly succumbing to my own mortality. My skin, like the other's skin, wrinkles with age. In this manner, I can find myself treating the face before me as an analogy for myself. Or, in reciprocity, I can find myself to be an analogy for the other before me. In both these instances, one uses a method similar to Aquinas's notion of analogy in order to bridge a difference between beings although one that is horizontal rather than vertical. Regardless of our differences, I and the other share in the same being, because we use the same terms to understand who we are.

But the significance that the wrinkles cannot translate into one's own terms is the vulnerability of the other to succumbing, the other's susceptibility.

For whatever similarity between the other and oneself in terms of respective vulnerabilities might be established, the *suffering* of that vulnerability remains infinitely untranslatable. One cannot suffer the other's ageing as one's own. To do so would be to live within the arrogant and self-serving posture of the pathetic fallacy. One would begin to imitate Hitler, to be swallowed up by a narcissism pushed to moral psychosis: one would act *as if* the face were nothing more than a mirror for one's own suffering.

In the suffering of the other, the utter passivity of the other's face before its own undoing, its "abandon of self," articulates a significance that is otherwise than intentional. The other's ageing presents me with a past "not *in* the present." The past held in this face *as face* resists any interpretation of it that would have it translated into a presence of what is now the case or even might be the case for me. One can choose to comprehend the other's ageing in terms of an analogy based on images, memories, stories that could be held in common between the other and myself. But this comprehension would lose precisely that manner in which the other's ageing is not mine. Rather than giving me access to a past outside of the present, the other's ageing presents me with the impossibility of his or her past becoming my present. The other's ageing submits me to a time that could never be mine, not even in sympathy. Rather than understanding this past, I must let it speak to me. But even to claim I "let" it speak to me already goes too far. For in its interruption of my confidence of being able to understand it, this past has already addressed me. Only because of a prior, immemorial past, can I now proceed to construct an account of the other's past that is accessible to me by means of an analogy.

In *Totality and Infinity*, as well as in several essays leading up to that work, Levinas explicitly outlines a scene in which the face-to-face encounter with the other not only reveals the other face's vulnerability to my violence but also resists that violence paradoxically by means of its very vulnerability, its nudity. Before the nudity of the face, Levinas argues I find "I am not able to be able."[7] Or again: "The absolute nakedness of a face, the absolutely defenseless face, without covering, clothing or mask, is what opposes my power over it, my violence and opposes it in an absolute way, with an opposition which is opposition in itself" (FC, 21). These statements claim that in spite of all the power I might exercise upon or against the face, its vulnerability to suffering at the hands of my power utterly escapes my power. The suffering that I encounter in the other I cannot take as my own. I utterly fail to translate the other's nudity into an intentional structure within my own consciousness of him or her.

Nudity involves an exposure of being exposed. One can perceive the surface of the face, one can find it exposed to one's line of vision, but this does not render the face nude. The face's nudity is that disruption of its appearance before me in which its *sensitivity* to exposure utterly exceeds my capacity to make it my own. This sensitivity is rendered in the expressiveness of the face, its address of me. Chosen by this address, I am submitted to a revelation that is incommensurable with my consciousness or perception of it. Thus, "the being that expresses itself, that faces me, says *no* to me by this very expression" (FC, 21).

But I can still strike out at the face and in so doing kill the other. The face remains vulnerable to my power, even as it exceeds it. Thus, murder emerges as an attempt to negate where no negation is possible. Murder is by implication a delusion—one strikes out at the other *as if* the other's face could be touched by one's power, but all this act accomplishes is to reinforce how absolutely this face in its very weakness transcends one's power. Certainly, Levinas argues, one can oppose the "intransigent *no*" of the other, his or her intentional resistance of my violence, by means of a sword or bullet that touches "the ventricle or auricles of his heart" (TI, 199). In doing so, one attacks the autonomy of the other. One interrupts the beating of the human heart in order to demonstrate to the other by means of a *force majeure* that the other's autonomy is fragile and susceptible to manipulation. But in the attack upon the autonomy of the other, what one can never cancel is the other's cancellation of my capability to possess her or him. Lying beyond what my power can appropriate or undermine in the other is the expressiveness of that face. The other resists me not by his or her force but by an openness to suffering that involves a passivity beyond the opposition of passive and active. In the grimace of pain, or even in the emptiness of the broken victim's eyes, one encounters an expressiveness that breaks open the face's surface, that interrupts its phenomenality and reveals an order of significance that can never be touched by means of force.

In being vulnerable to my power, the other negates absolutely my possible negation of her or him. In Levinas's words, "The face to face situation is . . . an impossibility of negating a negation of negation" (CP, 43). This impossibility is not given in terms of a perception of the other, of some appearing of the other in one's consciousness that could then become the instigation for a knowing of the other *as other*. If I could directly perceive the nudity of the face, the infinite disruption of my consciousness that the other instigates would somehow be made immanent within my consciousness. But the disruption that the other provokes in me in his or her nudity is incommensurable with my consciousness of it. The impossibility of killing *the other* can only be registered as a command to respect the other, precisely because one absolutely cannot contain the other. The very revelation of murder is synonymous with its prohibition. To encounter the "possibility" of murder is to be commanded by its impossibility. In the wake of this command, a command that was always already given, what appears as a "possibility" is revealed to be in fact a delusion, a possible that is actually impossible. In Levinas's words, "the face is the fact that a being affects us not in the indicative, but in the imperative, and is thus outside all categories" (FC, 21).

Implicit in Levinas's analysis of the face is the introduction of two modalities or modifications of reality heretofore neglected by much of the modern philosophical tradition: temptation and delusion. While Levinas does not develop this point in detail, it deserves consideration, particularly in relation to the scene initiated in Auschwitz in which the face of the other was to be rendered faceless. For in so doing, human beings succumbed to the *temptation* to treat the impossible *as if* it were possible. One acted *as if* one could kill the other with impunity. In so doing, one became subject to a *delusion*.

The modality of temptation involves the consideration of an impossibility *as if* it were possible. Only a creature capable of self-deception to the point of delusion, to the point of willfully losing track of what she or he is really engaged in doing, is capable of being tempted. Further, only a creature made vulnerable by an investment in the other exceeding any security found in his or her own identity would be tempted to slip surreptitiously from the impossible into the possible, to confuse the susceptibility of the face to violence with the capability of violating the face. For in doing so, one would forget the traumatic insecurity of one's own identity, as well as the priority of one's assignation[8] to the other, and would act *as if* one were given in oneself the measure of all that would command one to act. The delusion involved in the attack upon the other involves acting *as if* one were indifferent to the other, *as if* one were already implicitly oneself before one came before the other. One forgets in this delusion the derivative nature of one's own identity. Or in Levinas's terms, one forgets one is a creature. One forgets that being itself does not arise out of its own principles, that each entity is in fact creaturely, beginning in an anarchy, arising out of a generosity without a precedence.

The forgetfulness of the perpetrator is implacably self-defeating, for its very structure is built upon a prior assignation of oneself to the other, an assignation that one cannot defeat no matter how much one resists it. One cannot defeat it, because it has claimed one before one even began to be who one is. In the other's face, one confronts the truth that one finds an identity, a return of the same to the same, only in the wake of anarchy. One confronts how one comes into one's identity only after one has been made responsible for the other. One is revealed in the face of the other to be a *sub-jectum*, a being-thrown-under, whose involvement in the other transcends the warlike play of force and counterforce, of identity and counteridentity. Because one is always already involved in the other, any attack upon the other comes only at the expense of ignoring the very structure of one's own singularity as a subject. One is not truly an identity, a return of the same to itself, but a singularity, a node of responsibility for others whom no other can replace. Yet one's very involvement in the other is by way of her or his vulnerability to one's power. Thus, the face of the other tempts one "to a total destruction," even as it registers "the purely ethical impossibility of this temptation and attempt" (*TI*, 199).

In the wake of the face signification no longer functions in a declarative or descriptive discourse. One no longer has the time to talk *about* the other, since one has already been commanded to listen *to* the other. One finds before the declarative statement could have been uttered one was already subject to an imperative signification, a claim on the part of the other that leaves one no room but to listen to the other. To act *as if* the other were not to be listened to already presupposes that one has no choice but to listen to the other. One can pretend to negate the impossibility of this negation, but this pretense is simply that.

Rausch and Feigned Sincerity

Having given a sketch of one's singularity before the face of the other, the argument now needs to return to the scene of Auschwitz, where Borowski, as well as Levi, have witnessed the rendering faceless of the *Häftling*. But how exactly is this return to occur? For if Levinas's claim concerning the absolute resistance of the face to its violation is correct, then the very occurrence of Auschwitz must be *prima facie* an impossibility. Yet one has been called upon by Levi and Borowski to imagine as fully as possible the very instantiation of what Levinas argues is an impossibility.

One needs to keep in mind the paradoxical nature of Levinas's claim. Precisely through the vulnerability of the face to violation is given its resistance to violation. The face's resistance does not prevent the acting out of a violation but renders its intent futile. The face resists the intention of the violator from outside of intention. *It does so by having already claimed in its nudity the singularity of the perpetrator before he or she could resist this claim by means of an intention.* Yet the face, even as it resists absolutely the intention of the perpetrator remains vulnerable to agony, to a suffering to the point of abnegation. The face does not reveal an infinite autonomy, nor even a finite autonomy anchored in the absolute stability of its reason, but an "abandon of self." As was mentioned above, even if the face resists the perpetrator by means of its vulnerability, it still remains vulnerable to the perpetrator.

Thus, the face is open to attack but is incapable of being rendered faceless. In fact, the very rendering of the face *as if* it were faceless, *as if* its suffering were utterly without significance for the perpetrator, actually involves an act of self-deception on the part of the perpetrator. The perpetrator must strive to forget what is impossible to forget—that he or she is subject to the command not to murder. In attempting to forget this command, the perpetrator resorts to indirection, to a dishonesty taking place at the very borders of intentionality. One acts *as if* one were so innocent that the question of one's complicity in violence could never arise. Or one looks for complicity everywhere except where there is complicity.

Consider, for example, Andrei's attack upon the mother in Borowski's story. One might paraphrase the story this way: *Andrei accuses the mother of "running out on {her} own child." In the light of this accusation, he becomes enraged, calls her a "whore" and then murders her.* But the story might also be rendered in this manner: *Before Andrei ever encounters the woman, he is already in a state of fury. In his fury he need never look into the eyes of the woman. She is already annihilated and he simply carries out the sentence without allowing himself to notice what he has done.* In this second account Andrei's rage preexists his encounter with the woman and becomes a surreptitious means of pretending the woman's face is never encountered. One acts *as if* the command held in the nudity of the face has never been registered. In doing so, one allows oneself to become morally outraged at the mother's conduct, even as one engages in conduct even more outrageous but all the while remains indifferent to this hypocrisy.

Andrei looks for complicity everywhere except where his complicity is evident. But the very intensity and uncanniness of his acting *as if* he were not complicit becomes the indicator of a claim that persists no matter what his reaction to it might be. Andrei's rage is not a reaction to the mother's infidelity but is the symptom of his own infidelity. Even as he ignores the face of the mother, the very articulation of his indifference shows the impossibility of its success. Part and parcel of the *Rausch* reigning within the camps was a rage at any inmate who dared to question the ongoing business of annihilation. Acting as if one had the right to ask why, or to make any objection to the manner in which the business of the camp was being conducted brought immediate reprisals. While Arendt points to the lack of emotion people such as Eich-mann demonstrated in regard to their duties in the carrying out of genocide,[9] Herbert Kelman opts for a model of aggression in which rage is also pro-foundly at play, particularly in the day-to-day activities involved in mass vio-lence: "Hostility also plays an important part at the point at which the killings are actually carried out, even if the official planning and the bureau-cratic preparations that ultimately lead to this point are carried out in a pas-sionless and businesslike atmosphere."[10] Borowski, Levi, and Wiesel all confirm this point in their testimonies.

In Kelman's view this rage was not the true cause of the violence against those who were victimized in its wake. One did not lash out at the victim be-cause she or he had done something to make the perpetrator angry. Rather, anger "provided the perpetrators with an explanation and rationalization for their violent actions and appropriate labels for their emotional state" (VM, 291). Rage became a ploy to simplify the carrying through of one's victim-ization of the other—one could more easily kill those for whom one's only feeling was contempt![11] Preceding any anger against the victim was a surrep-titious closing out of the victim from the realm of feeling, as well as the realm of address, altogether.[12] But this very rendering of the face as faceless only re-inforces how the face persists in its commandment of oneself in spite of one's actions against it.

Borowski's narrator mirrors these sentiments when he observes: "I don't know why, but I am simply furious with these people [the *Häftlinge* arriving on the transports]—furious because I must be here because of them. I feel no pity. I am not sorry they're going to the gas chamber. Damn them all! I could throw myself at them, beat them with my fists" (*TB*, 40). Just as Kelman sug-gests, rage infects the narrator for no reason at all, or at least for no reason stemming from what the *Häftling* has done to deserve this reaction. What the rage actually entails is the desire of the narrator to harm the other *as if* it did not matter that he was doing so. If one is enraged, one can remain indifferent, one does not have to feel pity. But the failure to feel pity does not annihilate pity. It only thrusts one into a delusional state in which one acts *as if* an im-possibility—to be without pity for the other—is possible.

Andrei's rage, as well as the narrator's, is revealed in the course of the nar-ration to be a surreptitious ploy, an attempt to assert one's innocence in the murdering of the other even as one is commanded by the other's face not to murder her or him. The rage is a symptom of self-deception. Its intention is to act under the delusion that one can violate the very articulation of one's singu-larity as an involvement in the other with impunity. One acts *as if* one were not a creature, *as if* one were not claimed in one's very entrails by the nudity of the other's face. In order to kill the other even more efficiently, the perpetrators at Auschwitz resorted to a series of such ploys, all of which were designed to cover over a prior involvement in the other that persisted in mutated forms in spite of the consciously cultivated rejection of that involvement.[13]

One concludes that in spite of the rendering of the face as faceless in Auschwitz, the face continued to command those who rejected its commandment. The continuing effect of this command can be seen in the perverted modes of affectivity, as well as in the affected poses of sincerity that flourished within the camp. One not only acted *as if* one were sincere, but also *as if* one were so sincere that one's indifference to the other was a heroic burden. Levinas has called this condition "a ruse of innocence." In remarks delivered during a conference Levinas contends that National Socialism was an "obstinacy to be" so utterly taken up with its own survival, its own needs, that is became "contumacious and unpitying," resistant to "all kindness or mercy," and disdainful of any "sacrifice that would yield to the irreducible alterity of the other (*autrui*), who being irreducible, would be the singular (*unique*)."[14] Those running and manning the camps became adept at distancing themselves from any appeal to pity that the prisoner might make. These various strategies of perverted affect and affected sincerity were in actuality modes of repression of an already prior ethical feeling, namely pity, in which one is submitted to the other's vulnerability before one has any possibility of resistance.

Consider, for example, a passage from Rudolph Höss's autobiography, in which he remembers the particular day a Jewish mother was gassed in his presence. He writes, "My pity was so great that I longed to vanish from the scene; yet I might not show the slightest trace of emotion."[15] Höss's "struggle" gives an everyday account of what could be termed an instance of perverted sincerity. Having accepted the Nazi ideology concerning race and genetic purity as a "truth," one was supposedly submitted to a command to "dispose of" various individuals of supposedly inferior genetic strains. In carrying out this task, Höss claims he is struggling to be sincere, to admit his emotional reservations but to act logically for a good to which he also claims to be subjected unconditionally. Thus, in the name of sincerity, Höss sends a woman to a death so inhumane that no words can adequately characterize its heartlessness. In doing so, Höss feels sympathy for how he himself suffers because of the suffering of the other, *but he remains indifferent to the actual suffering of the other*. He acknowledges his pity only in order to deceive himself of its actual significance. Rather than submitting him to the other, Höss's pity becomes the ploy for self-aggrandizement and an implacable forgetfulness of what pity actually requires of one.[16] Philip Hallie refers to a similar instance in the testimony of Otto Ohlendorf who feels sympathy for the suffering of his own men insofar as they must endure the "terrible impression" made upon them as they opened up vans used to gas their victims and confronted corpses mired in excrement.[17] Ohlendorf is preoccupied with the psychological dimensions of these feelings, how they undermine the mental health of him and his men. What he remains steadfastly oblivious to is their ethical dimension—how this uneasiness suggests the suffering of the persons those corpses signify, persons whose interest was not to be identified with Ohlendorf's or his men's.

Here, in place of contriving a rage against the victim as a strategy of indirection, one finds a feigned commitment to rational discourse, as well as an inordinate concern for one's own well-being. The S.S. officer in Borowski's story serves as an example of this sort of strategy: *"Gut gemacht,"* he intones to Andrei after he chokes the mother. One becomes a pseudo-Kantian—one protests that one does the good thing no matter what the emotional cost. What one never considers is that the very disruption of one's emotions in the wake of one's violence signifies an address on the part of the other that absolutely prohibits that violence. One looks for complicity everywhere except where one is actually complicit. And as one does so, one congratulates oneself on one's struggle to be sincere.

Borowski's Witness: Paradoxical Discourse

The insincerity of the perpetrators is insincere precisely in its obsession to escape being rendered as insincerity. Paradoxically, the very gesture of insincerity is to profess its innocence, not only to be insincere but then to systematically forget what it has actually done. Thus, Eichmann is capable of arguing that although he carried out orders to murder millions of human beings, he himself is not actually guilty for having done so.[18] The person most deceived by this statement is not Arendt or the court before which he stood during his trial but Eichmann himself. Insincerity involves a doubled-forgetting, a doubled-deception. One not only forgets the face of the other, but one must also forget that one has forgotten.

This second forgetting weighs upon the insincere because of the very uncanniness of the face's claim upon the perpetrator. The perpetrator acts *as if* he or she is incapable of being incapable, *as if* he or she can act so decisively, so actively, that all that remains in the wake of that action is the purity of one's own decision. One tells oneself that one has erased the victim so the victim

can no longer matter. But the very intention to do away with the victim orig-
inates from beyond intention. This is what Levinas's account concerning the
transcendence of the face, of its command not to murder, would argue. One
does not own one's intentions when one is placed before the other, although
one is intensely responsible for those intentions. One's autonomy crumbles in
the anarchical and expressive gaze held in the other's face. One no longer is
able to be able.

In the manic, even psychotic obsession of a doubled-forgetting,[19] the victimizer would forget the other's face, would deny the priority of his own susceptibility to the susceptibility of its expressiveness, its vulnerability. It turns
out that to engage in this activity is *not* to forget the other's face but to become
deluded concerning one's own responsibility for the other even as the face of
the other continues to haunt one's every gesture. From the moment of the decision to murder the other, one becomes engaged in an ongoing structuring of
one's intentionality whose sole purpose is to forget what one could never make
one's own intention—the suffering of the other. The very act of assuming
ownership of one's decisions, of claiming autonomy, is repeated incessantly,
feverishly but uselessly. The authority of the face continues to command one,
even when one has seemingly rendered the face faceless.

In the scenes of Auschwitz that Borowski records, one finds in instance
after instance the refusal on the part of one human being to respond to another
human being *as if* he or she had a face, *as if* he or she were capable of actually
addressing one. But in turning to this refusal Borowski's witness does not
record the utter undoing of address, or the extinction of the face. The face
reemerges, the address of the other haunts the perpetrator, no matter what he
or she does to forget the other. In fact, the very activity of forgetting the other,
an activity that the perpetrator then had to attempt to forget that he or she
had forgotten, becomes itself an insistent witness to the contrary that the
other could not be forgotten.

The claim that the other cannot be forgotten, that the authority of the
face persists no matter what one does to it, should not be taken to imply that
one comes to know the face through a consideration of its image, through a
bringing of the face into a reflective play of memory against experience. For
Levinas, the face precedes memory, precedes what can be forgotten. Often,
Levinas will talk of the impact of the other upon one as traumatic.[20] By this,
he does not mean that sort of impact that humiliation of the other instigates,
an overwhelming of one's experience to the point that one's very suffering remains excluded from consciousness, so that one suffers precisely from the in-

ability to suffer what has been inflicted upon one. This too is an important part of the scene of Auschwitz and involves that crushing of autonomy that was so decisive in Levi's witness and commandment. But Levinas's sense of trauma doubles its articulation: one is not only capable of being traumatized but also has already been traumatized by the other's capability of being traumatized, of suffering. For Levinas, trauma involves how the face of the other already opens one up, already brings one into the scene of a suffering that is not one's own, so that one's very singularity or uniqueness is revealed to be already the undergoing of a trauma induced in oneself by the vulnerability of the other to suffering. Autonomy only follows upon anarchy and is eternally dependent upon it.

Before the humiliation of the other could have ever occurred, the perpetrator was already made humble by the other. In Borowski's scenes, perpetrators set upon their victims only to be wounded again and again by an insistence beyond memory that the other might yet speak in spite of all that one had done to her or him to prevent that speaking. Like Borowski's narrator, even Himmler swooned and became ill at one point when he witnessed the contumacious violence of mass murder.[21] His reaction to this incident, to increase the ration of vodka for his men, was an implicit acknowledgment of how incessant was the hold of the other's trauma upon one's own consciousness. In an effort to fight that trauma, one doped oneself up with consciousness-killing drugs or used other modes of achieving a numbing of one's emotions.[22] One literally traumatized one's own body in an attempt to cut off one's prior involvement in or proximity to the other. But the traumatizing of one's own consciousness so that one could protest the absoluteness of one's own autonomy in the face of the other is the most contradictory of gestures. One turns oneself into a servile consciousness in order to be able to crush the other's autonomy.

Thus, Borowski's witness, even as it draws attention to the crushed autonomy of the *Häftling*, does not accede to this humiliation. As Levinas would describe it, Borowski's narrative gives witness to the persistence of the ethical order in spite of everything that one does to crush it. This persistence is induced by a trauma that precedes memory and is the very condition by which memory itself signifies an involvement in another who would address one. One does not turn to the other because one has built up a repertoire of memories that slowly allow one to identify who she or he is in particular. Rather, the very movement to build up memories of another was already induced by the address of the other, by the sense that one had someone to answer to.

The fear that memory would only succeed in reenacting the trauma of a crushed autonomy, that a witness emerging from this memory would only demoralize those who remember, now finds an answer. For even as Borowski's witness demoralizes those who listen to it, its very structure also reminds the reader that this demoralization is only possible because an address persists in the face of the other no matter what is done to cut it off. The very cutting off of address uncannily witnesses to the persistence of address all the more. The question is not whether one should witness the victim but whether one is to embrace one's responsibility for that witness. The witness, according to Levinas, occurs whether one wills it or no.[23] But the taking responsibility for that witness, the affirming in one's own mind of an affirmation that was already imposed upon one no matter what one's response eventually was found to be, remains an issue.

In Borowski's infernal scenes, witness occurs mostly at the subliminal level, at the very margins of consciousness, precisely in the manner that the address of the other is being cut off and responsibility for the other is being denied. When a woman descends from a transport and looks for someone to whom she can speak, Borowski's narrator reports, "*Unknowingly*, I continued to stare at her until our eyes met" (*TB*, 44 [italics mine]). In the qualification of *unknowingly*, one finds the very articulation of Levinasian trauma. Beyond any intention the narrator may or may not have had to do so, he finds himself already staring at the girl, already obsessed by the gaze of another. Even as he refuses to answer, his very silence gives an answer in spite of himself. In this "unknowing" regard is registered the priority of an address that gives witness to the authority of the other's face regardless of one's assent to it.

What remains crucial for Borowski's narrator is whether he himself will now take responsibility for this face that has unknowingly seized his attention. The extremity of violence at work in Auschwitz gave very little space for gestures of effective resistance. Thus, the scene at the end of the story in which the narrator stumbles like a drunk and vomits in revulsion at the camp gives way to a realization that he will continue to be alive, that for him the camp holds the promise of oblivious survival, of "sleep among comrades who are not going to the gas tonight" (*TB*, 48). Even as he admits the horror of the camps, the needs of his own body assert themselves. In spite of what he has witnessed, he is glad to have survived, to have eaten his own piece of bread.

But miraculously even this moment of indifference to the suffering of the annihilated finds a paradoxical tone of outrage. For balancing the narrator's admission of self-absorption, of a capitulation to the betrayal of others lying at the core of life in Auschwitz, is his insistence on recording this very moment as a mode of witness for those whom he has failed to save. *"The 'Sosnowiec-Bedzin' transport is already burning"* (*TB*, 49). This ambivalent admission produces yet another moment of irreducible quandary. On the one hand, the tone implied is *Rausch* coupled with humor. *The whole mess is already behind me*, the author might say, *who needs these people anyway*! Here one encounters the fury the narrator feels for those who go helplessly to their annihilation. But the sentence also functions as an accusation, as the struggle of a conscience with its own failure to be effectively responsible, as well as with the outrageousness of a world indifferent to the demise of an entire village. For the death world is so mired in its rage to annihilate that a village goes up in smoke without a second thought. Carrying that thought into the world beyond Auschwitz, the narrator's witness finds in his very indifference to the other a disturbance, a restlessness that cannot be undone. The moment of triumph, of *Rausch* and humor, is subverted by accusation and outrage. But this accusation remains powerless to actually stop the ongoing violence. It resists without necessarily being empirically effective.

Useless Suffering and Gratuitous Witness

This last claim cannot be overemphasized. For the ethical command given in the face of the other does not necessarily protect the other from the rage of his or her would-be murderer. Nor can this command keep the generations from being swallowed up in aenocide. In characterizing ethical resistance in terms of the nudity of the face, Levinas opens up a characterization of the world in which history can become betrayal, and in which the face can be submitted to a consuming violence: The perpetrator "devours my people as if they were bread."[24] Paradoxically, precisely in the vulnerability of the face to those who violate it, a danger is revealed beyond that of "daytime wars," in which the attack upon the other is fueled merely by a desire to attain one's own end. In Auschwitz, one finds a war which "extend[s] into and enter[s] night, where reason is no longer mistress over the powers that have been unleashed" (*DF*, 189). In Auschwitz one finds an "extermination without justice" (*DF*, 189), a "world which has lost its 'very worldliness' " (*DF*, 191). For Levinas, the crushing of the other's autonomy already holds the threat of aenocide, of the submitting of the world to a violence without bounds. Further, the impetus driving those who would not only murder the other but would also erase the other's face is not merely rational. It is idolatrous as well. For the attack upon the face of the other would forget one's own initial poverty, the fragility of one's own autonomy, one's unrelenting restlessness before the other.

According to Levinas, one finds in the scene Borowski and Levi would witness a "great ambiguity." For Auschwitz maintains a question that Levinas claims cannot be resolved, that can only be underlined, a question that in the terms of the preceding chapters would be called a quandary. Levinas phrases his quandary in the following manner:

> Does the ultimate reason of the violence of war sink into the abyss of extermination coming from beyond war? Or does the madness of extermination retain a grain of reason? (*DF*, 187)

To be able to characterize war in terms of reason would be already to insure that war never enters into the night, the world-betrayed. For insofar as war follows the dictates of reason, it would find in the very dialectical nature of reason its own natural limit. The moment war threatened to become total, to deliver one over to a violence without constraint, war would cease to address one's own self-interest and would quickly be ended. As soon as Auschwitz became unprofitable, as soon as it interfered with other important objectives, one would give up its extravagant waste of time and materials. And yet, the Nazi war-machine increased its efforts to destroy Jews precisely when it needed the resources tied up in this effort to save its own existence from the Russian counterattack, as well as the Allied invasion. The "reason" motivating the camps turned out to be without reason.[25] Reason sank into that abyss of extermination exceeding war.

In the abyss of extermination, in the world-betrayed, one no longer acts according to the dictates of reason but in a mode of self-deception, of a forgetfulness of what reason could never justify, of a denial of the priority of the other's face. For this "reason," reason itself fails to limit the chaos unleashed by war. The conflict to which one is submitted transcends interest; beyond the reasons for which one fights is the uncanny persistence of one's submission to the other's vulnerability, as well as to the other's expression. In annihilation— as opposed to war—one does not attack the other for the sake of a possible good he or she might provide for oneself but on account of the very claim the other makes *as other*. One would forget that responsibility to the other that precedes one's very existence. One would deny that existence when shorn of justice is obscene.

But precisely by acting in this manner, one already gives witness to the face regardless of one's intention! The very threat of Auschwitz, of a descent into elemental darkness, also carries with it another sort of reason, a reason articulated by a responsible singularity who is addressed by the other before that singularity could ever justify its own existence. In the sections of *Totality and Infinity* following upon Levinas's account of the face-to-face relation, he argues for reason *as discourse*. Rather than being articulated as "an impersonal legality" that "absorbs the plurality of interlocutors" (*TI*, 207), discourse elaborates a reason that is always first involved in an address of another: "In speaking I do not transmit to the Other what is objective for me: the objective becomes objective only through communication" (*TI*, 210). In discourse, *signification*, the other's speaking to me, precedes reason, and reason is forever dependent upon this priority *of the other* for its own significance.

Yet one further twist remains in Levinas's quandary. Could the grain of reason, this *discourse* uncovered in the face and yet covered over and denied in annihilation, could *this other reason* ever bring annihilation back to its reason? Could the signification of the other's face finally offer a limit hemming in the virulence of the violence directed against it? Could one ever make an appeal to the glory or transcendence of the other's face in order to salve one's outrage that annihilation could ever have even been possible, let alone happen? Levinas refuses to resolve this question, "because the answer here would be indecent, as all theodicy probably is" (*DF*, 187).

What Levinas means by this remark is that in the wake of the other's face no time is left for self-justification but only for self-accusation. The face does not inspire wonder but shame, not a letting-be but an irritated restlessness.[26] My *interest* in a justification, in some sort of reason that could bring annihilation back into a functioning part of an interrelated series of events and entities, is revealed to be without justification: "For an ethical sensibility—confirming itself in the inhumanity of our time, against this inhumanity—the justification of the neighbor's pain is certainly the source of all immorality" (US, 163). By justifying how the other can be sacrificed for a higher purpose, one implicitly excuses oneself from how insistently the very scope of suffering in reality calls one *before all the others* to the real, gritty work of constructing a world in which justice is to be had here and now for all the oppressed, for the orphan, the widow, the stranger. In turning to theodicy, one ends up preaching to the oppressed that they should sacrifice themselves! This preaching, in which one calls the other to "a piety without reward," is scandalous (PM, 176).[27] One finds the other mired in a useless suffering, a suffering leaving them betrayed, and one suggests they accept this as their lot. This very attempt to justify violence retrospectively only furthers violence by furthering betrayal. One acts *as if* the other's pain is part of some scheme of reason in which what is useless, utterly gratuitous, finds a limit, a reason.

But the pain of the other exceeds any reason that could be given for it. For this "reason," one finds oneself already claimed by the other's susceptibility to pain to protest against it, even to put one's own pain in the place of the other's pain: "To be human is to suffer for the other, and even within one's own suffering, to suffer for the suffering my suffering imposes upon the other" (*DF*, 188). The same structure of asymmetrical obligation is expressed in *Otherwise than Being* when Levinas argues that I am not only responsible for the other but also for the other's responsibility (*OB*, 117). Levinas takes this priority so seriously that he is willing to argue that even the victim finds the pain of his persecutor prior to his own![28]

Paradoxically, "extermination without justice" remains a theme haunting reason in spite of the grain of reason at the core of extermination. For in rejecting theodicy, Levinas rejects any notion that the violence arising within history might find its natural limit by means of the very processes fueling that violence. For Levinas, no guarantee can be given that aenocide will fail to wipe out human history *unless that guarantee be that one enters into history oneself in order to resist violence*. But even this entry into history does not "guarantee" the success of one's intervention. Reason does not wait surreptitiously offstage only to step on to the scene of violence at the most opportune moment. Even one's entry into history on the behalf of the other exceeds reason. One finds oneself already before the face of the other and already inheriting a legacy of historical violence against the other without any guarantee that the crisis precipitated in this scene can ever be resolved. Levinas asks during an interview, "Doesn't a phenomenon like Auschwitz invite you, on the contrary, to think the moral law independent of the Happy End?" (PM, 176).

In fact, the question must be phrased even more accusingly: does not Auschwitz command one to act ethically in spite of the fact that "evil surpasses human responsibility" (*DF*, 193), in spite of the fact that the outcome of history may be aenocide, the very ending of the generations by means of which history finds its articulation? Levinas would have ethics think that thought in which one's very resistance to violence may ultimately be without effect but remains obligatory in spite of that. In the wake of Auschwitz, not only suffering but also goodness becomes gratuitous *but all the more commanding*.

In being commanded asymmetrically by the other face's vulnerability, one's responsibility is revealed to be gratuitous, without precedence, and without the security of a founding principle. With this claim one comes back yet again to the original question of this chapter, the question of whether one has indeed been taken in by morality and whether the very act of witnessing to the

Häftling does nothing more than to carry on the victimization that the witness would resist. To this threat of an annihilation without boundaries, Levinas proposes a goodness without justification. The issue is not whether one can justify one's response to the *Häftling* but that one has been called upon to respond to *the Nameless before any reason could have been given for doing so*. In fact, the very giving of the reason for one's response would already have presupposed the other's face, the one to whom my speech becomes signification. Rather than treating these quandaries as dilemmas capable of resolution by a more nuanced philosophical account, one must submit to them, live in their impossible tension, be commanded by them rather than mastering them. These others, *the Nameless*, leave no time for me to have considered my stake in the matter, my reasons for having responded.

One is in the impossible position of giving a witness that is gratuitous, without purpose, but all the same under the aegis of an authority *beyond question*. The very articulation of one's witness *for the other* leaves one in unresolvable ambiguity, in a quandary whose very insistence calls one to "infinite responsibility, to an untiring wakefulness, to a total insomnia" (*DF*, 193). But rather than signaling the defeat of reason, the quandaries of witnessing Auschwitz transcend reason and so call it into account. In them the grasp of reason upon its own intentions finds itself interrupted, already commanded to attend to the face of the other by an authority reason itself cannot establish even as it is subject to it. *The Nameless continue to command one even if the Nameless have been swallowed up in an irremediable and transcendent loss.* The gratuitousness of one's response to this command does not signify absurdity, the entertaining of a whim, but the priority of an involvement in the other that is commanded *for the sake of the other*, for no other sake than the other's transcendence of any plot or plan I may outline in which she or he might play a part.

In the end, one does not choose *whether* one will witness but *how* one will witness. In what could be termed an infernal witness, the witness of those like Andrei and the SS officer, one witnesses in spite of one's irresponsibility, in spite of one's subterfuges. In this witness, even the attempt to cover over one's witness witnesses. In ethical witness, on the other hand, in the witness of those like Borowski and Levi who would be commanded by the face of the other, one finds a witness of self-accusation, a witness unsure of its own sincerity, insecure in its own memory, but brought into insomnia, into a consideration of the other's plight that cannot be undone.

One also finds the witness of Frieda Aaron referred to in the last chapter, a witness not to betrayal in the face of the other's suffering but to fidelity.

Rather than allowing her daughter to die alone, a mother bribes herself and her other daughter onto a transport that seems destined for annihilation. Only by that arbitrary twist of fate that so permeated the death world of Auschwitz, did this transport turn out to have delivered the children and their mother to survival rather than annihilation.

What is miraculous in this story is not that the family found themselves delivered from death. As was pointed out in the last chapter, their very having been saved meant that two other women, with whom the mother had exchanged places, were delivered to death. To argue that this is miraculous would be to forget the indecency of any attempt at justification in the face of the other's suffering. But the fidelity involved in giving one's life for the sake of the other, in remaining true to the face of the other, even as one found oneself subjected to unbearable torment, is stunning. Michael Morgan has argued:

> The true Jewish vengeance, a Holocaust victim once wrote, is the power of the Jewish soul and its faith, an abiding trust that cries out "Hear, O Israel" in the face of guns and gallows and that cultivates dignity in the face of every imaginable assault on it. . . . The cases are myriad, cases of dedicated, intentional opposition, but for our purposes it is their common core and not their number that matters. Indeed in the midst of such hell even one such act would be sufficient encouragement for us.[29]

In the case of Frieda Aaron's mother, one finds an example of this dedicated opposition to an extermination without justice.

In discussing her mother's actions, Aaron remembers her having said: "We are more than human. And if we survive, and our truth is revealed and believed, others will want to touch us, for our suffering has sanctified us, rendered us inviolable."[30] Aaron in response to her mother's statement accepts at least one claim made in it—"namely, that we were more than human." For Aaron what is miraculous about her mother's resistance is how it saved all of them from madness. For if human beings were simply reasoning creatures, if something more than the merely comprehensible were not at work in their lives, then no mind could have undergone such cruelty and survived intact and no heart could have been so ravaged by betrayal and survived to care for others.

Yet Aaron also argues "our wounds have not really healed" (E, 198–99). The fidelity to which she gives witness is without a positive resolution. One does not emerge from the world-betrayed to find its trauma resolved by some "happy ending": "Grief like ours cannot be restoratively mourned" (E, 199). Yet one does reemerge from Auschwitz still claimed by the suffering of others, still engaged in a search for justice, still creative in one's response to the world. Like the witnesses of Borowski and Levi, as well as the witnesses of Andrei and the S.S. officer, the priority of the other's face is implicit within Aaron's testimony. Obviously much can be said about the distinction to be made between Aaron's epilogue and Himmler's speeches, but uncannily testimony is given in both instances regardless of one's commitment to making that testimony. In all cases, the priority of an ethical order transcending reason and its intentions leaves its trace in human discourse.

And he whom Levi termed "the Sómogyi-thing," in his last moments of capable resistance, gave food from his mouth for the sustenance of the others around him. One finds in the very collapse of this *Häftling*'s autonomy a commitment to the other transcending his own autonomy. For the sake of the other, Sómogyi makes provisions for a future that will not be his own. It is to this gesture and the ethical order it implies that Levinas would draw the reader's attention. One is not simply demoralized by the crushing of one's own, as well as the other's, autonomy, one is also inspired to an infinite, gratuitous resistance. Perhaps this is what Aaron's mother meant to suggest by stating "for our suffering has sanctified us, rendered us inviolable."

CHAPTER FOUR

Testimony and History

The Crisis of Address

Between the Other and the Other Others

B ut what is the situation of those who witness the *Shoah now, in this very mo-ment*, which paradoxically is to say, the situation of those who inherit the *Shoah* only in its aftermath? Left ambiguous in the preceding chapters is the distinction between those witnesses who actually have encountered the *Häftling* face-to-face in Auschwitz and the readers who receive the report of this encounter through the memory and testimony of those witnesses. For those who read Levi's text seem to be in a different relationship with the *Häftling* than Levi himself. Levi provides an account of the *Häftling* from out of his own immediate confrontation with her or him. He is commanded in regard to another who stands or has stood before him within the confines of Auschwitz. But we who live in the aftermath of the *Shoah* can come to the *Häftling* only through the mediation of a third party, of Levi, who as a witness necessarily must interpose himself between the *Häftling* and his reader, or the *Häftling*'s plight would fall into historical oblivion. Indeed, the very structure of witnessing commands that there be a *third* party, one who was absent or otherwise exterior to the immediacy of a dyadic proximity but who is nevertheless involved in the significance revealed in that proximity.

In the relating of his witness of the *Häftling* to a third party, Levi enters into a historical address, which is to say, an address that is given to those who inherit the plight of the *Häftling* without having been alive at the time of the *Häftling*. This address differs radically from that held in the face-to-face encounter, even as it finds itself commanded by that encounter. If one considers the manner in which Levinas composes that scene in *Totality and Infinity* in which one confronts the face of the other and in which one is addressed by the other's command not to murder, one quickly notes the scene takes place outside of any particular history or context. This exclusion of history, of a particular context in place and time by which the other might be given an identity, occurs even though the whole import of the scene of the face-to-face encounter is to articulate the particularity of the other *as other*. By setting up the scene in terms of a purely dyadic encounter that excludes historical or social specificity, Levinas implies that the other must be encountered *before* one can consider the third, that other other to whom one would give one's witness. This paradox must necessarily occur because Levinas's account of the face-to-face encounter reveals an expressive address on the part of the other that precedes or transcends whatever the addressee is to make of that address. The other *as other* is a particular other but not by the measure of her or his particular history or identity but by the measure of her or his susceptibility to *my* violence.

Further, in emphasizing the other's susceptibility to my violence, Levinas leaves unaddressed within the face-to-face encounter the distinction between those who actually undergo violence, who become the *Häftling*, and those who do not. In this regard, Levinas even goes so far as to argue that even if one is victimized, one is still in a face-to-face relation with the other who victimizes one. This suggests that whether the other whom one faces is a perpetrator or a victim, the relationship expressed in the face-to-face encounter is exactly the same. Only insofar as one's address enters into a social and historical world, insofar as one addresses the other others outside this particular face-to-face encounter, does the question of who is the victimizer and who is the victim become possible or meaningful. Only when one must compare between the various faces by which one is commanded, can the issue of justice, of a judgment about the degree of urgency of the various claims being made by various others, be raised.

Levinas's unwillingness to distinguish victim from victimizer within the face-to-face encounter does not mean he is indifferent to this distinction. But prior to any adjudication of where guilt might lie, one is already responsible for the other. Levinas distinguishes between guilt, which is the burden I or the other may carry for our specific actions or comportment in regard to the other, and responsibility, which is the burden upon me of the other's vulnerability to suffering. This burden imposes itself before any action on my part toward the other *as other* were even possible. Even if I am not guilty, I am responsible for the other. Or better: before I could ever become guilty, I was already responsible. In the face-to-face encounter, no time is given for me to ask whether the command of the other's face is justified. No matter who is the other I encounter, that other's suffering commands me. If I begin, within the very commanding of responsibility in the face-to-face encounter, to distinguish between victim and perpetrator, between the innocent and the guilty, the very height or asymmetry of the other's command of me is interrupted. Suddenly, some of the others command me more than the rest of the others. But if this is the case, then alterity itself no longer transcends reason, no longer involves the authority of an absolute command, and some sort of rational criteria is necessary after all to establish the ethical standing of any particular human being. One moves from an irenic to a polemic discourse in which only the others who fit these criteria would command me to responsibility.

On the other hand, in the wake of the face-to-face encounter the issue of who is guilty and who has been victimized is absolutely critical. For without a rational determination of how the other has treated all the other others, I am unable to be responsible for his responsibility. My interaction with the victimizer should not entail his dehumanization, but this does not mean I am without a voice to question his or her treatment of others *for her or his sake, as well as for the sake of the others.* Precisely because I have been so radically commanded to responsibility before the other, I must search out every way I am capable of responding to the other's violence as much as to the other's victimization.

Given these considerations, one must end up by arguing the genre of historical testimony arises in the wake of rather than in the midst of the face-to-face encounter. Or better, that historical testimony is continually interrupted by the face-to-face encounter in a manner for which history itself cannot account. Given the manner in which Levi or Borowski's testimony concerning the *Häftling* focuses on a particular other caught up in a historical situation in which he or she is also found in relation to other others, their witness cannot be characterized simply in terms of the face-to-face encounter as occurred in the last chapter, *as if* all that were involved in witnessing was a dyadic confrontation.

Indicative of this wider, secondary circle of responsibility was the manner in which the discussion of the encounter of the *Häftling* in the previous chapter jumped from Levi's or Borowski's voice (an autobiographical "I") to an impersonal voice (the reader, that "one" who at any moment could become the singular "I" of Levinas's text) to a unique voice, which is to say, my own voice (this "I" who could only be he who is writing this sentence and undergoing Levi's command at this very moment). The instability of reference in that analysis was a symptom of the infectious or transitive quality of their witness. Borowski and Levi's witness and the responsibility held in that witness commands *me.*

Borowski's "I" is also by its transmission in his witness *my* "me." This "me" in turn can be thought of in terms of all the other others who also are to be addressed by Borowski or Levi's text (not to mention the text "I" am now writing about those texts). Thus, "I" becomes "one."

But "one" must also remember that in the face-to-face encounter the only possible pronoun one can truly use is the first person: *I* am commanded by the other's nudity and in being so commanded *I* cannot find another to stand in my own place. In *Totality and Infinity*, as well as in *Otherwise than Being*, this *I* is in actuality Levinas himself. The autobiographical stance of Levinas's writing is not a stylistic idiosyncrasy but the inevitable outcome of the priority of the face-to-face encounter, in which *Levinas* finds himself elected, called out uniquely. To be called as Levinas is called, one must write the text again for oneself. No one can write it for anyone else, since the very urgency of the relationship precedes its thematization. Only because I stand in the face-to-face relation with the other am I uniquely commanded by that other.

In writing for those who come after them, on the other hand, Levi's and Borowski's testimonies invite or command the reader to substitute his or her own singularity for Levi's or Borowski's. This command, unlike the command of the face-to-face encounter, is mediated within history by means of language and is subject to the issues raised when one considers how the context in which one writes influences what one has said. Levi's very command is that his reader *consider* and *imagine* the *Häftling* by means of a text that has been provided for that reader and only in terms of which can occur that imaginative act on the part of the reader concerning the plight of the other. The text is delivered to the reader in order to substitute for the face of the other! But the text is as well an interpretation, an imaginative ordering and arrangement of events, facts, impressions, emotions, images, symbols, and so on, whose representation of the faces of the other others, of the *Häftling* as well as her or his victimizers, can no longer address the reader with the same authority as the *Häftling* her or himself. One's reading of the text is as well an inheriting of it.

Levinas treats this matter of inheritance in the latter part of *Totality and Infinity* by elaborating a notion of history in which the other's *works*, his or her stories, artifacts, labors, and so on are handed over to a succeeding generation without the other being there to express her or his own will concerning those works.[1] One could argue that the face of the *Häftling* in the writings of Borowski and Levi is no longer an actual face but an imaginative re-creation of their impressions of that face. And even the authority of that re-creation becomes compromised insofar as both Borowski and Levi are themselves dead and no longer remain to guide the reader's own interpretation of their interpretation of the *Häftling*. One is in the position of taking over a representation of the other's face without the other there to express his or her will in regard to that appropriation. In this manner, Levinas argues, the works of those who have been alienated by history can actually come to be used against their intentions.[2]

Thus, with the very first word of one's witness, the authority of the face-to-face encounter to which one would give witness is thrown into a crisis. For one translates the proximity of the face into a literary artefact. This crisis is doubled when one must also consider that the one for whom one gives one's witness is the *Häftling*, that is, one who is not only susceptible to violence but also has been actually violated. The very act of violation implies all the other others involved in that violation. To witness the *Häftling*'s violation one necessarily must witness for these other others as well. But this plural responsibility also means that the very inviolability of the face-to-face encounter, in which the other commands me from beyond any particular context, in which the face's authority is otherwise than its being, still finds itself inextricably interwoven with the fragility of a finite particular identity in a particular social and historical situation. One cannot deliver the victim from the confines of history or the realm of the *Shoah* even if the face of the victim addresses one from beyond that history or death world.

Lang's Rejection of Figurative Discourse

In his *Act and Idea in the Nazi Genocide*, Berel Lang is so perturbed by the crisis in authority instigated by artistic representations of the *Shoah* and its victims that he argues for a writing about it and them shorn as much as possible of artifice, of an interpretive or imaginative *poiēsis*. For Lang not literary but historical writing is the morally significant mode of responding to the *Shoah*. While Lang is more interested in delineating the severe limitations of literary accounts of what he terms the *Nazi genocide* than in describing the exact nature of the historical writing that would be appropriate to this event, his approach to this analysis is haunted by the following ideal of historical writing: "where the facts speak for themselves, anything a writer might then add through artifice or literary figuration will appear as a conceit, an obtrusion" (*AI*, 116). Given this ideal, the voice of history in response to the Nazi genocide would strive to become an anonymous writing—one would write in order to let the facts speak *for themselves*. In turning to historical writing, Lang would repress or severely constrain the singularity of the writer, as well as of her or his audience, so that the event itself rather than those who speak about the event remains the focus of one's historical and moral concern.

Thus, Lang argues that one is *obliged* in the aftermath of the Nazi genocide to avoid or diminish the importance of all forms of discourse about that genocide in which the writer's personal feelings or impressions play a leading role. In his words: "the most significant and compelling . . . writings about the Nazi genocide appear in the forms of historical discourse" (*AI*, 123). Even diaries written in the midst of the ghettos under Nazi control suffer from being too subjective in their perspectives and so vulnerable to misreporting actual occurrences (*AI*, 128). One can use the journals as source materials, in order to report what this or that group of people was perceiving at that moment in that situation, but the ultimate writing of the Holocaust must free itself from any influence that would stand between the reader and the event itself. One is obliged to represent as accurately as possible the true situation of those delivered to genocide without the interference of a text which draws attention to itself. For this reason, Lang would be led to object to the reliance upon Levi's and Borowski's writings, writings in which figurative discourse and the author's own subjective state of mind play deciding roles, as the exemplary sources for the account of the *Shoah* that is being elaborated here.

At the core of Lang's objections against the writing of witnesses such as Borowski and Levi lies the contention that such writing inevitably involves the creation of a *literary* as opposed to *historical* space of representation, a space in which one calls attention to the figures of speech and tropes constituting the body of one's writing (*AI*, 123ff.). The resulting metaphors and ironies (among other constructs) dominating this literary field only serve to emphasize that a specific writer has formulated her or his discourse in such a manner that his or her decisions as to how the discourse has been written become the preoccupation of that discourse. The articulation of this figurative space in turn leads to an emphasis upon the writer's particularity, that is, upon the particular author who created this particular figurative space as opposed to any other one that might be possible. Thus, Lang concludes, the poem is that literary space that would "personalize" the events it would represent historically (*AI*, 144).

Any attempt to personalize the events of the Nazi genocide is morally repugnant for Lang. He argues that the most distinguishing quality of genocide, its impersonality, is diminished by any poetic writing in which the particularity of one's voice comes to be the issue of one's writing. The extremity of the Nazi attack upon the humanity of its victims leaves those who would publicly institute the memory of that victimization in an extremely difficult position. Any attempt to call attention to the particularity of one's representation of the act of genocide can detract unforgivably from the dehumanization of its victims and encourages the reader in one manner or another to forget or repress the reality of that dehumanization (*AI*, 144–45).

In a corollary to this argument Lang claims that the literary author's struggle to personalize his text also leads to the phenomenon of "literary abstraction" (*AI*, 146) in which particular events, once they are represented in an imaginative, figurative manner, lose their contingent historical quality. In making this argument, Lang adopts an Aristotelian analysis of literary writing, but only so that he can end up reversing Aristotle's conclusion that literature is an intrinsically more serious form of writing about human beings than is history. Like Aristotle, Lang argues that insofar as the author tells a story for the sake of the story (and not for those to whom the story refers) she or he constructs a "fictional narrative" that is best "judged at least minimally by criteria of plausibility and consistency" (*AI*, 147). In emphasizing the plausibility of its narrative representation, literature in general and tragedy in particular emphasizes the motivations and choices humans make to act in a certain manner. Only insofar as a character's motivations fit her or his actions (i.e., insofar as he or she acts plausibly) can one say the narrative structure has been well constructed. Thus, at the core of Aristotle's argument for the superiority of literature to history is the claim that literature presents us with human agents whose actions become the dramatic focus of the audience's attention.

But, as Lang points out (as do paradoxically Levi and Borowski in their own "literary" narratives!), "the Jews did not become victims as a consequence of their own decision or choices" (*AI*, 148). In Lang's view, to translate specific victims of genocide into a figurative discourse would amount to forgetting that genocide, in adopting a policy of the annihilation of its victims, denies them any possibility of agency. In the world instituted by genocide, the victim does not exist to be struggled against. Further, the victim's actions have nothing to do with why the victim must be eradicated—the victim is to be disposed of simply because of the victim's so-called racial or biological characteristics. History, on the other hand, levels no requirement for a narrative plausibility that is intrinsically evident. Thus, the lesser form of writing for Aristotle becomes the morally superior one for Lang, at least insofar as one writes about the Nazi genocide.

The Sincerity of History

Lang proposes a writing of history within history that is itself ahistorical. Lang is disturbed by those who would argue that the hermeneutical instability of history means that writing about any event is always shadowed by the threat of a further revelation, of a yet-to-be-determined significance that heretofore has gone unconsidered. At a certain point, Lang argues, the facts have been determined and to encourage a suspicious attitude about them, as in the case of revisionist thinkers who argue the *Shoah* did not occur, undermines the very stability of any moral judgment that can be given about a historical event (*AI*, 156ff.). If nothing can ever be unproblematically characterized as having actually occurred, then no moral judgment about what occurs could ever matter. Without the stability of facts, of objectively established quanta of truth, the world becomes morally incoherent. These considerations become especially relevant when the event is as morally urgent as genocide. When so much harm has been inflicted upon so many, one is obliged to resist any deflection from a direct and unremitting consideration of its occurrence.

But Lang fails to take into account the priority of the rhetorical situation by means of which a historical discourse, even about facts, is established. Historical writing is not a machine in which words are produced so that various praxes of processing those words might then be employed to produce yet more words. Historical writing first and foremost would *express* its knowledge to an audience. Prior to the establishment of any historiographical discourse lies the rhetorical situation in which a writer addresses an audience and the audience responds. One can only establish Lang's ideal of historical truth if those who write that history are willing to act in such a manner that the others to whom that history would speak can trust what has been written. In historiography, the reader's trust in what he or she is reading hinges on the question of both the reader's and the writer's sincerity.

But how does one establish the sincerity of one's discourse? Lang implies that the various modes generally accepted by historians of using evidence in order to establish the shape of an event should suffice in this matter. Historical discourse is superior to literary discourse precisely because it invokes disinterestedness on the part of its practitioners. Given time and reliable praxes of analysis, objective truth inevitably emerges from this stance of disinterest. Yet experience has taught us again and again that historians misrepresent what they set out to picture based in part upon biases of which they are not yet aware, as well as the transcendence of any given person over whatever can be represented about his or her experiences.[3] Simply because the Nazi genocide involves an event of enormous moral import does not mean that such misrepresentation will not again occur. In fact, in spite of the urgency for an accurate depiction of genocide, one is obligated to assume that misrepresentation will occur and to admit that various modes or styles of representation will cede to yet others as the interests and world of those writing about the *Shoah* undergo historical change.

The history of the *Shoah* will inevitably have its own history. In the elaboration of a variety of responses to the *Shoah* that will occur through its transmission from one moment to the next, from one generation to the succeeding one, the issue of how and why one is taking up with that history will inevitably surface and should surface. One should not study the *Shoah* as if one were simply repeating *ad infinitum* a series of words about a specific occurrence. The question of how one is affected *in one's soul, which is to say, in one's humility before the other's face*, must also be part and parcel of a response to the *Shoah*. To ask this question does not necessarily introduce an unwarranted personal element into the account of how the Nazi genocide crushed the autonomy of a mass of human beings. Certainly, to use the Nazi genocide as an excuse to parade one's own particular capabilities or sensibility as a writer is itself inexcusable. But this very activity reveals an indifference to those who suffered annihilation that is itself worthy of discussion. As the witnesses of all the authors considered in the preceding chapters suggest, the other who is victimized commands one to resist his or her victimization. This command is not general or abstract but specific and singular. To undergo it is to find oneself in a struggle to articulate *in sincerity* one's concern for the other's plight. No one who writes or reads a history of the *Shoah* should be or ultimately can be without this struggle.

Levinas speaks of that mode of history written securely within the worldview of those who survive as "historiography." Historiography "recounts the way the survivors appropriate the works of dead wills to themselves; it rests on the usurpation carried out by the conquerors, that is by the survivors; it recounts enslavement, forgetting the life that struggles against slavery" (*TI*, 288). Like Lang, Levinas is uncomfortable with the idea that those who inherit the Nazi genocide (or the *Shoah*), or any other event of history (including an implicit reference to the Egyptian bondage among a multitude of other events in the mention of slavery) will not only ignore the suffering of those who have been rendered silent but will use that very silence to victimize yet again those who have suffered. Here history becomes a profane form of theodicy, in which victimization is justified retrospectively or at least is ignored or downplayed.

While Lang would write a history that resists "historiography" by emphasizing facts that speak for themselves, Levinas worries about a history "seen from the outside" (*TI*, 243), that is, a history that has become so obsessed with its objectivity that it demands the "depersonalization" of the one who writes it. This Levinas cannot abide, since the pivotal resistance to historiography does not stem from my disappearance "into the totality of a coherent discourse," but from my willingness to be accused of having been untrue to the historical other who has suffered in the very writing of my account of her or him. History is, to use an expression of Kristeva, in process/on trial. Before one is guilty, one is already uniquely and irreplaceably in a position of shame in regard to those about whom one is to write. Judgment here is predisposed against those who write history, even those who simply write down its facts. To resist the misuse of history, to refuse it "its [so-called] right to the last word" (*TI*, 242) (a word that Lang himself seemingly insists upon), the writer must write in such a manner that her or his very writing undergoes an incessant judgment. This judgment can only be articulated in terms of a unique and particular subject who "could defend itself during the adjudication and through its apology be present at its trial" (*TI*, 242).

The question is not simply one of finding out the facts, nor even of determining the most elegant representation of those facts. One must also position oneself within this writing in a manner that makes one uniquely and particularly responsible for how one characterizes those who have actually suffered. For instance, Saul Friedlander complains about how in the revisionist histories of contemporary German scholarship, "the history of National Socialism is no longer repressed; it has instead degenerated into dreary required reading" (*MHE*, 87). If one wishes to undermine the *Shoah*'s historical veracity, one need not deny it occurred. One can also adopt a style of writing about it that renders it insignificant even as one reports the actual facts of its happening. One adopts the indirection of a consciousness that considers all the relevant data except those that would burden one with responsibility. One poses in the mask of objectivity as one pursues one's self-interested agendas. Friedlander speaks of how "various forms of avoidance, and particularly the splitting-off mechanism (in which perfectly well-known facts such as the existence of Auschwitz were split off from the main argument of a historian's thesis), have led to a growing fragmentation in the representation of the Nazi epoch" (*MHE*, 126). One finds "ever more minute research into various aspects of everyday life and social change during the Nazi era, without any compelling overall interpretive framework" (*MHE*, 126).

Thus, the writing of the *Shoah* must involve a continuing discourse about the inadequacy of the act of that writing. Sincerity in this manner is not exhausted in giving a positive account of the facts of the case based upon what one has concluded are the most reliable sources. As Levinas argues, sincerity involves not only an exposure of one's thoughts and motivations before the other but also an exposure of that exposure.[4] In this vein, one is obligated as an historian not only to engage in a discourse about the *Shoah* but also to engage in a discourse about one's discourse, an act in which Lang himself is engaged by his very writing of *Act and Idea*. This discourse about discourse, in which one incessantly considers the inadequacy of the means by which an account concerning genocide is given, actually ends up emphasizing rather than diminishing the role of the writer who would witness to what has occurred. Lang himself gives proof of this by the amount of attention he pays to writers such as Borowski or Celan in the very act of considering their shortcomings as writers of the *Shoah*. Further the very breadth and details of Lang's analysis command a hearing in its own right from those (such as myself) who read him. *But this emphasis upon the writer as witness does not stem from an interest in his or her creation of a figurative space but in her or his commitment to those who have suffered.*

In considering the issues raised by the inadequacy of any representation of the *Shoah*, Saul Friedlander argues for a history fashioned as commentary. In commentary one does not write a straightforward version of the facts but fashions a discourse that "disrupt[s] the facile linear progression of the narration, introduce[s] alternative interpretations, question[s] any partial conclusions, withstand[s] the need for closure" (*MHE*, 132). This notion of commentary is not so far from Levinas's own description of a witnessing before the other in which one would avoid the enrapturing cadences of poetic discourse in order to fashion a *prose* of "rupture and commencement," a saying that involves the "breaking of rhythm" (*TI*, 203). One would search out a discourse in the face of the other that "preserves the discontinuity of a relationship, resists fusion and where response does not evade the question" (*TI*, 203).

As Friedlander points out, to carry this notion of ruptured discourse to its rhetorical extreme, as occurs in some deconstructionist approaches to history, "would exclude any ongoing quest for a stable historical representation" (*MHE*, 131).[5] This too would be unacceptable. One must finally argue for "the simultaneous acceptance of two contradictory moves: the search for ever-closer historical linkages and the avoidance of a naive historical positivism leading to simplistic and self-assured historical narrations and closures" (*MHE*, 131). Could not one call the submission to this unresolvable contradiction yet another quandary? In this quandary, commentary becomes a sort of writing that opens up historical texts by showing the complexity and necessary indeterminacy of any attempt to make clear and distinct what has actually occurred. Yet commentary must also close these texts by means of an evaluation or judgment of the materials one has been given, so that the victim might be rendered at the very least the justice of her or his victimization having been acknowledged for what it was.

Thus, when one writes about National Socialism, a moral burden is placed upon one that prohibits one from simply viewing the events of that time in a merely neutral manner, even as one strives for objectivity. One does not write *as if* one is simply listing a series of facts regardless of what one's commitment to those facts happens to be. In the wake of Nazi cruelty to other human beings, one discovers objectivity can only be instituted *after* one has been already claimed by a command to resist this cruelty one would picture or represent. *Before history can begin, one must have already protested its victims.* One *ought* to write in the following mode: "My stance of disinterest does not signify indifference. If what I picture before you occurred, as I now find it to have occurred, the very picturing of that occurrence comes already too late. I have adopted the stance of a disinterested observer in moral outrage over what I fear will be shown only too well to have been the case. Because what occurred is so morally outrageous, objectivity can never be more committed to any other perspective than that of articulating the victim's voice. My disinterest is already claimed by the victim. Further, this claim is so pressing that I must incessantly bring my own presentation of it to trial." This claim does not mean that one unjustly accuses the innocent, or that one ignores various facts and events that might put the victim in a less than positive light. Further, as one begins to consider one's representation of historical fact, one must yet again determine who the victim is and in exactly what manner. One must strive to be sincere in one's objectivity. But objectivity is not ultimately neutral, since it has already been commanded to speak as a mode of resistance against those who victimize.

This is the point of Levi's command and the claim made early in the first chapter that before one could have known about the *Häftling* one was already commanded by her or him. The claim made by the victim is not ontological but ethical in its structure, as is one's own commitment to the victim in response to this claim. This commitment leads to an epistemological vigilance, not for the sake of some abstract ideal of objectivity, or for the wonder of simply letting what exists appear as such, but for the sake of those who have *truly* been wronged. In particular, the "objective" historian ought to continually question how her or another's perspectives upon the *Shoah* might be undermining the priority of the commitment to the victim. One fears the surreptitious denial, the change in emphasis, the coining of a new term (*Resistanz*) that displaces accusation (*MHE*, 78).[6] One fears as well the settling into formulaic responses that would dull the urgency of one's responsibility in these manners, and so one engages in an interminable process of "working through" that tests "the limits of necessary and ever-defeated imagination" (*MHE*, 133).

Witness and Figurative Discourse

But one still needs to consider Lang's original thesis that *literary* (as opposed to historical) writing is not only an inadequate but also morally dangerous response to the *Shoah*. For it appears that Levinas as well is suspicious of "poetic" writing, a writing dominated by rhythm, which is to say by the manipulation of a textual field so that one is taken up in a field of writing purely for the sake of the manipulation of that field.[7] The image of the living entity given in this field is depicted in one of Levinas's essays as a "puppet" or "a caricature of life."[8] The face's smile or grimace in a work of art, Levinas notes, is suspended in time, unable to become expression and caught up in an aspiration for life that can never become an inspiration. In this manner, the imaging of the face becomes a form of idolatry. One forgets the priority of the face's susceptibility to suffering and becomes obsessed or fascinated with its image, with an appearing for the sake of appearing. In its disengagement from the face's expressiveness, art constitutes for Levinas "a dimension of evasion in a world of initiative and responsibility" (RS, 12).

Yet Levinas finds in the writing of the poet Paul Celan a mode of address that is "the interruption of the playful order of the beautiful" and in which occurs "the interrogation of the Other, a seeking for the Other."[9] Levinas also argues in an interview that among others the poets and writers can fulfill a prophetic role by putting into question whether the justice institutionalized within a society "really *is* justice" (RM, 19). These comments imply that literary writing, like the prosaic discourse described in *Totality and Infinity*, is capable of a self-critical awareness in which the insufficiency of one's own representation of the other is brought into a discourse offered to the other for the sake of the other. Put in other words, the poet, like the historian, is capable of a writing that would critically engage rather than enrapture its audience. Levinas mentions at the end of his essay attacking art as a form of idolatry that "modern literature, disparaged for its intellectualism, certainly manifests a more and more clear awareness of [the] fundamental insufficiency of artistic idolatry" (RS, 13). The self-conscious artist, like the critic, lives in doubt before artistic images and finds her or himself obligated to construct an image that is also a criticism of the image. While Levinas leaves this thought undeveloped, it at least implies that the artist, as much as the critic, might be able to articulate a discourse about discourse within the very confines of the art work in which the sincerity of one's discourse rather than a fascination with it becomes one's concern.

Could not this claim be carried a step further? For one can also argue that the figurative space opened up in literary writing might articulate a particular sense of the ethical that is actually covered over in critical or historical prose.[10] Further, this writing is not a newfound accomplishment of modern poets and novelists but stems from the prophetic traditions of Hebrew culture that Levinas has found to be most deeply allied with a purely critical, as well as immediately ethical, notion of discourse.[11] Yet Levinas's own characterization of prophetic discourse often ignores the vital role that images, rhythms, and poetic tropes play within its textual field.[12] Indeed, one can go so far as to argue that in prophetic writing one confronts another sort of historical writing than that discourse of prosaic representation which dominates contemporary elaborations of historical awareness. In this other form of historical writing, responsibility for the past is articulated by means of a figurative language in a manner that is extremely intimate and yet overwhelmingly ethical.

Yosef Yerushalmi argues that from the viewpoint of the Hebraic tradition its most historical writers were not the compilers of chronicles or the composers of great narratives but the prophets.[13] For a prophet, history involved more than the determined preservation of a memory that would have otherwise been lost in time. The prophet was also extremely interested in how particular memories had claimed her or him, so that her or his having a history implicitly carried with it the responsibility to be answerable to those others whom she or he remembered. The issue of truth for the prophet was not simply whether he or she had given a factually true account of an event, but also and more importantly whether she or he had been true to (faithful to) the memory of those who had lived out that event. In particular the prophet was concerned for the victims of history, for, in the words of Psalm 12, "the poor [who] are plundered and the needy [who] groan." In their memory, the prophet comes to resist in her or his writing "all those evildoers who devour my people like bread" (Psalm 14).

As these citations amply illustrate, prophetic writing is permeated with the very tropes and figures of speech that Lang argues are so damning in contemporary attempts to address the Nazi genocide in literary testimonies. John Sawyer comments that the biblical prophets showed "considerable skill in handling sophisticated literary techniques, drawn from various sources:

poetic, didactic, liturgical, or the like."[14] Abraham Heschel goes so far as to argue, "the prophet is a poet."[15]

But one would be mistaken to think that the prophetic uses of poetic language to write historically signals a simple repudiation of Lang's thesis concerning the nonpoetical nature of historical writing. In fact, the prophets often made the same critique of their own writing that Lang makes about poetry. André Neher discusses one such critique[16] from the Book of Ezekiel involving the crowds that would gather excitedly around the prophet in order to listen as he read his newly fashioned verses. Under the sway of "the word of the Lord" (Ezekiel 33:23), the prophet describes their attentiveness disparagingly. G-d complains that the crowds listen to the prophet as if he were "like one who sings love songs with a beautiful voice and plays well on an instrument." Particularly disturbing to G-d is how these admirers "hear what you [i.e., Ezekiel] say but they will not do it" (Ezekiel 33:32). Here one finds precisely that sort of distraction that Lang fears—that one not only forgets the ethical exigency of the victim's plight in the wake of the artfulness of a description of that plight but also ends up sustaining the apotheosis of the poet who writes that description.

Neher also points out that, according to the talmudic tractate Sanhedrin 93a, G-d not only allows but also commands Ezekiel to continue to write poetically, in spite of the susceptibility of the prophetic genre to this mode of misprision (E, 76f.). The prophet finds himself both outraged by the impotence of his poetic response to the suffering of others and yet obligated to continue its practice. Neher would interpret this paradoxical situation in terms of a dialogical initiative *(jeu)* on the part of G-d that would entice or seduce the prophet's auditors to an awareness that is paroxysmic, in which the very sense of what one's awareness means and where it leads one is shaken to the very core. In Neher's words G-d is telling Ezekiel: "One day, they will understand that My Word is not a fiction but a detonator of reality" (E, 76). The aesthetic address of the prophet becomes a surreptitious mode of involving his auditors in a conversation that exceeds their own sense of themselves, their unquestioning poses of self-sufficiency and self-satisfaction. The prophet exploits an uncanny, disturbing fellowship between fiction and G-d's word—both deprive their auditors of their normal, secure notions of the real.

One could also interpret Ezekiel's reversion to poetry in a manner that is more immediately ethical. Precisely because poetry is a form of writing in which pathos is at issue, in which one is to be shaken beyond one's own ken, its figurative language may be especially suited for that address that would call its reader into a paroxysmic affectivity before the suffering of others. As Emmanuel Levinas argues, "the Divine can only be manifested through my neighbor."[17] In this version of prophetic witness, G-d is revealed in the others one confronts, particularly those who are in need. In speaking of this revelation, Levinas would emphasize the vulnerability of the other over the figuration of G-d. The other's vulnerability, the nudity of the face, institutes a necessary atheism, in which G-d steps aside, is emptied out or contracts so that the one can come before the other as this particular other.[18] In making this argument, Levinas refers to Jeremiah 22:16: "He judged the course of the poor and needy; then it was well. Is not this to know me? says the Lord."

In G-d's address of Ezekiel, one hears a similar theme in the outrage of G-d over how the "shepherds of Israel," these very crowds flocking to hear the prophet's words, feed themselves on the sheep for whom they were to provide sustenance:

> Should not shepherds feed the sheep? You eat the fat, you clothe yourselves with the wool, you slaughter the fatlings; but you do not feed the sheep. The weak you have not strengthened, the sick you have not healed, the crippled you have not bound up, the strayed you have not brought back, the lost you have not sought, and with force and harshness you have ruled them. (Ezekiel 34: 2–4)

"Should not shepherds feed their sheep?" In this question G-d is not insistent upon G-d's own epiphany but upon the epiphany of the widow, the orphan, and the oppressed (see, as well, Isaiah 1:17). The indifferent crowds listen to Ezekiel's words but "their heart is set on gain" (Ezekiel 33:31). The condition of the heart, then, is what obsesses the prophet's address. The hardness of his audience's hearts, their indifference to being moved by the suffering of others, is what the prophet seeks to resist. In Levinasian terms, "the words of the Lord" would have the prophet call his audience back into the face-to-face encounter with the other in which the susceptibility of the other to violation commands one not only not to harm her or him but also to take the bread from out of one's mouth for the sake of the other (*OB*, 15).

Prophetic and Deliberative Witness

Thus, prophetic discourse is not primarily imaginative but elective. One addresses one's audience in order that it undergoes a command to which it is then called upon to respond. The command is articulated in the other's vulnerability that Ezekiel renders in the image of "the hunger of sheep." But the call to respond to this command occurs on two levels. On the first level one is called into an immediate relation with the other's vulnerability. This level involves what Levinas would term *prophetic witness*. In being called to this witness, one finds oneself reawakened to a responsibility that one could never have forgotten. That one has attempted to forget it, to live in what was termed "delusion" in the preceding chapter, or what the prophets might term "hardness of heart" is revealed as an utterly empty ploy.[19] At this level of response, the articulation of one's responsibility before the face of the other is, to use the term from Neher, paroxysmic: the very recoil from the other's claim upon one only makes the claim more acute. In the wake of this claim, any hope for a contentment founded in a concern for one's own needs and one's capabilities to provide for those needs is "devastated" (*CP*, 166). One finds that one is real only because of one's responsibility for the other. The world of safe homes and warm meals is detonated. One is helpless, "unable to be able," and yet also profoundly restless. One is not simply before the other but is in the very heart of one's "identity" an articulation of responsibility for the other.

Paradoxically, insofar as the prophet's address inspires his audience to this first level of response, the audience's very response replaces the call of the prophet and becomes its own command. Not the prophet's authority, not G-d's authority but the very proximity of the other's susceptibility is the authority by which one is commanded. This proximity, in which one is involved in the other before one could have chosen it, calls forth the authority of the other in the very articulation of one's own subjectivity. The command, no longer coming from the prophet, "sounds in the mouth of the one that obeys" (*OB*, 147).[20] This authority sounds in one's mouth as Isaiah's "*hineni*," a response to G-d's address that could be translated as "*here I am, already at your disposal*." At this level of response one's witness of what commands one involves an exposure to the other from which no recourse can be given.

In this exposure one's very psyche is revealed to be animated by exposure, by one's signifying-for-the-other.[21] Only because the other's face already claims one, because one finds one has already been addressed, can one find oneself articulated as a singularity, a unique node not of identity but of responsibility. In the *hineni*, one gives a sign "of this very signifyingness of exposure" (*OB*, 143). In finding oneself sounding the *hineni* in one's mouth, *one not only is exposed but must also be exposed in one's exposure*. Exposure is doubled and redoubled, paroxysmic. In being so exposed one is not confused with the other but in continual recurrence to oneself for the sake of the other. One's subjectivity is articulated as an "incessant signification, a restlessness for the other . . . cellular irritability" (*OB*, 143). In the wake of exposure to the other, one "becomes a heart, a sensibility, and hands which give" (*CP*, 168).

Thus, the literal heart of one's subjectivity is a doubled passivity, an undergoing of one's undergoing, in which affect rather than concept is singularly at issue. At this level of affectivity, one undergoes "a trauma that could not be assumed" (*CP*, 166), as one is struck open to the very core of identity, of the return of one to oneself, by the other's infinite resistance in his or her vulnerability to any appropriation of it that one might attempt. In this being affected for the sake of the other, which transcends an emotional life centered in the privacy of one's feelings, one experiences "the impossibility of indifference . . . before the misfortunes and faults of a neighbor" (*CP*, 166). In this sensitivity to the plight of the other is found Levinas's philosophic translation of the prophetic notion of heart.

In being called to one's heart by prophetic discourse, one is exposed in that call to the very exposure of one's exposure before the other. One is called, in other words, to sincerity. In sincerity one is involved in an affect, a "fear for the other" that is "my fear, but there is nothing in it of fear for myself" (BC, 39). In this fear one is assigned to being responsible for what might have harmed the other *no matter what one may have intended*. One lives in "fear of all that my existing, despite its intentional and conscious innocence, can accomplish of violence and murder" (BC, 38). One is *"accused without guilt"* (BC, 37), which is to say, one is accused of all that can befall the other regardless of whether or not one has initiated any of it.

In addressing the extremity of passivity that is undergone in one's sincerity before the other, Levinas contrasts it with the sort of passivity found in the existential thrownness of Heideggerian *Geworfenheit*.[22] In *Geworfenheit* one finds one has already been implicated in a scene, that one is already in debt (*Schuld*) before one could have decided for oneself what one's response was to be.[23] But *Geworfenheit*, one's having-been-thrown, also becomes the condition by which one finds one's significance in relation to oneself. At the ontological level of Heidegger's analysis, *Geworfenheit* ends up articulating a significance *about* a having been thrown *for the sake of* he or she who was thrown. Thus, in one's anxiety, one's being-toward-death, one finds one moved *about* one's finitude *for the sake of* one's finitude. The movement of being brought out of oneself ends up in articulating the significance of who one was already given to be.[24]

But prophetic affectivity is paroxysmic rather than ecstatic. Here affectivity "takes shape as a subjection to the neighbor" (*CP*, 166), in which no time is given for one to return to the question of one's own being. In sincerity, one is an effacement of one's presence before that other that must be rendered more and more acute. Before the nudity of the other's face, one is paradoxically "denuded of all attributes" (BC, 37). Even sincerity itself cannot be treated as an attribute of one's response to the other but rather is that response, that *saying*, in which one is opened up to a giving *"without being able to dissimulate anything"* (OB, 143): *"hineni,* here I am, already at your disposal."

Prophetic writing then begins in a nonintentional affect. Its saying, in this mode, is restless and ever self-effacing. One could characterize it as the addressing of one's address, although an addressing that is not active and intentional but commanded and undergone. Because this addressing of address cannot be for oneself but already must be for the other, prophetic discourse is perpetually insecure about whatever comes to be said in its saying. One finds oneself commanded not only to respond to the other but also to accuse one's response to the other, to expose one's exposure before the other. In so doing, one would undo "the alienation which saying undergoes in the said, where, under the cover of words, in verbal indifference, information is exchanged, pious wishes are put out, and responsibilities are fled" (OB, 143). Certainly this is the case in Ezekiel's discourse, in which the very words he uses to signify the vulnerability of the other settle into the consciousness of his audience as a thematic structure that they are now free to interpret or speculate upon. What was given as a traumatic imposition of responsibility is now betrayed as his listeners hear the prophet's address in terms of an intimate and private discourse of lovers. The members of the audience transform G-d into a mirror that uncritically affirms the priority of their own needs and self-complacency. In doing so, they flee their troubling responsibilities for the other, for the oppressed, the orphan, the widow, the stranger.

As the complexity of the audience's reaction suggests, simply to find oneself exposed before the other does not exhaust what responsibility for the other entails. The second level of the prophetic call to respond occurs when one finds that one must in turn witness the first response of sincerity before the other to all the other others surrounding one. The very call of the prophet to the first level of response, to sincerity, was in fact the articulation of this second level of response as well. The prophet addressed his audience in order to bring them to a consideration not only of the face-to-face encounter but also of their judgments and actions in the wake of this encounter. In doing so, the prophet was already witnessing the face-to-face encounter to all the other others. As a result, he had to make judgments about to whom he should witness and in regard to what actions. In doing so, he could not simply be sincere but must also have articulated a vision, a figure, of justice.

In this articulation, the prophet must move from *hineni*, from an unmitigated saying before the other of one's being addressed by the other, to a saying that falls more fully into a said, which is to say, a saying that becomes an
artefact, a discourse, with discrete claims about the truth of the social and historical situation in which one now finds oneself. But this fall into the said
would also keep its commitment to being animated by a saying before the
other. One might term this second level of response deliberative witness.
While prophetic witness "is humility and admission, kerygma and prayer,
glorification and recognition" (*OB*, 149), deliberative witness involves one in
the asking of questions. In the asymmetrical relation before the face of the singular other, one's exposure before the other preempts all questions. One can
never be right enough, assured enough in one's innocence, to demand an answer of the other. But in deliberative witness, one is asked to compare incomparables, in order that justice might be rendered. Here one asks questions of
the other but only in relation to all the other others.

In this second mode of response, one is called to an "incessant correction" (*OB*, 158) of the responsibility articulated in the first mode of response.
In the wake of one's proximity to the singular other, one's "*hineni*," one is
called upon to represent this other to all the other others. But this representation does not involve the reduction of one's witness to an account of the
other that is total and impersonal—one does not simply let the facts speak for
themselves. Ezekiel's representation of the oppressed, even as it speaks about
their plight, even as it portrays the reactions of those who ignore that plight,
also continues to speak in a mode of emphatic or exhortatory address. The
most pressing issue of his discourse is how those to whom he speaks will answer his question to them: "Should not a shepherd care for his sheep?" In posing this question, Ezekiel is reminding his auditors that, as Levinas puts it,
"justice is impossible without the one that renders it finding himself in proximity" (*OB*, 159). The prophetic question is not asked indifferently or arbitrarily or even disinterestedly but in exhortation for a response that would in
turn be a witnessing for the other. In this second level of witness, one's obsession by and for the other is not broken up but is now articulated in a representation of the other in which "the contemporaneous of the multiple is
tied about the diachrony of the two" (*OB*, 159). One adopts a mode of repre-
sentational speaking in which "the equality of all is borne by my inequality,
the surplus of my duties over my rights" (*OB*, 159). By implication, one can
address to the other others the burden of this same surplus, a burden announced not in one's own name but in the name of those who are most susceptible to violence.

Textual Affectivity and Tonality

One can mark within this second level of witness, within the call to delibera-tion, to the comparison of incomparables, the continuation of an emphasis upon affect and by implication the need for a discourse caught up in a certain mode of using literary figures and tropes. While a nonintentional affect tran-scending even the distinction between the intentional and the nonintentional dominates the saying of prophetic witness, the complexity and complexes of intentional affect, as well as its unconscious dimensions, become an additional consideration in deliberative discourse. This claim seemingly flies in the face of Levinas's own emphasis upon deliberative witness as a mode of *rational* dis-course in which straightforwardness and disinterestedness seemingly would play deciding roles. One might think here of a discourse that Levinas at one point terms "philosophic criticism" in which one "speaks in full self-posses-sion, frankly, through concepts, which are like muscles of the mind" (RS, 13). Would not the intensification of the image in the "allusions," "suggestions," and "equivocations" (RS, 13) that open up and characterize the artistic and lit-erary space lead one astray from one's witness, one's assignation to the other? Deliberative witness should lead one to the other, as closely as possible to the *hineni* that in its signifying is a one-for-the-other, a "pure transparency" (RS, 6). Discourse that becomes preoccupied with its own text seems eminently questionable in this context.

Paradoxically, the very notion of incessant correction may require an in-tensification rather than effacement of the figurative. For incessant correction need not and should not occur only at the level of one representation versus another. At times, Levinas's description of incessant correction suggests a dis-course in which various notions of or perspectives on what is at issue are each given their respective representations. One would then supposedly listen as each representation spoke its version of the question. In the outcome of this listening, no single representation would predominate but each would serve to limit and inspire the versions given in all the other representations. This discourse, like Lyotard's dissensus, would lead to an intensification of the problems that call for social responses. As a society became increasingly just, one would become increasingly sensitive to the extent and diversity of injus-tice. Hence, Levinas's dictum that "the more I am just the more guilty I am" (*TI*, 244).[25]

One can also imagine a mode of representation in which an incessant cor-rection is already articulated at the very level of representation itself. This genre of representation would turn to the very modes of discourse that Levinas has sometimes criticized—allusions, suggestions, metaphors, equivocations—in order to open up a given representation to an infinition of address and addresses. In the articulation of the poetic figure, language is doubled over itself, so that it no longer signifies a signified in a straightforward manner. In its doubling and redoubling of language, the figure complicates signification, renders it, to use the terms of postmodern discourse, "indeterminable." But this destructuring of the representation by means of a complicating or doubling over of signification does not necessarily involve the writer in an evasion of responsibility. The writer does not necessarily write in figurative language because he or she would avoid the straightforwardness of truth.

Paradoxically, straightforwardness or sincerity also requires that one submit the very intention to write an account of the truth to the question of all the other possible accounts of the truth addressing that account. The very words one uses to construct one's account are already doubled over into a plurality of other accounts expressing the views of a series of other voices. For this reason, even before one has begun to give the structure of one's own account, its very constituents have already been claimed by these other voices. In whatever one says, the trace of other sayings are at issue. Thus, one writes in "ambivalence" (*OB*, 162). One does not so much invent the doubling over of one's words into the voice of the other as register it. Creativity here is a receptivity to what Levinas terms the trace, to the transcendence of the other's voice as it is registered in one's discourse. In hearing that trace, one speaks not only for oneself but also for or in response to the other. This doubled speaking saddles one with a writing that finds itself incessantly interrupted and redirected.

Among others, Handelman has noted how the lexical instability of midrashic discourse, in which puns and allusions are so predominant that, as Levinas, in keeping with the Jewish tradition, once put it, each word of the Torah has seventy interpretations, offers a prototype for a writing of incessant correction.[26] In his essay on Celan, Levinas speaks of a citation of Malebranche made by the poet ("Attention is the prayer of the soul") but only by way of "a text by Walter Benjamin on Kafka and Pascal, according to Leon Chestov" (*PN*, 42). Consonant with a Levinasian understanding of midrashic discourse, Malebranche's statement is submitted to a plurality of citations by means of which it is given multiple readings and contexts. The destructuring or displacement of meaning that occurs in this shifting of voices is neither anonymous nor simply indeterminate. Because textual indeterminacy arises from the intertwining of singular, transcendent voices, of nodes of address, the issue of how a text registers the various responses of a plurality of speakers becomes its preoccupation.[27] This registering, in which the text is inflected[28] in the other's voice, as well as all the other others' voices, is a rendering traumatic of the text. The text carries more than can be said, because the saying of multiple voices intervene in every said. The instability of the traumatized text is not so much hermeneutical, in which one thinks of the inexhaustible variety of interpretations it elicits, as it is ethical, in which one is confronted with a plurality of addresses, of other expressions, that dispossess the subject of its own intentions and meanings and breaks open any possible closure of the text.

In its inflection of the other's and all the other others' voices, the prophetic text is affective in its structure. Its indeterminacy does not simply arise from the indeterminacy of boundaries, from the impossibility of ever totally fixing a meaning in terms of all the other meanings in the text. Textual indeterminacy also arises because texts carry the voices of the other and all the other others. This ethical burden enters from beyond the text, overwhelms it, and compels it to carry within the limitations of its discourse a significance it has not been nor ever could have been prepared to accept. In Susan Handelman's words, "Signification here is not Barthe's 'pleasures of the text' but rather pain as 'pure deficit, an increase of debt in a subject that does not have a hold on itself' (*OB*, 15)" (*FR*, 256).

This burden of meaning, this trace of the other, leads to a logos, which, according to Krzysztof Ziarek, is lateral in its articulation.[29] One does not simply leave the text behind in search of the infinitely transcendent other but is submitted within the text to a proximity of the other that obsesses the meanings of the text and so already has claimed whatever one might say about the text. In Ziarek's words:

> Laterality does imply absolute separation, but a separation that already designates an "obligating" direction. This direction lateralizes the said in a manner radically different from polarization, for lateralization implies not only difference but the enveloping in non-indifference. It is lateralization that makes all language, all atoms of the said, at each and every moment, marked with the saying, with the non-indifference toward the other. (*IL*, 97)

To read the text is to find oneself always already engaged in responding to a series of interlocutors, to diverse sayings whose address of one is prior to and incumbent upon whatever one might make of that address. One finds one's own discourse is continually effaced by this priority of the other. Thus, Levinas writes of Celan's multiplicity of citation that it "obeys no norm." One must "listen to him more closely" so that one hears how his poem "already speaks *with* another" (*PN*, 42). Further, this priority is articulated even when a node of saying is not indicated. Whether one consciously cites the saying of the other or not, that saying is always already at issue.

Thus, the preoccupation of poetic discourse with the articulation of its text, with the individuality of its saying, need not lead to narcissism, a fixation upon self, but to responsibility, an obsession by and for the other. The very fact that one's subjectivity is already traumatic, already caught up in a nonintentional having-been-affected, demands that one's writing and reading, no matter what the text, is already burdened by the saying of the other. One's very words already are claimed by other voices, already burdened with a debt to the other, so that one's response in language to the other is not at all unlike "a tearing away of bread from the mouth that tastes it, to give it to the other" (*OB*, 64).

Rather than taking up with one's words *as if* they were one's own, one offers them to another. In the very movements of allusion, equivocation, and suggestion, one signification is interwoven with another so that one's own meaning, one's intentional grasp of the text is always in the process of being effaced. This effacement or offering involves not so much a rupture of one's language as a "baffling" of the text, in Ziarek's terms, so that "the language mesh is ruffled by the passing-by of the other" (*IL*, 96). This ruffling or traumatism leaves the text overdetermined, weighted with a having-been-affected that cannot be directly translated into a prosaic, thematic statement. In being baffled, the text's signification is revealed in terms of its being addressed by another.

Put otherwise, the language of this text signifies not so much in terms of its indexicality as of its tonality. In the tone and tones that a given text takes on or registers is given the mode of address by which the text approaches an other, as well as all the other others. Tone is not in the first place the registering of one's own state of mind (although it encompasses this as well) but of one's expression in regard to another who has addressed one. In expressing one's thought to that other, the same words can take on a variety of often contradictory meanings through a change in their tone. For example, in his *Meridian* Celan points out how Lucille's "Long live the king" in Büchner's play on the death of Danton is given an entirely different meaning from its denotation by means of her tone, her mode of addressing her auditors (*CPr*, 39–40). The source of this tone can in part be located in various clues given in the contexts from which a specific expression arises. But at its source, one's tone transcends the resources of language as a having-been-said and resides in the situation of address, of saying. In its tone, one's language shows itself to be a sensitivity, a vulnerability to the other. One's words do not belong to oneself but have always already been offered to and claimed by another. In being offered to and claimed by that other, one's expression must in the first place respond to and register the meaning of that offering and claiming—whether it be in scorn or compliance, indifference or enchantment, dissimulation or sincerity.

In one's tone, one's affect is revealed. But, as the discussion above has indicated, affect for Levinas, as for Celan, is not primarily to be articulated as the ecstatic return of the self to its self. One's tone can reveal one's state of mind, the particular subtleties of one's own sensibility. But the very tonality of one's tone reveals that in one's saying the very exposure of one's exposure to the other is at issue. Tone always implies a struggle to be sincere (or to avoid sincerity).[30] In tone is given how language is always already a registering of the other's address of one. Whether one acknowledges it or not, one's expression to the other, one's saying, is already possessed by the other. Otherwise, one would merely be talking to oneself or to no one at all. Whether one wills it or not, one is called upon to reveal to the other the affect of one's saying, one's traumatism. Speaking renders one naked. That some choose to cover up this nudity, or to deny in their tone that they were ever vulnerable to the other only emphasizes the priority of their vulnerability. The Nazi disdain for Jewish persons, as well as their Judaism, was in fact underlain by a helplessness before these Jewish others from which the Nazi could never have recovered. Thus, tone is in the first instance not a modification of what is to be said but the very saying of the said—in one's tone one's language already is submitted to another, is already an expression rather than a thing or a work.

Further, a history of tones already resonates in the language to which one turns in order to address the other. For instance, in the wake of Nazi practices within German of greeting and addressing others, one's writing or saying of *Heil*, the German word for health and flourishing, is hardly the innocent act that a simple consideration of the word's indexical meaning might suggest. Before one could say it as one's own, the word already carries a tone that affects whatever one wishes to say. One finds that the words one uses accrue a meaning not only in terms of their indexicality, of what they refer to, but also in terms of their locution, of how they have been used to address others. One's use of a word to address others already carries the history, the burden, of all the other acts of address that have been carried through that word. Words register the tone of their address. As the next chapter suggests, Celan is particularly disturbed at how an entire history of malice against Jews is registered in the German words he must now use to witness to the *Shoah*.

Prophetic Affectivity

In adopting figurative language, the prophet would speak to her or his audience in terms of their hearts, hearts set on gain, hearts hardened against the vulnerability of the other to violence. These hearts, knotted up in delusions of self-sufficiency, in rebellion against their own powerlessness before proximity, consumed by what Levinas has called (in regard to National Socialism) an "obstinacy to be" (*AS*, 61), protest their lack of affect or their outright hostility in regard to those who suffer. As uncomfortable as Ezekiel might be with the poetical dimensions of his discourse, the very misprision of that discourse by his auditors becomes the sign, as well, of the traumatic dimensions of the crowd's involvement in all the other others. Underneath and prior to its disdain for the oppressed, the crowd has already been affected by the other. In resisting this having-been-affected, the crowd constructs its own version of its affect: one interprets the urgency of G-d's address, its paroxysm or acuteness, in terms of a lover's discourse in which one yields to what one claims is a call to ecstatic and even orgiastic interplay with G-d. In fascination with this figuring of G-d, the crowd forgets G-d's own abhorrence of idolatry and obsession with righteousness and loving kindness, with modes of affect in which justice before the other, especially the other who is disenfranchised, is urgently at issue.

But while the crowd is busy dehistoricizing and desocializing the affect of the prophet's discourse, that affect continues to be in command. As Neher would argue, the urgency, the paroxysm, of G-d's address continues to be at issue, even as the crowds repress it. If the prophet would revert to a purely intellectual approach at this point, his address would cease to render the immediacy of involvement, that traumatism of the other in one's own identity that Levinas emphasizes to be the heart and soul of ethical responsibility and political justice. For this "reason," the prophet refuses to abandon ethical affect and continues to write poetically as well as prosaically. At the same time, the prophet's address must resist the ecstatic notion of affect that dominates the crowd's response to him. This secondary affect, in which one's being moved becomes the articulation of one's ownness, of Heideggerian *Eigentlichkeit*, is subjected to an interruption, an effacement, a paroxysm. In this manner, the impact of the prophet's address serves to destabilize the normal affective import of poetic writing. No longer simply aesthetic, prophetic poetry leaves both its reader and writer in a state of mind in which one questions the priority of one's own feelings, in which one returns to an affect in which feelings are no longer felt for the sake of oneself but as an effacement before the other.

This feeling for the other is not to be thought of in terms of a cathartic release or some form of sympathetic empathy, a *Mitgefühl*, in which one feels the other's suffering *as if* it were one's own. In the prophetic articulation of affect, what one must feel as one's own is how one does not feel the suffering of the other, even as one is moved to some representation of it. The other's suffering is precisely not one's own suffering and for that very reason leaves one in a state of uneasiness for the sake of the other. In the prophetic moment, one finds one is animate precisely in being effaced before the other. In confronting the other's suffering, one's own "anguish" is felt insofar as one "is immolated without fleeing [oneself], without entering [oneself], without entering into ecstasy, without taking a distance from [oneself]" (*OB*, 108). Sincerity, in which the inability to flee the other or one's own responsibility for that other is registered, prohibits any cathartic release from the other's plight.

This obsession does not confine itself to sincerity. Beyond one's sincerity in the face-to-face relation are the complexes of feelings that are instigated when one must compare one's sincerity before the other with one's concern for all the other others. One could argue that the "incessant correction" of which Levinas speaks above (in regard to what has been termed deliberative discourse) involves one's representation of the other not only in concepts but also in affects. Sociality is not indifferent to affect but immersed in it. As one struggles to represent the other to all the other others (and vice versa), one must continually reconsider how each of these others suffers uniquely and individually. While one can offer oneself in the place of any given other and so resolve the crisis posed by the other's suffering through suffering in the place of the other,[31] one must also consider how all the other others' suffering also matters, also claims one's substitution. One must make judgments about the relative urgency of pain and anguish, and one must also forge a discourse in which the other is given the opportunity to represent her or his own versions of his or her suffering. Without a discourse in which the full range of the other's emotional life is given nuanced and detailed consideration, one could hardly say one is being responsive to the other's call for justice.

The claim is that prophetic discourse takes upon itself to engage in a representation in which judgments about the weight and importance of the other's affect, as well as the sincerity with which one is claimed by that affect, plays a decisive role. In elaborating this representation, one is called upon to consider how one's preoccupation with one's feelings, with affect articulated as an ecstatic involvement in one's own being-moved for the sake of being so moved, is interrupted incessantly by another sort of affect. In its paroxysm, in which the other's suffering is rendered with greater and greater acuity, one's feelings are broken open and one is submitted to an ongoing critique concerning their relative importance.[32] In the process of discerning one's feelings, one turns to figurative language, to metaphors, allusions, equivocations, and so on, as the indirect means of evoking affect, of signifying that passivity in which one's intentional life is already caught up in a situation. But then the very turn to these modes of representing affect is itself subjected to an ongoing critique, an incessant correction. This correction occurs not merely by a conceptualizing of affect, by placing footnotes in one's poems in which one comments on the rational implications of what one has just evoked, *but by letting intentional affect be struck open by an address that is not one's own.* In this address, one is inspired to a feeling about the impossibility of feeling the other's feeling rather than to a feeling that simply feels for oneself or in place of the other's feelings.

It can be claimed that in deliberative witness a third modality of affect emerges. In his essay, "G-d and Philosophy," Levinas distinguishes between two types of affect: intentional and nonintentional. Intentional affect involves an ecstatic return to oneself in which whatever lies outside of one's subjectivity reenters into it as "experience," or even perhaps as the question of the Being of one's being. Intentional affect signifies the "incessance" (*CP*, 157) of one's identity, of the return of one's attentiveness to its very articulation in the same. On the other hand, nonintentional affect has been characterized as traumatic, an imposition of the infinite into one's psyche that cannot be assumed. Here the depth of one's emotions is no longer capable of articulation even in an ecstatic play of absence in presence. Thus, one can characterize the infinite resistance of the other's face to my power over it as imposing "a depth of an undergoing that no capacity comprehends, that no foundation any longer supports, where every process of investing fails and where the screws that fix the stern of inwardness burst" (*CP*, 163). In this affect, the face has already affected me, its address has already been placed in me, before any recollection of it could ever have occurred. Levinas also characterizes this affect in prophetic terms as "a devouring fire, catastrophying its site." (*CP*, 163)[33]

But in deliberative discourse one must slip between intentional and nonintentional affect. In so doing, a third modality of affect is articulated in which intentional affect serves as a mode of representation for the ethical urgency of nonintentional affect, even as intentional affect is "destructured"[34] by the nonintentional affect it seeks to mediate. In destructured affect, one's intentional feelings, one's fear, anger, elation, or even anxiety become specific modes of signification for one's inability to feel the other's feelings. This third notion of affect is not a Hegelian synthesis of the other two in which a higher, more complexly determinate reality is achieved. Nor is it caught up in a dilemma in which one must choose one alternative or the other—one is either in one's own feelings or one is traumatized by the other's vulnerability, the other's transcendence of my own self-presence. Rather, the trace of nonintentional affect disturbs intentional affect, renders it in constant perturbation for the other's affect. One lives in the ambiguity of an enigma in which the very feeling of one's feelings is already involved in a prior commitment that incessantly puts one's feelings into question. One's intentional affect is denucleated. One's feelings become a pluralism, a variety of addresses that now confront one with a social and historical world in which the feelings of all the other others must also be rendered in one's discourse, even as one's discourse is addressed to them.

The feeling for the impossibility of feeling the other's feeling leaves the figurative space of the literary work in crisis and in quandary. As the preceding chapters have indicated with increasing urgency, in the face of the other, and in particular, in the face of the *Häftling*, one's imagination works negatively rather than positively. In following out Levi's command to imagine the suffering of the *Häftling*, one is not so much concerned about the picture one can paint of her or his situation as how that very picture fails to render the other's situation in terms of the other. But this phrasing of the quandary of the limitations of the imagination in terms of a negative versus positive characterization of imagination is itself deceptive, for it suggests that one has some sort of mystical ken beyond that of one's normal conception of imagination, some "negative capability," in which the other's feelings as such are finally registered in one's own. This is precisely what cannot occur if one is to be serious in one's claim that the suffering of the other truly transcends one's own. Instead of speaking of a negative imagination, one should now refer to an effacement of imagination that is paroxysmic, a rendering acute of the limits of imagination through a limitless intensification of its helplessness before the other. In this intensification of effacement, one is incessantly put into question in regard to one's feelings, even as one pictures as well as one can what one thinks and feels the state of mind of the other might involve. One's affect is rendered ambiguous—one feels one's feelings in order to feel that one cannot feel the other's feelings. One does so because one is obligated to speak to all the other others for and to whom one is also responsible.

In technical terms, one could characterize the prophetic use of figurative language as one that inevitably is dis-figuring, that is to say, a figure is introduced only to be emptied out by the intrusion of a troubling excess that defies any space for a claim of mastery on the part of the prophet/poet who authors the figure, or the auditors who hear the figure. Thus, poetry in the prophetic mode is written under a trope of countering, of resistance, in which all the varied and elaborate attempts of writing to give the figure of the other are disrupted. This trope is established in The Book of Ezekiel by the prophet's appeal to "the words of the Lord." In this particular mode of address is registered the entrance of an infinite disturbance into one's discourse, in the wake of which discourse has no means of remaining or restoring a tranquility or confidence in its representation of the other. This trope of countering is in reality a metatrope, since it gives the condition under which all the other figures and tropes of prophetic writing are to be heard. After its introduction, all the other tropes become paroxysmic—their revelation occurs in the acuity of their attention to an address coming from beyond any possibility of being given a figure. Yet this acuity can only be revealed insofar as one has already committed oneself to figurative discourse, to a text in which the very mode of how the text figures the world is itself opened up to incessant critique.

The Figurative Space of Witness in Borowski and Levi

The discussion in the foregoing sections advances an alternative to Lang's thesis that historical writing necessarily de-emphasizes its figurative space. Just to the contrary, in prophetic and deliberative witness, one finds a particular sort of historical representation in which the figurative nature of one's writing is magnified infinitely. The mode of this magnification is the manner in which the address of the other slips into one's discourse and yet also remains outside of it to trouble its figuration, to call the text to greater and greater attentiveness to a voice whose saying can never become a said without a certain betrayal[35] or contradiction[36] having occurred. For this reason, one writes in incessant correction of what one has written. This mode of writing seems quite different from that authoritative, magisterial accumulation of facts and insights that Lang's own notion of historical discourse would instantiate, at least in relation to the events of the *Shoah*.

In emphasizing *address* over *explication* or *explanation*, the prophets articulate a historical witness in which one is called upon not to indifferently accumulate facts but to remain true to those about whom these facts are accumulated. The instability of one's representation of the other, the fact that it will be subject to limitless revision, does not mean one gives up any hope for facts. But one must also be wary of an obsession for facts that would allow one to forget the priority of responsibility over certainty in one's ethical relation with the other. The witness of Levi and Borowski, even as it translates the proximity of the other's face into a representation of that face for all the other others, for all those who inherit the memory of the *Shoah*, calls one into a responsibility for that face that transcends its translation into any specific said. What is expressed in Levi and Borowski's discourse is the trauma of a responsibility that claims one from beyond one's own resources to justify that claim. This trauma does not remain contained within a specific moment or figure of what is written but infects discourse at every turn and leads to a writing that is metatropic, open to incessant correction, to an ongoing self-accusation.

Several moments of metatropic signification in Borowski's witness were already considered in chapter 2. For instance, Borowski writes the scene in which a mother possibly betrays a child so that the text must be read against itself in what was termed a "doubled narration" tormented by a "doubled affect." In adopting this mode of representation, the writer both mimics *Rausch*, the elation of mass annihilation, and yet gives this mimesis a sarcastic tone that speaks against its abandon or bacchanalia. In this doubled consciousness, one finds an undercutting of consciousness by means of consciousness that would constitute an incessant correction of one's representation of that event. The authority for this doubled representation, as was explored in chapter 3, stems from the manner in which the face rendered faceless still speaks, still unsettles those who murder in spite of themselves.

In his remarks directed in particular to Borowski's "sequence of stories," Lang emphasizes how Borowski employs devices of representation important to historical writing, namely, chronologies and enumerations, even as he resorts to imaginative writing in order to suggest history as "a lived experience" (*AI*, 136). But, as Lang himself points out, the very trope of imagination, in which the lived-quality of history finds its textual expression, is played against itself again and again as the very facts that Borowski records outstrip the imaginative capabilities of his discourse. In Auschwitz, the ordinary is so morally outrageous that it puts to shame the hyperbole and self-referential creativity of the surrealist pose. Only in an event so morally outrageous, one that exceeds the human capability to imagine, could surrealism come from finding events that "could not be exaggerated" (*AI*, 136) Precisely in this outstripping of the imaginative by the everyday is found the source of the narrative tone of sarcasm discussed in the preceding paragraph.

Lang would concede that writers such as Borowski can give his or her readers important insights into the events of the Nazi genocide. He also argues that any writer who would address the moral enormity of genocide must labor within a moral space of discourse that severely constricts or challenges the limits of imaginative discourse. The discussion above of Ezekiel's prophetic discourse shows the same quandary being wrestled with millennia before the *Shoah*. But what Lang fails to communicate and what Ezekiel must also struggle with is the *necessity* of imaginative discourse in one's witness against victimization. The affect carried in this discourse need not be forgetful of the other, need not be an instigation to catharsis, to a cleansing of one's own emotions at the expense of a merely fictive figure who suffers only within the text. Nor need the "personal" involvement of the writer in a text signal self-aggrandizement and moral indifference. In prophetic discourse the articulation of affect occurs as an effacement before the other who is vulnerable to suffering. Here affect magnifies rather than detracts from one's singular responsibility before the other. As was explored in the preceding chapter, precisely because the Nazi genocide is so unremittingly impersonal and heartless, so much an extermination without justice, one is stirred in one's very heart to speak out against it. Being stirred in one's heart, a state comparable to the prophetic call to *teshuva*, to a response that returns, that answers to an imperative without bounds, is a far cry from the modernist stance of a poet-genius articulating the intensity of his thoroughbred sensibility with little concern for the audience whom he or she addresses or for the manner in which his or her use of figures within the work of art involves him or her in a responsibility for others.

Borowski's or Levi's testimonies do not merely supplement historical writing, or offer it a particular sort of archive, but are themselves a unique and irreplaceable species of historical writing. In making this claim, one must understand that history is more than a memory of the past and more than a global representation of that past produced by the sifting through and processing of innumerable resources (documents, objects, interviews, testimonies, etc.) in order to provide a coherent and totalized temporal field of interrelated events, institutions, intentions, and personalities. One cannot read Borowski's and Levi's testimonies *as if* one could reverse the flow of time, *as if* one could live the other's time as one's own. "The time that marks historiography," argues Levinas, "is the recoverable time, the lost time that can be found again" (*OB*, 36). But the time that is witnessed by prophetic writing exceeds memory and its capabilities. Prophetic writing provides one with a transcendent witness, a witness otherwise than a straightforward representation of what can be said to have occurred.

Borowski's and Levi's testimonies, among others, reveal that in its initial response to the past, history is accusation of oneself before the other who is vulnerable and who suffers, whose very appearance before one signals a break or rupture in time that can never be undone. The other's proximity can be neither summarized nor diminished in the passage of time. The very urgency on the part of Levi and Borowski to witness the collapse of autonomy, as well as the extermination without justice, that characterized the death world of the camps is an expression of this rupture and of the burden it places upon all who inherit the *Häftling's* persecution. While these two writers certainly attempted to give an empirical account of the everyday life of these camps, the more pressing responsibility was to express how one was commanded by a suffering that ultimately escaped all efforts at representation. As Levinas puts it:

> The witness is not reducible to the relationship that leads from an index to the indicated. That would make it a disclosure and thematization. It [witness] is the bottomless passivity of responsibility and thus sincerity. It is the meaning of language, before language scatters into words, into themes equal to the words and dissimulating in the said the openness of the saying exposed like a bleeding wound. (*OB*, 151)

That "event," in which one was commanded in spite of everything to testify to the suffering and annihilation of *the Nameless*, can be (and ought to be) given a prosaic representation within the various historical accounts of the *Shoah*. But to confine this event to that sort of representation would be to cover over the paroxysm, the acuity, the moral urgency that Lang himself so insistently argues is an essential feature of the Nazi genocide. Witness involves sincerity-before-the-other as well as disclosure and thematization. One should remember that Levi himself was a chemist who became a writer only because of his experiences in the camps. For him the urgency of the command to consider the *Häftling* demanded a writing that was more than prosaic, in which affect was brought to the fore, in which his address of his readers would interrupt the accumulation of empirical details and memories that also occurred in his texts.

In the context of prophetic witness, the very meaning of the terms Lang would use to criticize the moral capabilities of imaginative literature undergo a paradoxical rereading, a metatropic turning. The "personal" quality of Levi's text, the fact that it transmits an address from one singular and irreplaceable person to another,[37] articulates an entirely different sense of the personal than that denoting an emphasis upon one's own private and intimate domain to the exclusion of others. In prophetic witness, writing is personal because one finds oneself commanded to a responsibility for whom no other can serve as a substitute. When my students read Borowski's and Levi's testimonies they in turn testify to having undergone an election in which their response to Levi's or Borowski's response becomes a pressing and unavoidable concern. What one now feels and thinks about these events, how one now chooses to inform oneself about them, how one lives one's life in response to these events, obsesses them.

In a similar manner, the movement toward literary abstraction that Lang decries, in which the particularity of contingent historical truth is repressed by an obsession with plausibility, with a movement toward a universal truth, is also transformed. In deliberative witness, figurative discourse no longer centers on plausibility and coherency but engages in complication, interruption, and ellipsis. In doing so, this discourse would represent incommensurable points of view across a difference (namely that of proximity, of the face-to-face encounter) that can never be integrated within one's discourse. The very form of one's discourse involves one in that incessant correction, in that breaking open of closure, that Friedlander would call "commentary."

Shoshana Felman and Dori Laub argue in their reading of Claude Lanzmann's *Shoah* how the incommensurable perspectives and acts of representation characterizing the film's text call the reader into an incessant reconsideration of exactly how the history of the *Shoah* ought to be configured:

> It is because the film goes from singular to singular, because there is no possible *representation* of one witness by another, that Lanzmann needs us to sit through ten hours of the film to begin to witness—to begin to have a concrete sense—both of our own ignorance and of the incommensurability of the occurrence. The occurrence is conveyed precisely by this fragmentation of the testimonies, which enacts the fragmentation of witnessing. . . . But the collection of the fragments does not yield, even after ten hours of the movie, any possible totality or any possible totalization: the gathering of testimonial incommensurates does not amount either to a generalizable theoretical statement or to a narrative monological sum. (*T*, 223)

They then quote Lanzmann himself: "You cannot do such a film theoretically. . . . You build such a film in your head, in your heart, in your belly, in your guts, everywhere."[38] In doing so, one's attention is continually called to those lapses of memory, to those failures of witness in which history itself can be shown to be "a historical (ongoing) *process of forgetting*" (*T*, 214). Figurative discourse in this mode actually intensifies the attentiveness on the part of the reader concerning the particularity, contingency, *and transcendence* of historical events involving other human beings.

CHAPTER FIVE

Witnessing Trauma

Suffering the Perpetrator's Address

The Scene of the *Häftling*

How then *ought* the encounter with *the Nameless*, with those who suffered the *Shoah*, be staged or represented? At times, this text has adopted Levi's command—to consider the *Häftling*—as if this scene were primordial in regard to *the Nameless*. One presented the scene *as if* it revealed the full weight of the suffering involved in the *Shoah*, *as if* in this one scene the very essence of the *Shoah*'s violence might be best rendered in graphic, phenomenological terms. Further, this scene of the *Häftling* was composed in such a manner that one stood reflectively before the *Häftling* who in turn displayed her or his wounds before one. The scene was rendered in terms of one's confronting the other in such a manner as to determine the impact of that scene upon one's subjectivity. The scene was composed *as if* one were asked the following question: in what manner have I already been submitted to this particular other before whom I find myself?

As in the scene of the face-to-face encounter in Levinas, the scene of the *Häftling* makes one aware that one has *always already* been under a command to be responsible to the other, a command that is not dependent upon the other's forcing one to listen but upon one's *already* having listened *in spite of oneself*. In this listening before comprehension, the very structure of one's own subjectivity is revealed to be a traumatism, in which the voice of the other has already addressed one before one's own thoughts and one's enjoyment could have been articulated as one's own. No matter how one reacts and no matter what one experiences, one has already witnessed the other's vulnerability before one could have chosen otherwise. That one might then choose otherwise, or might be rendered incapable of sensing this trauma at a particular moment, does not change the traumatic impact of the other upon one. Even if one does the best one can to delude oneself into thinking one can act *as if* one were utterly independent of the other, that gesture has always already failed and only reemphasizes the priority of the other.

Up until now, the unfolding of the meaning of this trauma has passed over too quickly the particularity of the other before whom one has found oneself. This has occurred because at times the analysis has functioned too much as if the mode of priority it was attempting to articulate were transcendental in nature. The very structure of one's subjectivity was revealed to be a traumatization by the other *no matter who she or he is*. To be traumatized by this only vaguely singular other seemingly became the *a priori* condition of being a subjective node of responsibility. But in this mode of thought, the other addressed one *as if* he or she were independent of any historical or social specificity. The scene of the *Häftling* became interchangeable with the scene of Levinas's *face-to-face* encounter, a scene that seemed to transcend any particular context in order to articulate an absolute and universal claim about the structure of being claimed. It was *as if* the scene of one's encounter of the other required at some point that one must let go of the historical particularity of that encounter. But the face-to-face encounter described in Levinas does not ultimately take place in general, sheared away from the actual face of the other and only considered in the abstract, textual simulacrum of that face. If this were so, the singularity of the other would be a parody. One would not undergo the necessity of turning toward the actual face of the other; one could be comfortable in considering simply a face in general.

One comes to admit that the very scene of this non-scene, the face-to-face encounter with the other, is inevitably a constructed scene. No matter how absolutely the scene may be rendered, it is rendered in language and so is already caught up in the tones of discourse involving all the other others who also speak language. The urgency of the singular other, the other for whom no other might be exchanged, the other to whom I am submitted without reservation, this other can never be given in the manner in which she or he is being elaborated in this moment of writing. One announces one's *hineni* in an utter lapse of the scene, in a turning toward the *singular* other whose impact has already been *singularly* registered and whose *singular* reality has already escaped my capacity to comprehend it, to grasp it in my own tongue. One should never have ignored the *singularity* of the other's suffering in order to speak of it in general. To do so is to participate in the blasphemy against the human that Levinas terms theodicy. Even these words *here and now* are subject to this criticism.

Yet one must speak anyway. And in the very speech that takes account of the nonaccountability of that speaking, one has betrayed necessarily she or he whom one has been called to witness. And yet one betrays in this saying, which always too quickly and too finally becomes a said, not because one is remiss, not because one has chosen not to be responsible, but because the very urgency of one's responsibility commands that one say something, that one respond.

Under the weight of this urgency, the discussion turned in the concluding sections of the last chapter to a notion of deliberative witness in which the trauma of the other's suffering is registered in terms of all the other others one is also called upon to address. This trauma, insofar as it is brought into a saying before all the other others, a saying that must also become a said, an artefact of language, seeks to bring the suffering of the singular other into a historical and social context. One constructs in deliberative witness a posing of the question of the relative weight and significance of a multitude of human experiences. Here, one can begin to find how the trauma that was registered at the supposedly transcendental level also holds a specifically historical significance in which singular human beings are addressed. The scene of Levi's prologue, in which one stands before the *Häftling* who "fights for a scrap of bread," whose eyes are "empty," whose womb is "cold like a frog in winter," is such a construction.

Given these considerations, the status of the *Häftling* insofar as he or she is the figure of a scene rather than the *singular* other referred to in that scene becomes a pressing concern. Is there a limit to the confidence one can have that this scene or any scene truly addresses the suffering undergone by the *singular* other, this other who is truly *the Nameless*? How primordial is this scene after all? No matter how effective a particular figure of *the Nameless* might be (and one must also keep in mind that *the Nameless* is yet another figure that must undergo this critique as well), its very command that one is to have listened to *this* other requires that one become sensitive to the tones in which this command is given, to how its very figuring of the absolute command to have responded is itself set under a commandment of incessant correction. As one comes to inhabit Levi's scene, as one takes it on as a manner in which one might best articulate the significance of the other's suffering in terms of all the other others, one is also submitted to a disturbance of the said in which the voice of the other and all the other others is always already interwoven with and incumbent upon one's own saying. In registering this laterality of one's text, one is confronted with how even a particular representation of the world, or, more specifically, of the suffering of another, is already a construction dependent upon other voices whose saying already commands one before one can determine what is being said. For this reason, the text is always already a destructuring of its structure, an incessant correction of its having-been-said. The scene in which Levi constructs his version of the *Häftling* is itself a multiplicity of saying, a pluralism of citation.

Yet one more reservation about the construction of Levi's scene must now be reemphasized. For the scene pictured in the first chapter assumes that I come before the *Häftling* already established as an independent human identity. The scene, so to speak, only takes place after I have taken my place before it. But the very notion that I preexist this scene, that I have already come into it as a sovereign being who only now must be cracked open like an egg is itself a fiction. Robert Bernasconi speaks of how Levinas's later writings must "combat the ingrained presumption that the story that must be told is that of how an already formed subject turns toward the neighbor."[1] The traumatism of my identity does not only occur retrospectively, after the fact of my identity, but has always and already been involved in the very fabulation or constitution of my identity. My very saying before the neighbor is revealed to implicate me in a said where the other's voice has already made its impact, has already disturbed the very possibility of any straightforward presentation of myself as a node of responsibility before the other. The *Häftling*'s impact upon me is more involved, more disruptive, and more *uncanny* than the staging above of the scene of Levi's *Survival in Auschwitz* can in its own terms suggest.

As Bernasconi reports Levinas himself must do in his move from *Totality and Infinity* to his later *Otherwise than Being*, one must also here at this moment in this argument aim "to move away from the 'narrative, epic way of speaking' (*OB*, 13)" (*OP*, 81) that the face-to-face encounter, as it has been articulated from the beginning of this text, sometimes involves. In doing so, the argument being constructed here seeks humility. For the thought that one could offer a phenomenology of the face-to-face encounter, especially with that of the *Häftling*, already assumed that one could incorporate that description into a life otherwise complete and sufficient unto itself. One acted *as if* one were already who one was, regardless of what the description of the *Häftling* might uncover. Certainly, one might have suspected that some hidden dimension of one's existence was yet to be uncovered, an ecstatic return of an absence into presence, but the analysis itself seemed to neglect that the very words one was using to formulate it were already haunted by the voice and voices of *the Nameless* and all the other others involved in one's historical inheritance. The very voice established in this text, *the one who is now speaking*, was not constituted from the vantage point of a particular identity self-sufficient to itself but was already intertwined with and suffering under the address of the other and all the other others as well.

In a similar manner, the move to a transcendental level of analysis in regard to one's submission to the other is also suspect. The priority of one's responsibility to the other is yet more prior than the *a priori* of Kant. At times in the preceding chapters, particularly in the analysis of nonintentional or traumatic affect, as well as in the face-to-face encounter, the discussion proceeded *as if* one's submission to the other were a *logical* precondition for one's identity, *as if* this submission took place outside of the particular histories and societies in which one then only afterwards found oneself. The implication of this analysis was that the *a priori* conditions for the constitution of one's subjectivity must first be addressed before the particular dimensions of one's singular subjectivity and responsibility could be given any significance. In doing so, an illusion was cultivated that one's subjectivity was articulated without regard to one's actual particularity or to the time in which one lives. The turn to the structure of the face-to-face encounter articulated what seemed to be an eternal exemplar of ethical significance, *as if* this very scene were not also a thematization of what ultimately transcends all thematization.

In moving to a notion of persecution, Bernasconi argues that Levinas would suggest an involvement in the other that "is not a generalization but is always rooted in a certain specificity" (OP, 83). One implication that could be drawn from this claim is that the very elaboration of the scene by which the other is incumbent upon one cannot be resolved in a single or terminal philosophical analysis. Just as nonintentional affect came to be interpreted in terms of its disturbance or denucleation of particular intentional affects in the previous chapter, one must now consider how the traumatism associated with nonintentional affect, that submission to the other that leaves one already under the burden of responsibility, already offered in place of the other, comes to be interpreted in terms of the particular situation of persecution in which one finds oneself. Here too one finds the priority of the other articulated as a denucleation of one's intentions, experiences, and especially of one's language. The face-to-face encounter no longer stands outside of historical or social contexts and texts but must continually be re-articulated with reference to them.

In doing so, one would do well to consider that the priority of one's subjection to the other is neither temporal nor logical but ethical. Only because one is already burdened with responsibility for the other does one even turn to a scene like that of the face-to-face encounter in order to make a limited philosophical sense of one's condition. The issue is not whether this scene must or can actually occur as it is pictured, or whether the transcendence it articulates must or can precede the drama of the constitution of one's own identity. The other is already incumbent upon one; one already suffers a burden of responsibility that is utterly gratuitous and without an origin. The priority of the other is registered as a disruption that has already been articulated before it could have been accounted for. Whatever one might do to make sense of this responsibility (and one is certainly called on to make sense of it), one cannot escape its burden. Further, the reasons one gives for the insistence of this assignation or burden can never be the justification for it. Responsibility precedes justification to the point that it precedes even the structure of the *a priori*, of a constructing of the conditions for the possibility of something having significance. Even in this sense is the significance of responsibility without conditions, without limitation.

The very progress of this *book*, this ongoing narrative of the fate of Levi's initiative, of his scene in which we confronted the *Häftling* pictured as he "who fights for a scrap of bread," has implied a gradual revelation of the meaning of that scene. One wrote *as if* Levi's command concerning that scene might finally be rendered in an account that would reveal its truth if not once and for all then at least for oneself and for the time being. But this very gesture of philosophy, in which the nonthematizable is rendered as a theme anyway (whether the theme be absolute or temporary) is done so "*at the price of a betrayal which philosophy is called upon to reduce*" (*OB*, 162, italics mine). Philosophy is constituted by means of a necessary betrayal and must remain ambivalent in its conceptions of what is to be said, if that betrayal is to remain less than virulent.

Citing and Siting the Scene of the Other in Celan's Poetry

"To conceive ambivalence and to conceive it in several times" (*OB*, 162) becomes the theme and burden of the discussion of this chapter and the next concerning the witness of Paul Celan. The problematic, multiple thematization of the unthematizable particularly haunts the poetry of Celan, who seems burdened more than almost any other writer by the transcendence of the other's address, as well as the multiplicity of all the other others' addresses at issue in any witnessing of any historical event, let alone of the *Shoah*. Levinas himself remarks that in Celan's poetry "the fact of speaking to the other—the poem—precedes all thematization" (*PN*, 44). For Levinas, Celan's poetry, precisely in being a poem, turns language from the imaginative articulation of a confident and luminous sensibility toward a reticence in the face of the other. The poem "adjourns its acumen" as it "goes toward the other" (*PN*, 43). Levinas argues in regard to Celan's writing: "the poem leaves the real its alterity, which pure imagination tears away from it" (*PN*, 44). The poem restores a regard for the other that its imaginative capability is always in danger of undermining. The poem is a "*turning*" toward the other, in which ecstasy, that affect caught up in its own coming back into itself, is "postponed."

The poem is tied to imagination yet also radically reorients it by means of what Levinas might term a "denucleation" of its powers. Thus, one is called upon to use one's imaginative capabilities in the poem but only under the aegis of an addressing of the other. In this address, the poem is engaged by that which transcends its own having-been-said. Yet this transcendence of the said, of language as an artefact, does not lead one to a truth shorn of ambivalence and multiple times. The poem of a denucleated imagination would not simply present its reader with facts about the other that would speak for themselves. In fact, the Celanian poem fears the fact that speaks for itself utterly shorn from the ambivalence of multiple times and sayings as much as the imagination, which would overwhelm facts with its self-consuming playfulness. In either situation, one is in danger of turning away from that prior subjection to the address of the other that is the very condition for the signification of the poem. Celan, perhaps more than any other writer of the *Shoah*, makes his readers aware that witnessing the other is not only *not* an event of playful imagination but also *not* an indexical event, not the matter of pointing to various facts that have already been given their place within a scene, or even a blunt pointing out of the victim her or himself.

Beyond the seductive clarity and immediacy of the index, the poem engages one in witnessing the other *as other*, which is to say in the words of Levinas, in an "openness of . . . saying exposed [to the other] like a bleeding wound" (*OB*, 151). One speaks not so much *before* the other as one speaks already *obsessed* by her or him. Poetry is a submitting to language as "contact," as "the obsession of an I 'beset' by the others" (*CP*, 123). One's speaking in this obsession is, as Bernasconi points out, "persecuted," and Celan's thematization of the other is itself persecuted and persecuting. The poem's thematization, its offering of figures that move toward another, leaves one in a singular uneasiness for the other, ready at every moment to drop all that one is, so that the other's address might be addressed.

The poem, in its speaking toward the other, becomes the scene of the setting of the scene of the other's address, of the other's proximity. In Levinas's words, the Celanian poem "already speaks . . . *with another who would even be close*, who would be *very close*" (*PN*, 44). In its approach of the other, the poem remains radically attentive, hypersensitive, to its own incapability of rendering in any actual terms the scene in which the other is to be con-fronted. The poem "adjourns its acumen." The scene remains figurative, not because it is unreal but precisely because its reality not only transcends what can be said about it but also is ultimately betrayed by any translation into discourse, into a "speaking-about." The poem, Celan tells us, *"persists at the limit of itself"* (PN, 43).

The setting of the other's scene always already involves the priority of the other's address, a priority that itself escapes any thematization that would simply picture that priority, render it in terms of a having-been-said. The scene is permeated by Ziarek's "laterality," yet this permeation cannot itself be figured in any straightforward matter. The very articulation of laterality is itself "lateral." Thus, Celan's poetry would teach its readers that to speak to the other others in response to the singular other's transcendence does not en-title one to have already determined the scene of that speaking, let alone the facts that would emerge in relation to that scene's horizon or background. The very setting of the scene becomes itself a question to be submitted again and again to the priority of the other in one's discourse.[2] The poem, like phi-losophy, is called upon to reduce its thematization, to remain ambivalent in the saying of its said.

Part of the method of the poem's reduction of its thematization involves its articulation of what Levinas terms its "figures." Rather than considering Celan's poems in terms of the *beings* or *entities* they name, Levinas cites Celan's own words in speaking of the poem's language as offering *"figures for that poem, of the other."* These figures, within the context of the poem, are offered toward the other. They hold the very movement of transcendence that renders all that is said in the poem an exposure to the other and an obsession by her or him. These figures should not be interpreted as representations or even indexes of the other, but as nodes of attending, of attentiveness, of subjection to the other who already matters before the poem could ever have been spoken. What the poem names is precisely not the other but a mode of speaking that would be already commanded by the other. In this mode of speaking, all that is named is named for the sake of the other. In being denucleated, in being rendered in "terms" of the other, names become figures. These names carry an ambivalence that can never be undone. They cannot simply stand for themselves, for their own naming, for their own being or Being, but must already be caught up in a signification for the other.

In what figure or figures then ought the address of the other find its am-bivalent thematization? And more particularly, in what further figure might she or he who is named as the *Häftling* become the obsession of the poem, of that saying that "goes toward the other"? Why even the word *Häftling*? And why should one already expect that the scene involving the *Häftling* should consist of a presentation of the *Häftling* before the mind's eye so that his wounds might be indexed and numbered? Such a scene at times characterizes the Gospel narratives in relation to the historical Jesus. For example, believers who read those narratives encounter the suffering of Jesus through the perspective of his mother Mary (as well as his apostle John), who stands before her dying son, or through the apostle Thomas, who probes the wounds of the resurrected Jesus with his own hands. These two citings and sitings of the other's suffering are sometimes interpreted in order to emphasize an indexical relationship between the witness and the victim. One witnesses that Jesus really existed, that he really was upon the cross, that one could number and point to the wounds he suffered, that one actually saw and buried his dead body, and so on.[3]

It is not immediately obvious that this scene is any more applicable to the situation of the *Häftling* than other manners of providing a context for the other's address. Indeed, in its very dependence upon a Christian source, the scene may have already troubled an address that comes from beyond a Christian context. Further, the emphasis upon indexicality (an emphasis that is implicitly criticized in the very construction of the Thomas narrative in the Gospels) is in danger of allowing one to become obsessed with the signs of suffering to the exclusion of the one who suffers. Lang's desire for facts or numbers that speak for themselves is a similar instance of indexicality that may quickly lead the reader from a concern for the other who suffers to the fetishization of numbers and facts, *as if* these alone would be sufficient to address what the *Häftling* or *the Nameless* entails. One must begin with the presumption that no matter what is the scene one sets, it will have already come too late to have been the other's scene. One must beware of an idolatry of the scene, of setting down in words a primordial event or appearing that only afterwards can come to question. Not only the content of the other's saying but also the very mode of characterizing the articulation of the unfolding of the other's priority has already always been in question.

Could not Levi's own turn to the figure of the *Häftling* itself already be a writing of multiple times, a reduction of thematization in ambivalence, of a common figure (along with its scene) that is used to render the generic victim in palpable terms? The very phrase, "if this be man," which served as the original title of Levi's book in Italian, alludes to a Christian response to Jesus's asserted divinity. The phrase, "if this be man" would lead one traditional line of interpretive reading to the phrase, "then G-d is incarnated upon the earth."

In this reading, the disbelief in Jesus' humanity articulated in this conditional phrase ("*if* this be man") is revealed paradoxically to be to the credit of all human beings. Further, the suffering of this man Jesus, abominable as it may seem, is redemptive in its divinity. It would not be an exaggeration to say that Christians read Jesus' suffering as the type for all human suffering. In Jesus' suffering, human suffering is rendered significant.

Yet Levi's formulation of the phrase "if this be man" uncannily shifts or turns the expected sense of his allusion. In asking whether the *Häftling* is human, Levi, rather than raising one's expectations concerning human dignity and the significance of human suffering, demoralizes them. Like the *Häftling*, Jesus also was incarcerated, executed as a common felon. But in calling Jesus a *prisoner* or *felon* or even *blasphemer*, one cannot signify exactly the same movement, the same terminus of address that the figure of the *Häftling* provides. One's address becomes complicated by the interference of two distinct although respectively immemorial times. By bringing Christian allusions into the siting of those who suffer within Auschwitz, Levi speaks "in several times." One can neither dismiss nor naively affirm the characterization of the *Häftling* in terms of Christian accounts of Jesus' suffering. Instead, two times, two distinct modes of proximity, neither of which can be given a straightforward thematization but both of which claim the reader's attentiveness, are brought into affinity. One must compare incomparables. One must be wary of reducing one incomparable to the other.

And could it not be argued that Levi submits Christian language to this turning or shifting, because of the insensitivity he must presume in the audience he addresses, an audience already in the throes of Christian expectations, Christian allusions, Christian techniques of narrative interpretation? This turning does not involve the erasure of Christian rhetoric, a submission of it to an annihilation that would simply end up repeating the Nazi's original attack upon Judaism, but calls attention to the reader's inattentive expectation that the figure of Jesus, as well as the particular notion(s) of redemptive suffering that this figure implies, would be a sufficient translation of the suffering that occurs in Auschwitz. The suffering of Jesus (even if only by implication and by allusion) must now be brought before another, this *Häftling*. And the *Häftling*'s name, being that name that the Nazis literally used to list the victim's identity, that name by which the very praxis of rendering the other's face as faceless occurred, that name whose very calling out involved the erasure of any sense that the name called could also be an address, that name must both be differentiated and yet compared to the name(s) that call(s) out "Jesus."

In the following chapter, Celan is found to have engaged in a similar but much more thematically self-aware destructuring of the modes of signification concerning the Christian representation of suffering, as well as a variety of other modes of representation. In doing so, he will not abandon Christian formulations of suffering, *as if* the suffering in Auschwitz and the other death camps were an exclusively Jewish event calling for a purely Jewish typology or figuration. Rather, the very figures used in formulating the scene of suffering, figures that within the German language, at least, have been long influenced by the address of Christians, are troubled by other addresses, other times.

Celan's poetics often reverts to a strategy of citation when it seeks to render the transcendence of the other's address. Important in a Celanian poem is not only what is said, but who or which tradition says it, as well as how it is listened to and how other traditions are addressed in its saying. Celan is obsessed by the issue of multiple or layered citations, of how a citation from one voice, from one vector of address, is altered, is given another time, when it finds itself cited and sited in yet another voice. Levinas's own citation of Celan's multiple citations of Malebranche's "attention is the prayer of the soul," which was cited in the last chapter, is an example of how this poetics is articulated. Obsessed by discrete voices, by incommensurable addresses, all of Celan's poems can be associated with the description Levinas gives of Celan's speech, *The Meridian*: "An elliptic, allusive text, constantly interrupting itself in order to let through, in the interruptions, his other voice, as if two or more discourses were on top of one other, with a strange coherence, not that of a dialogue, but woven in a counterpoint that constitutes—despite their immediate melodic unity—the texture of his poems" (*PN*, 43). One finds in Celan's poetics of citation a rendering in ambivalence of differing voices, of differing times.

Submitted to multiple times and voices, the poem is more the instigation for the construction of a series of scenes than a scene in itself. Amy Colin's reference to Celan's poems as "holograms of darkness" alludes to the fact that the poem does not so much present a scene as it provides a mode of constructing scenes of "strange, disturbing shapes, depth and colors, which often change dramatically with the spectator's angle of view" (*HD*, ix). Celan's poems resist a cursory first reading, much as a holographic plate would resist a cursory first viewing. One must construct the viewing, one must place the plate within an apparatus that then allows it to project an image that in turn can only reveal certain aspects of the scene dependent upon the point of view of the observer. For Celan, one's very subjectivity, the "acute angle of one's existence," serves as the apparatus of projection. But Celan's poetic holograms are not so much an imaginative projection as a traumatic submission, a hav-ing-been-addressed by the other in which the multiple times of multiple ad-dresses inspire in the subject a variety of readings, each of which exceeds any thematization that can be given of it. The poem serves as the instigation of or inspiration for the construction of a thematization, of a scene, in which the ef-fort of construction, and the submission to the multiple times that this con-struction involves, is the "focus" of the poem. Further, the very scene that is to be constructed is itself open to divergent times, divergent modes of exceed-ing its thematization.

Not just a point of view upon a scene is at issue, but the very siting and citing of the scene itself. The Celanian poem's ambivalence about its scene, which is sometimes interpreted by critics as a hermeticism, would seem at first glance to repudiate the historical nature of its witness. For the reader can barely guess at the events that the poem intends to index. Often one must turn to biographical details, to notes scribbled in the margins of a manuscript, to insider knowledge, to abstruse references or citations, in order to determine the poem's historical reference points. In adopting a midrashic approach, in which one must continually move to other texts, to other citations, in order to make sense of what one has just read, the poem refuses any conception of organic unity or immediate presentation. One's siting of the *Shoah* involves one in an incessant labor, a listening to singular witnesses and particular modes of address that lead to yet other witnesses and modes of address. These singular times cannot be collapsed into a uni-fied poetic field, but must remain interruptions of one another, even as they address one another. One can no more read these poem's "theoretically" than one can view Lanzmann's *Shoah* in a similar mode. In the language of Lanz-mann, one must "build" the poem in one's head, one's heart, one's belly, one's guts, everywhere.

For Celan nothing could be more historical, which is to say, nothing could be more implicated in a witnessing across generations, between in-commensurable times, than the crisis this witness precipitates in this siting of the poem. For this crisis, kept in its ambivalence or quandary by the very complexity of citation that is the obsession of the poem's writing, submits the poem to a series of addresses by multiple pasts and futures that the poem through its own resources could never have remembered or expected. Noth-ing is said that has not already moved laterally, that has not already found it-self in the mouth of yet another saying, of another scene. Celan's poems continually speak in deference to another whose very being-addressed in the poem continually obligates the poet to reevaluate his siting of the appearance of that address. Like Levinas's philosopher, the poet is called upon *to reduce* the betrayal of thematization, to render its impossibility in ambivalent terms:

> To stand-for-no-one-and-nothing.
> Unrecognized,
> for you
> alone.
>
> *(PPC,* 225)

Plagiarism and False Prophecy in "Huhediblu"

To begin to articulate the hermeneutical complexity and moral urgency of Celan's poetics of citation, the discussion now returns to a consideration of the objections treated in the previous chapter to poetry as a means of historical writing about the *Shoah.* In doing so, the notion of prophetic witness elaborated in the last chapter is to be articulated in relation to that particular moment of history that is termed the *Shoah* and in which the *Häftling* has emerged as a particularly compelling although highly problematic figure of the other. Further, how Celan himself takes up with the notion of prophetic writing as providing one means of siting and citing the suffering of the *Häftling, the Nameless* is to be considered. The manner in which Celan's poems become the scene of a persecution is given particular attention in this process. The following stanza from the poem "Huhediblu" will serve as the instigation for these reflections:

> *Und—ja—*
> *die Bälge der Feme-Poeten*
> *lurchen und vespern und wispern and vipern,*
> *episteln.*
> *Geunktes, aus*
> *Hand- und Fingergekröse, darüber*
> *schriftfern eines*
> *Propheten Name spurt, als*
> *An- und Bei- und Afterschrift, unterm*
> *Datum des Nimmermenschtags im September-:*

> And—yes—
> the poetasters' bastards
> lurk and vesper and whisper and viper,
> epistles.

What is foreboded, out of
hand and finger entrails, above
scriptfar
the name of a prophet traces, as
on- and by- and slander-script, under the
date of the nevermansday in September–:[4]

Lang, in his discussion of Celan's poetry, would be thinking of exactly such lines when he points out that "the more consistently figurative or 'imaginative' it [a poem by Celan] is, the greater the distance between it and the claims of historical reference or authenticity" (*AI*, 140). This poem, on first reading strikes one as intensely imaginative; any sense of reference to the Nazi genocide seems at best fragmentary and elliptical. These traits, which are characteristic of Celan's writing in general, caused him to be misinterpreted early in his career as a surrealist poet of strikingly original but unworldly and even nonsensical imagery.[5] Should one not fault a poem about the *Shoah* whose very obscurity, despite Celan's intentions, causes readers to become utterly confused about what it actually represents?

The issue of the poem's relation to the victims of genocide becomes even more problematic when one learns that the poem is at least at one level Celan's response to a charge that he had plagiarized the poetry of Yvan Goll, a deceased friend, in order to create his unique style of writing. This charge, concocted by the deceased poet's wife, Claire, haunted Celan throughout the fifties and early sixties. The accusation was made and then resurfaced only to be soundly refuted each time not only by Celan but by a variety of critics.[6] Celan himself was deeply stung by these charges when they continued to plague him in 1960. In a letter quoted by Felstiner, he describes Claire's attacks and the vitriol it inspires as "machinations" stemming from "neo-Nazis" who are involved "in an attempt to destroy me and my poems" (*PC*, 155). Celan is particularly and understandably upset at how Claire Goll describes the actual murdering of his parents by the Nazis as a "sorrowful legend" (*PC*, 154).[7]

In arguing for the originality of his voice, even if it is a defensible claim, Celan's poem seems to become precisely what Lang fears most—the opening up of a figurative space in which the style of the poet becomes the decisive concern for both writer and reader of the poem. But within his poem Celan is careful to pose the issue of plagiarism in prophetic rather than poetic terms.[8] For Celan, the charge of plagiarism is dangerous not because it might undermine his personal fame or poetic mastery but because it might discredit his address of and by the victims of Nazi genocide. To accuse Celan of plagiarism is to accuse him of having betrayed these others for whom his poems profess such a troubling and distressed concern. Or even worse, the charges of plagiarism can function to discredit the very witnessing of the occurrence of genocide. Such charges ring out even more ominously when they are considered against a background of renewed outbreaks of anti-Semitism both within Germany and abroad, as well as reports of the survival of Nazi war criminals in Arab and South American countries (*PC*, 154). For this reason, Celan fears neo-Nazi machinations.

For Celan the charge that his poems are plagiarized would imply that his poems are in some sense a false prophecy—that they misguide and deceive their audience, that they betray their own alleged call to sincerity before the other. Further, this alleged betrayal would be reminiscent in Celan's mind of the yet earlier betrayals enacted by the Nazis themselves, betrayals that often included the use of lies and propaganda to distort language and to manipulate an audience's emotions. Ironically, those who ought to be most concerned about this background of plagiarism, about the Nazi's defamation of the Jewish other, as well as all the other innumerable categories of others with which Aryan ideology was obsessed, are those German voices who now refuse to consider the full implications of that betrayal. As Celan himself hints, Claire Goll's charges give Germans an excuse not only to deny the full implications of the violence that occurred but to excoriate those who would remind them of that violence. In this vein, at least one defiant German editor uses the furor raised up by Claire Goll's charges in order to report how he refuses to "lick Herr Celan's ass" (*PC*, 154). The very use of such a figure of speech in regard to a poet who writes in the wake of both personal and historical betrayal is morally outrageous. That this figure be addressed to him by one who was at the very least a fellow citizen of those who engineered his parents' murders is doubly outrageous. One could argue that this taunt involves a form of blasphemy paradoxically directed toward the human rather than the divine.

In alluding to such difficulties, a series of figures is given within "Huhediblu," including the figure of a prophet, that suggest on multiple levels how the poem, a speaking toward the other, can become instead an act of betrayal, of prophetic desecration. This approach is unsettling, for in prophetic discourse it was more likely that one would excoriate those who sought to undermine sincerity, to speak duplicitously. In so doing, one drew a decisive boundary between the false and the true prophet. But in Celan's poem, the poem itself is submitted to duplicity, even possessed by it, as a soul might be possessed by a demon. *The poem is not only about persecution but finds itself persecuted.*

In rendering this uncanny scene, Celan makes use of rhetorical techniques traditionally used by the biblical prophets. The verse is organized as an invective against false prophets. The mentioning of pagan modes of foretelling the future, methods that require the disemboweling of animals, gives an explicit example of a practice any biblical prophet would have abhorred. In the alliterative "vespern und wispern and vipern" is a word play not unlike those Sawyer claims lie at the core of many prophetic oracles.[9] And the notion of an oracle, of a speaking out to others on the basis of an authority transcending one's own, is at least implied in these lines. The implied oracle even attempts to name a date, "a nevermansday in September."

Unlike biblical prophetic utterance, Celan's poem never allows a divine authority to explicitly emerge. Indeed, insofar as communication with G-d is hinted at in these lines, it becomes demonic—*vespern* decomposes into *vipern*, the worshipful tone of evening prayers becomes the hissing of a snake. Even in the verb *vespern* is already found a possible allusion to Will Vesper, "the Nazi poet whose writings were infused with fascist venom" (*HD*, 128). The very use of the word for an evening prayer in this context finds the word itself to be already defamed or polluted. The indeterminateness of reference as to who the prophet might even be—"the *name* of a prophet"—suggests both traditional exemplars of the prophetic (such as Samuel, who is actually named as the prophet in drafts of the poem [*HD*, 122]) and contemporary exemplars of the false prophet (such as Vesper, or even Hitler). The remaining verses of the poem enact this same sort of pollution and decomposition—from divine to demonic—in a variety of figures stemming from a variety of languages, histories, and traditions. Rather than excoriating its enemies, or at the very least exhorting them to act otherwise, the poem is in danger of being possessed by them. Its last mode of resistance seemingly becomes its own scornful witnessing to its inability to resist, its weakness before that other who would destroy its saying.

Key to a reading of these lines is the realization that the naming of poets as *Feme-Poeten* implies far more than the English translation of "poetasters," those who write trashy verse. As described above, Celan's poetry inevitably becomes a line of citations, a movement of a figure through multiple utterances and times. In this instance, *Feme* (which comes from the Old German root *vehme*, meaning judgment or punishment) alludes to the "*Feme-Gericht*," a secret German court of the fourteenth to eighteenth century responsible for condemnations and executions (*HD*, 121f.). The use of this term in connection with poetasters in turn alludes to the poets, such as Will Vesper, officially sanctioned by the Nazi party. These poets were part and parcel of the politics of secret denunciation and terror by which the Nazis organized the life of the Third Reich. Because their poetic voice was so thoroughly and intentionally deaf to the voices of those who were suffering, these poets, from Celan's viewpoint, were not only incompetent writers but also false prophets. Thus a line of citations leads one from trashy poets to star chambers to Nazi collaborators to false prophets to the very writing of Celan's poem in the wake of the accusations of Claire Goll. In the background as well are the renewed machinations of neo-Nazi anti-Semitism. In the interweaving of these citations, in the multiplicity of their utterances, the poem resists a straightforward siting of the other's suffering or of her or his betrayal. The reader is brought to consider all the shadings and nuances of signification that accrue as the figure leads one through a multiplicity of voices and their histories.

In this instance, the voices to whom one is led are those who, like Borowski's *Kommandant*, would not only persecute the other but render her or him faceless and voiceless. The laterality of the poem's text, its texture of citations, is troubled by a countermovement, a blaspheming or collapsing of its ethical asymmetry, in which the ethical other, the one who is weak or dispossessed, would be utterly shorn of his or her voice. Celan's poem is haunted by the rhetoric of those who would systematically deny the claim that is made by the other's suffering. That this countermovement is the expression of the delusion that one can live *as if* one is not already commanded by the other's address does not keep the delusion from engaging in its malevolent work. In the playing out of the delusion that the other's address does not matter, the very integrity of language is at issue.

One particular manner in which this integrity is undermined involves using words so that the significance they are purported to carry is betrayed by the tone in which they are addressed to others. For example, the word *Feme* (in Celan's locution *Feme-Poeten*), which originally signified "justice" or "punishment," has come to suggest "conspiracy" or "repression" in contemporary usage. While the courts of justice once termed *Femegerichte* may have been signified in public as the scene for the meting out of justice, in their secret workings they became a scene for the playing out of coercion, revenge, and vendetta. In their aftermath, the very meaning of their signification, their *Feme* or "justice," was perverted and its original sense was lost. The degradation in meaning of *Feme* shows how even the word "justice" can signify nothing more than coercion and betrayal when it is put in the mouth of the persecutor. The heritage left by these courts makes it impossible to say the word "justice," the Old German *Vehme*, without its already having betrayed its meaning.

Nor can one say the German word *Prophet* in Celan's contemporary situation without the same effect. The corruption of this word through insincere address is given an especially powerful example in a speech delivered by Hitler:

> In the course of my life I have very often been a *prophet*, and have usually been ridiculed for it. During the time of my struggle for power it was in the first instance only the Jewish race that received my prophecies with laughter when I said that I would one day take over the leadership of the State . . . and that I would then among other things settle the Jewish problem. Their laughter was uproarious, but I think that for some time now they have been laughing on the other side of their face. Today I will once more be a *prophet*: if the international Jewish financiers in and outside Europe should succeed in plunging the nations once more into a world war, then the result [will be] . . . the annihilation of the Jewish race in Europe.[10] [italics mine]

And one must consider not only these words as they are written down but also their delivery and its reception. Victor Klemperer comments on Hitler's style of oratory and its effect upon his audience: "I understood only occasional words. But the tone! The unctuous brawling, true brawling, of a priest." And again: "The Nuremberg Party Rally has just been raging. The press worships Hitler like G-d and the prophets rolled into one."[11] Whether or not Celan is aware of the particular speech cited above, he is certainly aware of this Hitlerian tone and the tendency of the German citizenry to view Hitler as prophetic. Celan's own citation of the word "prophet" inevitably carries the burden of this genocidal mode of address.[12]

In this vein, "Huhediblu" articulates the betrayal of language that occurs when the address of one's prayer bears the desire to annihilate the other and when the addressing of letters has become the means of denouncing one's colleagues.[13] Like the biblical prophets, Celan is concerned with the sincerity of one's address. In particular he would ask whether one's response to the other who suffers remains true to that suffering. Celan himself is painfully aware of how, in the wake of the Nazi possession of the German language, the very words of the German language have become so defamed, so corrupted, so interwoven with an extermination without justice, that the writing of German poetry, whose inspiration in some part must be taken from language itself, now threatens to reinscribe annihilation rather than to resist it. In the German language, one cannot speak of "prophets" or of the "justice" they would "in-spire" without already alluding to and being burdened by a betrayal.

Yet Celan's "Huhediblu" is purposefully interwoven with the citations of Hitler, of Vesper, and of all their genocidal colleagues. The poem attends to the address of those who would annihilate the other (as well as the poet) by rendering her or him voiceless. In spite of the anguish it causes the poet, his poem does not turn away from the speech of those who would manipulate their words in order to render the murder of Celan's parents and all *the Name-less* as that "sorrowful legend" cited by Claire Goll. Celan's poem at times mouths the very address of those who annihilate his own address, who would defame his own language. That Celan's own work should now be interwoven with these duplicitous voices, becomes unendurably traumatic, an imposition of misreading upon a text already overwhelmed by the ambivalence of what it says. The text is, as suggested above, persecuted.

The Equivocation of Persecution in Levinas

In being submitted to persecution, Celan's poem brings into focus and also de-mands further clarification of exactly what it is that Levinas suggests when he states that witnessing is "a saying exposed like a bleeding wound." For one could think of one's traumatism, that exposure to the other that must expose its exposure, as involving one in a sacrificing of one's own means and nourish-ment for the sake of another who is vulnerable. One takes the food from one's mouth for the sake of the other who starves. One puts one's life in danger for the sake of the other whose well-being is threatened. Or one even offers one-self in the place of the one being persecuted. In these instances, one submits to being wounded for the sake of another who is weak and perhaps innocent. But in broaching the issue of persecution, Celan also brings both himself and his reader into contact with that other who is not powerless, who is not the victim of history, but who willingly uses his or her power to attack another's or even one's own integrity.

In being interwoven with the citations of the persecutor—with the voices of the Nazis and their historical precursors, with those voices who have in a manner also possessed the voice of Claire Goll when she charges Celan with having fabricated the murders of his parents or at the very least of having cultivated the "legend" of their murder as part of a poetic act of charlatanism—Celan's very act of writing resubmits him to that destructive trauma that occurred when he too, a survivor of the *Shoah*, had been treated *as if* he were faceless. In this form of trauma, Celan is in danger of being overwhelmed by the other's delusion that he and those whom he loved no longer signified anything. This being-overwhelmed, this persecution, threatens to debilitate the very possibility of Celan's response to the other. Celan's discourse is infected by a wounding that renders him speechless, or even worse, that possesses his saying to the point of demonic possession, of blasphemy, of obsession by that particular other who would trick him into a delusional state.

The instability of Celan's own mental state becomes an extremely important issue when one considers this particular inflection of trauma. For the onset of Celan's psychosis, which increases in intensity throughout the writing of *Die Niemandsrose* (in which the poem "Huhediblu" is found), becomes an important element of his poetic address. In Celan's own life, the very attempt to communicate his suffering, particularly with Nelly Sachs who is undergoing a nervous breakdown at this time as well, only manages to reinscribe the trauma. In Felstiner's words; "The two Jewish poets' anxieties proved mutually contagious" (*PC*, 159). In a particularly telling moment, Celan confides to Sach's companion a story of what he terms the "betrayal" of his father, when (in Felstiner's words) "he had let go of his father's hand through barbed wire and run away" (*PC*, 159). Fearing for the effect of this revelation upon Sachs's own precarious mental health, Lennartsson exhorts Celan not to retell this story to Sachs, a request that Celan evidently honored.

This traumatism of persecution, this possession by violence that leaves Nelly Sachs enveloped in "Dante-hells" and "Hieronymous Bosch images" (*PC*, 161), that leaves Celan driven to paranoid fantasies, is among other things an infection of the imagination. The imagination is seized, although in a manner that at least initially seems different from the traumatism of saying before the face of the other. The traumatism of Levinas's prophetic witness is precisely not a seizure intentionally inflicted upon one by another in order to violate the heart of one's singularity or identity. In prophetic witness one finds that the articulation of one's very subjectivity is already an obsession for the other that is also already a command to irenic discourse, to self-effacement, to responsibility for the other. Further, Levinas, when he comes to speak of persecution as a suffering for the other, insists that it "does not make up the content of a consciousness gone mad" (*OB*, 101). The significance of one's persecution is not that one suffers to the point of madness, of incapability, but that one's suffering offers an address of the other who persecutes one.

In the traumatism of persecution articulated by Celan's poems one is left so overwhelmed by the images of one's memory, by the past that is part of one's intentional affect, that one's hold upon one's intentional world is in danger of dissolving. To Levinas's claim of a persecution without madness, Celan might answer that each word he writes is owed to "destruction" (*Verderben*).[14] Further, this state of being in which one finds oneself in thrall, in which one is compelled to be affected, is itself that which is most generally recognized as the trauma of persecution. Here one undergoes an *attack upon* (in addition to an obsessing of) one's consciousness that leaves one simply without capability rather than paradoxically incapable in one's capability.

The distinction between being without capability and being incapable in one's capability is important. Levinas's discussion of one's powerlessness in the face of the other, at least as it was articulated in the earlier *Totality and Infinity,* never presumed one's psyche to be rendered impotent by the other but only that it find in its potency an incapability it could not master and that undermined the very notion of mastery. Paradoxically, Levinas's analysis required that one must be capable in order that the priority of an unmitigated passivity, of a submission to the other without qualification that *transcends* the tension between capability and impotency, between freedom and compulsion, might be registered. Further, in finding oneself powerless *beyond* (rather than in resistance to) one's capabilities, one is given over to an irenic saying, to that sign of pure exposure before the other in which all of one's capabilities are put in service of the other: *hineni.* In this service, not less but more capability is required. One's very restlessness before the other, an affect that has been characterized as articulating the very structure of one's animation, does not deny one's capabilities, does not refuse one's intentions, but stirs them up from the depths of their inescapable insufficiency.

So far the discussion reflects more closely the language of Levinas in *Totality and Infinity,* that work in which the scene of the face-to-face encounter does not leave the identity of he or she who is submitted to the other so radically in question. As Bernasconi notes, only in *Otherwise than Being* does being submitted to the other involve not only a command in relation to the other but also a suffering to the point of persecution for the sake of the other (OP, 79). In spite of Levinas's statement that his notion of persecution should not be confused with one in which one is rendered incapable or mad, this secondary or "ontic" notion of persecution remains an inescapable and even significant aspect of that Levinasian persecution which suffers for the other. If Levinas were to articulate a notion of persecution that utterly dismisses how being persecuted involves at the very least the threat of an attack inflicting pain to the point of madness, to the point of the collapse of one's autonomy, or to the point that history itself would collapse in its wake, he is in danger of dismissing as well the very specificity of the persecution to which *the Nameless* were submitted.

As suggested in chapter 1, the greatest trauma registered by the *Häftling* was not the pain induced by a purely physical assault upon her or him but the act of betrayal that the incessant attack upon the autonomy of each *Häftling* involved. The very numbness of the *Häftling's* pain that ensued when his or her suffering reached traumatic proportions in the collapse of autonomy only intensified his or her betrayal. In betrayal one suffers beyond suffering. This betrayal, along with its intensification of suffering, constitutes the very structure of what is normally meant by persecution: to pursue (or be pursued) with hostility, malice, or enmity.

What distinguishes persecution from a more generalized notion of trauma is malice, a desire expressed on the part of the other that pain *should* be inflicted upon one. This malice in turn doubly traumatizes: one suffers not only the pain of suffering directly inflicted upon one but also the pain of knowing that one's suffering is being imposed upon one with the assent and willful participation of another human being. One's very contact with the other, as well as the other others, is attacked in this second realization. The torturer makes use of this doubled traumatization to intensify yet again the painfulness of his or her victim's suffering in order to augment its destructive power. At the core of one's persecution is the presentation of the other as having the intention to persecute. The presentation of this intention, often carried as much in the tone of address as in the information it conveys, is itself enough to traumatize, as name-calling, baiting, and other forms of malevolent speech themselves continually make clear.

Levinas's interpretation of persecution in *Otherwise than Being* utterly transforms its meaning from a suffering under malevolence to a suffering transcending malevolence. Levinas speaks of a revelation in which the malice expressed in the face of the other who tortures one obsesses one "as something pitiful" (*OB*, 111). This revelation occurs because the other who persecutes, in spite of his or her hateful intentions, is still engaged in an address of she or he who is persecuted. As Borowski's account of the face suggests, even the intention on the part of the persecutor not to be addressed by the face of the one who is persecuted is already a-being-addressed by that face. In spite of itself, the hateful expression expresses an address of the other. In being addressed by the other's hatefulness, the persecuted one bears witness to a dimension of the persecutor's involvement in persecution that transcends the very intention to hate. The persecutor's hatefulness is revealed to be in utter futility—even as the persecutor intends to never have been addressed by the persecuted, he or she is already betrayed by the persecuted's (i.e., one's own) being addressed by those intentions.

This revelation of futility involves the denucleation of intentional life discussed at the beginning of this chapter. Levinas could be interpreted as arguing that the attack of persecution is itself always already subject to a denucleation, an interruption of its self-confidence, that renders its significance otherwise than as a attack. In being so rendered, the malice of the other's expression does not disappear, although it is now registered in one's witness of it as a delusion about rather than a commitment to one's reality. In this fashion, the face contorted in destructive rage inspires pity rather than a blind hatred from she or he who is the object the face's wrath. Yet the face overwhelmed by its delusions of violence can still carry through its intention to harm. One's pity for the persecutor does not prevent him or her from either the threat or the realization of the undoing of one's autonomy. Human beings in Auschwitz and the other extermination camps were susceptible to violence to the point of being rendered a *Häftling*. But even in succumbing to the onslaught of this violence, the very suffering of that violence continues to address the annihilator. In spite of itself the face of the persecutor is revealed as pitiful.

By "pitiful" is meant not that modern sense of the word in which one becomes condescending toward another because of the meagerness of her or his resources, or the small-heartedness of her or his actions. "Pitiful" here would call forth a pity that hearkens back to the Shakespearian sense of the term, as in his *King Lear* IV.vi.200–201: "A sight most pitiful in the meanest wretch / Past speaking of in a King"; or again in *King Lear* I.vii.53–54: "I should e'en die with pity / To see another thus."[15] This notion of pity involves compassion and grief: one is moved by the harm another suffers for the sake of that other.

Because the hatred of one's persecutor is revealed to be pitiful, one does not dismiss the other in contempt or disgust but finds oneself, in Levinas's words, "liable to answer for the persecutor." This formulation is startling, since it suggests that persecution entails an increased rather than diminished responsibility for the other who persecutes one. In answering one's persecutor, one is called to a patient enduring of one's suffering whose very endurance is also an offering back of that suffering to one's persecutor for the sake of that persecutor. This enduring does not occur by means of one's own resources, or by reference to any other form of external power or compulsion, but out of one's unique vulnerability to the other. This vulnerability, in which one's very subjectivity is revealed to be "as *the other in the same*, as an inspiration" (*OB*, 111) is what makes one liable for the persecution worked by the other in the first place. What one's endurance offers to that other is an exposure to the suffering inflicted upon one that reveals its shamefulness.

One finds oneself filled with shame for the sake of one's persecutor: "To tend the cheek to the smiter and to be filled with shame." This biblical verse, which Levinas notes in a footnote is taken from the Book of Lamentations (3:30), differs from the more renowned Gospel version (at least within the Christian canon) in that one does not turn the cheek for yet another blow but endures in the first blow upon the cheek that suffering to which one has been submitted. The verse from Lamentations suggests that one's enduring of a specific act of persecution is an explicit moment of revelation in which the other who persecutes is invited to find his or her way back to animation and createdness, to soul or heart. One bears witness to the persecutor by offering her or him the possibility of confronting the shamefulness of what he or she has worked. Suffering is not a kind of magical redemption (*OB*, 111), or even a taking on of the other's rage in such a way that the other can be protected from its full implications. Rather, one's suffering gives one a chance to address the other in a manner that breaks through his or her delusions about the false priority attached to his or her identity and intentions. One offers the other another way of seeing the relationship between the other and oneself, as well as the other and all the other others.

If one chooses to vilify the other, to remain enmeshed in one's outrage over the other's actions, then one remains enmeshed within the plot of violence that the other's persecution of oneself has already instigated. For Levinas, in persecution one passes "from an outrage undergone to the responsibility for the persecutor": one resists the dynamics of hatred begetting hatred by means of a patience that exceeds beyond any accounting the very gesture of hatred or the play of intention and counterintention that it instigates. In being obsessed by the other's hatred as pitiful, one's suffering is transformed into "expiation." In expiation, one's resistance to the other's persecution is articulated otherwise than as a violence countering violence. Instead, patience renders the violence of the other helpless by one's enduring of one's very helplessness before the violence of the other.

Infectious Persecution in Celan's Poetry

In "Huhediblu," as in many other poems in *Die Niemandsrose*, the reader is submitted to the scene of a persecution in which what is suffered is simply undergone rather than explicitly and willfully resisted. As in Levinas's notion of persecution, Celan seems insistent on tending a cheek to the smiter that reveals how one is filled with shame. Yet this strategy of poeticizing, if one may call it that, raises the question of whether the poet is engaged in a praiseworthy activity or in a dangerous and ultimately self-destructive repetition of his victimization. As pointed out above, Levinas explicitly argues for a persecution that "does not make up the content of a consciousness gone mad" (*OB*, 101). Yet the poet of "Huhediblu" seems in danger of cultivating his own mental torment to the point of utter despair rather than in resisting the other's hatred by rendering it as one's own shame. Further, the tone of Celan's voice, in which prophetic modes of address degenerate from a "*vespern*" into the hissing malice of "*vipern*," leaves in question whether the poet is truly registering the pitifulness of the face contorted in malice. One senses instead within the other's address a hatefulness that overwhelms the poet's vulnerability and leaves his own sensitivity to the other paralyzed. Is this paralysis in turn an ironic mode of expressing outrage? And if the poet is enmeshed in his outrage over what has occurred to *the Nameless*, then can he ever move beyond being enmeshed in the cycle of violence instigated by the persecutor? And if he cannot, does not Celan's poem merely function as a reinscription of a perverting or destructive trauma that yet again traumatizes?

To answer these questions one must consider more exactly how Celan undergoes the persecutor's address in "Huhdediblu." A paradoxically decisive feature of this suffering is its ongoing ambiguity or ambivalence—even as Celan seems to articulate outrage at the persecutor, he also endures the speech of the persecutor. The poem is caught up in that equivocation described by Levinas in which the hateful is also revealed to be the pitiful. But can one in one's movement to the pitiful simply set aside the hateful, *as if* it had never occurred? Does the movement from outrage to responsibility involve one in a forgetfulness of the other's hatred, like that suggested in the Blakean motto that to forgive is human but to forget is divine? Or is the expiation to which Levinas has referred more tortured, more absorbed in its suffering than a simple movement from hatefulness to the pitiful might suggest? One must remember that persecution is most destructive in the very articulation of its betrayal of the other. If this betrayal were not registered in he or she who is persecuted, then the very notion of persecution collapses. One could never be persecuted, if he or she who is harming one did not mean to harm one. The hatefulness of the other's face instantiates a betrayal that both wounds one and moves one to pity. This might be the point Levinas makes in speaking of a necessary equivocation. Expiation hinges on a doubled, equivocal significance in the other's face—a face that is *both* contorted with rage *and* an invitation to peace *in spite of that rage*.

Celan's poems are remarkably ambivalent in their attitude toward those who were and are betrayers of *the Nameless*. On the one hand, one cannot read the poem "Huhediblu" without quickly sensing its anger at and disdain for those who use ploys of speech to defame or convict the innocent. Yet, on the other hand, the betrayer or persecutor is not given a scene within the poem in which a line is drawn that simply and comfortably delineates betrayer from betrayed. This claim does not mean that the poem pictures the victim as inevitably a persecutor, or the persecutor as inevitably a victim, *as if* in the end all humans betray all other humans, *as if* all humans are both victims and persecutors. Such a brother and sisterhood of mutual malice would be nothing more than a conspiracy to persecute with impunity. But Celan's scene of persecution as it is rendered in the poem articulates a proximity between betrayer and betrayed that neither can evade. Due to this proximity, the persecuted remain obsessed with their persecutors.

Celan insists on a sort of infection of his poetic discourse by the betrayer that goes to the point of producing multiple scenes in which there is yet again and again a crumbling into powerlessness, into persecution, before the onslaught of the other's attack. Celan will not simply read out the names of his betrayers and index the site of their betrayals—*he insists that his poems be submitted to their address as well*. Celan remains committed to his poetics of citation, even when this means one must be submitted in the figures of one's poetic discourse to those who would annihilate one. This very submission in turn is either a self-destructive repetition of that betrayal, or an enduring of it in shame for the sake of expiation—or both.

Celan remains attentive to the tormentor's address not only for the sake of the tormentor but also for the sake of those other others who were also persecuted. As Celan puts it in an earlier poem already referred to above: "Whichever word you speak— / you owe / to destruction."[16] To present *the Nameless* in a scene in which her or his torment itself is utterly forgotten, or in which it (i.e. the torment) is subject to an apotheosis that renders its destructiveness irrelevant, would be to betray *the Nameless* by dismissing the significance of the very attack upon her or him that constituted the particularity of her or his suffering. As a result the poet must remain true to the agony of *the Nameless* and inevitably must "betray" those who would forget that suffering, who would deny persecution. Thus, the poem from which the lines above were taken continues by stating: "Whichever stone you lift— / you lay bare / those who need the protection of stones." These lines remind their reader that the perpetrator is the very first to cover over her or his deeds, *as if* she or he could confine the morbidity of his or her violence to the dark nether world on the underside of stones. The poem cannot tolerate this denial of torment, this rendering docile of destruction.

The meaning of these lines, of stones that protect, is rendered even more ambivalent as Celan intertwines one citation with yet others. For these lines can also be read as referring to the persecuted, the violated, *the Nameless*, who "need the protection of stones," the marking of their deaths, in order to be honored as being dead. In this rendering of the poem's scene, the poet denies the annihilated their death and brings them back, in a nearly blasphemous inversion of birth, "naked" into the world, where they renew the "entanglement," their being plaited into the braiding and interweaving that marks the reality of address, of the poem that goes toward the other. But the poem can also refer in these words to Celan himself, as well as to the other survivors, those who might wish for forgetfulness of what has occurred, for some possibility of having put behind one the destructive events one has witnessed. These too must bear witness.

In this plurality of citation one confronts multiple times, multiple vectors of address, that render the very words of the poem disturbingly ambivalent. Do "stones," in an address to the victims, refer to "tombstones," or, in an address to the perpetrators, to the "stones" one finds in every field lying about the earth (which in turn could refer to those fields in which thousands and tens of thousands of the exterminated were buried and then left *as if* nothing more than a rural field with a green prospect lay before ones eyes), or, in an address to both the reader and the poet, to a more abstract and less indexical stone that would be the sign of a repressed or traumatic memory of past violence? Celan does not resolve the ambivalence of these lines but intensifies them in order to render the poem a projection of multiple addresses through a single "figure." "Stones" names not so much an entity as a mode of articulating a plurality of addresses. Caught up in this plurality, in this interweaving of citation with citation, the poem's reader is submitted to Levinas's ambivalence in multiple times. In being so submitted, the reader cannot escape how the persecutor, even as much as the persecuted, is brought near by his saying.

Celan, like Levi, would not have his readers use poetry to escape the significance of persecution, in which one is not only commanded not to murder the other, but also to suffer for the sake of the other. One must give up the protection of stones, of those indexes of death that let one seal over the tomb, put to rest the "naked" dead. One must find how "they now renew the entanglement."

Yet this approach of the victim, Celan shows us, must also be an approach of the victimizer. One cannot delineate one from the other, *as if* only the victim and not the victimizer were significant. And yet, this bringing near of the victimizer does not resolve the act of victimization, *as if* one could now assume that persecution will end, that the victimizer will repent, that all will be revealed to have been an absurd game, a regretful misunderstanding. The harm that has been inflicted upon the persecuted is real and lasting. One cannot act *as if* it were otherwise without becoming a victimizer as well!

The poem struggles ambivalently with the following question: In what sense can one's persecution, which is to say one's submission to a suffering under malevolence, transform or transcend that malevolence? Like Levinas, Celan refuses to characterize transcendence ontologically. One cannot resolve the issue of suffering or of evil by arguing that it is part of a design or process in which the final outcome justifies what has occurred. One is called upon to witness the destructive impulses of others *without* any assurance that one will remain untouched by that malevolence. In fact, one witnesses the other's hostility through the very nakedness or exposure of one's vulnerability to her or him. If one were not exposed *to the point of helplessness*, then suffering could never have been said to have occurred. This is not to suggest that one is rendered evil by the other's doing of evil but that one can be crippled by the other's evil to the point of being rendered without one's autonomy. One's resistance to the other's attack is not assured at the intentional level, in that scene in which force is met by force. Yet even one's utter "capitulation" (in one's suffering) to the persecutor in that scene need not signify the annihilation of one's significance or one's dignity. For even in the collapse of one's life, one remains in an address to others that is inspiring to the other regardless of the other's intention.

How exactly should one interpret Levinas's claim that in expiation one moves from outrage to responsibility? One might explain that one simply leaves outrage behind—it is as if one were never outraged. But Celan's poetics of persecution, at least in *Die Niemandsrose*, suggests that in the movement from outrage to responsibility one carries with one the harm one has undergone. One's suffering was not an illusion but a reality. One cannot undo this reality. What one has lost in the deprivation that instigates the victim's suffering is not necessarily capable of being restored. Celan cannot undo the inexcusable deaths of his parents, or his own terrible wounding as he lets go the hand of his father. These realities must be respected, even if their very repeating in words presents a further inflection of irremediable wounding.[17]

But this wounding need not signify a yielding to malice, even as it involves a suffering under its yoke. In "Huhediblu," Celan may owe his words to destruction but his payment of them is in the order of creation, which is to say, in the order of a goodness that would remain attendant upon the voice of the other. Colin speaks of the poem as providing the poet with "weapons" that would "fight against those '*Beilworte*' that attack human life itself" (*HD*, 126). Paradoxically, the poet acquires these weapons by citing in his poem the very attitudes and uses of language that characterize this attack. The *Beilworte* become weapons against their own use because of what they reveal in their very use about those who use them. This revelation would not be so authoritative or so shaming if Celan himself did not take the address of the persecutor seriously enough to let it yet again find its target. Celan endures the words of the plagiarist in order to reveal their pitifulness. Yet the poet's very citation of the persecutor resubmits him to the other's destructiveness, to his or her attack upon him. The poem is in this sense a torture chamber, but one in which the poet insists on remaining true to his address of the other *and all the other others* in spite of his defamation by the one who persecutes him. In doing so, the poet remains in the equivocation between the hateful and the pitiful, although the pitiful here is undoubtedly more colored by a disdainful regard on the part of the poet than Levinas would perhaps allow. Yet what keeps this disdain from becoming overwhelming is the poet's own continuing vulnerability to the machinations of the plagiarist. By the poem's end, the reader feels both the hatefulness *and* the shamefulness of those who have played and still play the role of "*Schinderhannes*" (the name of an infamous anti-Semite from the seventeenth century), the persecutor who goes to work *as if* he or she were "legitimate," *as if* his or her "love" were not a collusion with others to pervert and destroy.

CHAPTER SIX

Blaspheming G-d

Facing the Persecuted

The Elliptical Address of the *Häftling/the Nameless*[1]

Celan's "Huhediblu" does not end upon that note struck in the poem itself as "the Oh-not-these-gallows-again, the Ah-it-prospers" note, that note of uncaring hypocrisy and posed insensitivity that characterizes the world of past and contemporary Schinderhannes. In spite of the insistent degradation of address within the poem, the seemingly inevitable corruption of *vespern* into *vipern*, the final words of the poem are given, at least in part, to Verlaine:

> *Oh quand refleuriront, oh roses, vos septembres?*
> Oh roses, when will your septembers flower again?
>
> (*HD*, 118, 120)

This final line's fluid expression of nostalgia and desire interrupts the nursery-rhyme rhythms and crude formulations of the preceding verse (lines obsessed by the hatred of the anti-Semite). In these previous lines, a mood of *Rausch* is at play in a manner not unlike that in Borowski's scenes of atrocity analyzed in chapter 2. The final line's change in prosody marks a turning in the poem's tone of address, a *teshuvah*, or what Celan might call a meridian.

The final line also reflects an earlier line within the poem, which was as well an allusion in German to the very line cited above from Verlaine:

When,
when do they, when
when do they bloom, hühediblüh,
huhediblu, those, yes the September
roses?

(HD, 119)

As is his practice, Celan's poetics is characterized here by complexes of citations in which the new context in which each citation finds itself becomes as essential to its meaning as the former context to which it alludes. The outcome of this process emphasizes how Celan, the poet, is both addressed by Verlaine and responds to this address. In his response, just as in his response to the plagiarists, to the proto- and neo-Nazis, as well as the Nazis themselves, the poet is also responding on behalf of all the other others, the persecuted of the *Shoah*.

Before the reading of this citation of Verlaine is given any further development, one needs to remember that the citation of the persecutors that characterizes "Huhediblu" does not take place purely in reference to their address. Like the prophetic witness explored in chapter 4, Celan's poetic witness is in the very first instance claimed by those who suffered at the hands of their persecutors. The siting of the other within Celan's poem is complicated by the fact that there are always the other others as well. Celan's response to the persecutor cannot merely suffer for her or his sake but must also suffer for those others (besides Celan) who were tormented by the persecutor. While their address of the poet within "Huhediblu" is overtly less articulate than that of the persecutors, their proximity remains crucial to the poem's search for not only an ethical but also political response to the *Shoah*. One cannot speak of the persecutors without also posing the question of how they have devastated and annihilated the lives of their victims. Like the prophet, Celan is obsessed by the injustice of the suffering he confronts. Obsessed with rendering justice to the victim, his very citation of Verlaine becomes a political act, a call to his readers and their traditions for a new order of poetry that addresses more responsibly and more attentively the play of violence characterizing history and its forgetfulness of its victims.

This turn to the persecuted, even as it seems, at least initially, more heartening, more just, and less troubling than one's obsession with the persecutor, is implicitly more devastating. In the previous chapter it was remarked how Celan's failure to have protected his father from the hands of his persecutors constitutes in Celan's own mind a telling betrayal on his part that haunts his life: "he had let go of his father's hand through barbed wire and run away." Certainly, one can argue that in Levi's "normal world" Celan should in no way feel guilt for what occurred to his father. But, as the analysis of chapter 2 has suggested, betrayal was woven into the very structure of the social relationships instantiated within the death world of the camps. And guilty or not, the very shamefulness of both his own and his father's helplessness before their persecution undoubtedly shadows his memory of this event.[2]

Celan's very impulse to share these feelings with Nelly Sachs, one who had suffered as he had, was judged to be a threat to Sachs's own well-being. The memory of the persecuted in this instance turns out to be even more threatening, more persecuting, than the memory of the persecutor. This particular rendering of the *Häftling*'s scene is amplified millions of times over as the poet considers the heritage of those other others also annihilated in the death world, as well as those who survived to witness that annihilation. In his poetry, as well as in his life, Celan is called upon to exercise a careful, even obsessive restraint as to how the scene in which the persecuted might be figured is to be constituted.

In "Huhediblu," the death camps and *the Nameless* are referred to in only the most elliptical and ambiguous of manners. For example, in the figure of "hands and finger entrails" (from the verse cited above in chapter 5), Celan ultimately alludes to the disemboweling not of animal bodies, as was common in the pagan practice of soothsaying, but of human ones. In this figure, Celan cites the Nazi praxis of the annihilation of Jewish bodies, the reduction of human beings to so much material to be disposed of. But this citation comes only by way of a figure ("entrails") that is in turn traced into the hands of the false prophets, the *Feme-Poeten*, who do not write with their hands but "forebode" the truth, as pagan soothsayers once did, in the entrails of these hands. If one reads the poem in this manner, the entrails that drop from these hands would be the starved, emaciated bodies of the *Häftling*. In this rendering of the figure, the *Häftling* are victims of an obscene and blasphemous sacrifice in which their dead bodies become the signs of National Socialism's ascendency, its thousand-year Reich. One can also read the figure as if the entrails were the poems written by the *Feme-Poeten*, poems whose denunciation of or indifference to the victims of the Nazi genocide becomes the manner in which the poet Celan forebodes both the hatefulness and the pitifulness of their poetic address. But the hands can also refer to Celan, whose citation of these false poets is written in a hand obsessed with and persecuted by their saying. In this interpretation of the figure, the entrails would refer to the disemboweling of Celan's own body for the purpose of exposing the "slander-script" of his persecutors.

These figures of the persecuted, once they are "projected" or "obsessed" into scenes (as in the amplified notion of Colin's poetic hologram introduced in the previous chapter), can become rather gruesome. This is often the case with Celan's poetry, particularly in those poems constituting *Die Niemandsrose.* For instance, in "Alchemical," Celan refers to the incinerated residue of the bodies of the annihilated emerging from the crematoria, along with their transformation into ash-laden gases, in the following manner:

Silence, cooked like gold, in
charred, charred
hands.
Fingers, insubstantial as smoke. Like crests, crests of air
around—

                                                (*PPC*, 178–81)

This figure of persecution persists at the very limit of the persecutor's destructiveness by means of an indirection in what it figures.

This indirection is necessary if the poet is both to reflect the extent of the destructiveness at "play" in the persecution of *the Nameless* and to respect the integrity of *the Nameless* at the same time. This strategy stems from the poet's refusal to engage in a straightforward, indexical witness that would simply count the victims, picture their wounds, and observe their humiliation. The hands of the poet do not point to the victims but are offered to them, often in a figure that suggests how the very writing of the poem in the poet's hand involves an uncanny and sacrificial mode of substitution. The poet's hands serve as a site of reception for the address of those who have been rendered faceless and voiceless. For this reason, they are charred twice in the passage cited above from "Alchemical"—once in the burning and a second time in the writing. In yet another poem, "Radix, Matrix" (*PPC*, 186–88), a startling figure for this substitution is given as the poet's hands no longer articulate his own intentions but are possessed by the "you" addressed by the poet. This vocative other moves the poet's hands so that they "grope" back toward a past, a beyond, that exceeds any straightforward indication. The very possession of the poet's hands by this shadowy figure (who could be interpreted as being, respectively, the poet's own parents, the anonymous masses of the *Shoah*'s annihilated, the generations upon generations of the Jewish faith, or the contemporary generation that inherits the *Shoah*) is used by the poet himself as pointing out "what is here" for the poem. This pointing out is denucleated—it points out by being overcome and possessed by the very figure one would have pointed out. One ends up pointing out the other by a groping "into there,/ and into nothing", which is to say, a groping that belongs to the other rather than to oneself and places one in an utterly ambivalent position in regard to the very act of pointing out the other: in order to point to "there," one finds one's hands are being used by another to point to "nothing." The figure indicated transcends indicating.

Celan's obsession with images of the hand can in turn be linked with that very empirical memory that he expressed at least once in his life: the hand of his father slipping from his grasp behind the barbed wire of a labor camp. This memory finds a citation in the following lines from "Radix, Matrix":

> At that time, when I was not there,
> at that time when you
> paced the ploughed field, alone:
> $\qquad$ (*PPC*, 187)

When one also considers how Celan refers to the poem as nothing other than "a handshake" (*PN*, 40), one begins to sense how Celan's poems would reach (literally and figuratively) beyond a mere pointing out of the victim to some significant contact or proximity with her or him.[3] But this contact does not bring the victim home to one's own body but functions to denucleate it, to render it a giving up of oneself for the sake of the other. All of these nuances in regard to the hand are implied in the figure of "hand and finger entrails" in "Huhediblu."[4]

The Heterogeneity of Dates

Returning to "Huhediblu," one marks in the ending line of the verse involving the *Feme-Poeten* that, in the manner of the prophet, a date is to be named, the "date of the nevermansday in September—:" The paradoxical setting of a date that suggests either/both its own nonarrival or/and the utter exclusion of the human (one can read the locution as both "*never* a-man's-day" and "never-a-*man's* day") leads to the questions of: (a) what is the event to which this date refers and (b) *will* this date *have ever arrived?* In the verse following upon this line, the date is given a further specification: it has to do with the blooming of September roses. This in turn leads the reader back to the last line of the poem quoting (but also altering) Verlaine in French: "Oh quand refleuriront, oh roses, vos septembres?"[5]

As can be expected in Celan, the date is itself a multiplicity of citations, in this case centering around the onset of persecution and referring one ultimately to the plight of those particular others who were persecuted. In the words of Colin:

> In September began those tragic events that were to overshadow not only Celan's personal life, but also the entire history of humankind. Hitler attacked Poland in September 1939 and World War II broke out; in September 1941, Nazis and Romanian fascists forced all Jews living in Czernowitz to move into a ghetto, deporting thousands of them to Transnistria's death camps. (*HD*, 123).

The date also refers to an event, actually a series of events, in Verlaine's life. The roses of September, at least within the poem from Verlaine's hand, likely refer to the year of 1872, when Verlaine traveled to England with his beloved Rimbaud. Their relationship, already tortured by arguments and outbursts of violence, came to an unhappy climax in the following year when Verlaine shot Rimbaud in the wrist. Sentenced to prison for this act, Verlaine underwent a conversion to Christianity and began to work on a series of poems with Christian themes. After leaving prison on the 16th of January in 1875, Verlaine almost immediately searched out Rimbaud. When he tried to convert him to Christianity, a fight ensued that reportedly left Verlaine knocked-out on the floor. After this event, Verlaine continued to edit the poems he had composed in prison and finally published them in a cycle titled "Wisdom." Celan's citation is from one of these poems.[6]

Thus, "Huhediblu" resides in the proximity of at least three sets of dates, one having a poetic significance, one having a personal significance and one having a world-historical significance. Each of these dates invokes a particular event in which particular others were involved. Further, each of these dates remind the reader of Celan's own claim in his *Meridian* speech that the poem is "mindful of its dates" (*CPr*, 48). For Celan the poem is in the first place neither a speculative praxis nor an aesthetic experience but the witnessing of the plight of a particular other who lives and suffers within a historical context. Just as Lang suggests (as reported in chapter 4), this witness requires that one remain true to the contingency of the other's existence. Not a universal truth speaking to the nature of all human beings but a particular truth addressed by a particular date and its particular other is required of the poet.

Yet, in spite of the uniqueness of each poem as a mode of witness and the uniqueness of each date for which it gives its witness, "Huhediblu" instantiates the anniversaries of several dates simultaneously. Several supposedly distinct moments when the memory of a series of respective others will "bloom again" are juxtaposed. Jacques Derrida argues that this juxtaposition indicates how the date is not only an indication of a unique event, of the time of the other, but also a part of a system of signs. The date functions as a node marking out a location on a gridding-over of time. Because of this structure implicit in dating, any particular event named by a date *will have always already* referred to other events named by the same date. No matter how insistently one speaks of a particular other, one's very words will involve one in all the other others as well. The laterality of Celan's text cannot remain isolated to a particular other but must open up a multiplicity of singular addresses, what Levinas might call a "pluralism." Thus, to speak of "the roses of September" is to name both a particular and unique event, as well as its intersection with all the other dates sharing that September. One cannot name the date without already sacrificing or effacing the date. The date remains, Derrida claims, "a kind of *hypothesis*, the support for a, by definition, unlimited number of projections of memory."[7] Thus, the dates named above are juxtaposed, even if Celan does not name them as such.

Because Celan does name them concurrently, he makes problematic in a thematized manner the very access the poem (which of course carries its own date in addition to the dates it names—*Die Niemandsrose* is published in 1963, but the date of its reading by a particular reader is yet another date altogether) to its dates, to the events those dates would name and to the human beings whose suffering and persecution those dates would register. But simply mentioning that the dates are juxtaposed does not resolve the ambivalence of the date. Derrida rejects any pose on the part of the Celan that would imply he "holds the key to the crypt" that could guarantee a "transparency of meaning" in regard to the date's significance. In Levinasian terms, the date is offered as an address (by the other) rather than as an indexing (of the other). One is submitted to the date, which is not in the first instance a number to be pointed out on a grid but a submission to an involvement (with the other and all the other others) that necessarily exceeds what can be named or pointed out in the poem or in language altogether. As in the setting of the scene, the setting of the date involves the poet in a writing of incessant correction, of writing ambivalently in multiple times. The poem becomes for Celan the particular way of registering the transcendence of address, of how at every turn its saying leads beyond the index to Levinas's "exposure of wounds." In Derrida's words:

> The crypt remains, the *shibboleth* remains secret, the passage uncertain, and the poem only unveils this secret to confirm that there is something secret there, withdrawn, forever beyond the reach of hermeneutic exhaustion. A nonhermetic secret, it remains, and the

date with it, heterogeneous to all interpretative totalization, eradicating the hermeneutic principle. There is no one meaning, from the moment there is date and *shibboleth*, no longer a sole originary meaning. (S, 28)

But the outcome of Celan's date is not merely a submission to indeterminacy, *as if* the poem were merely about the impossibility of naming the date. The poem is also about a date one is obligated to name for the sake of the victim, the date of persecution, that date that Derrida would name only paradoxically in his circumspect refusal to name it: "Forgive me if I do not name, here, the holocaust" (S, 50). Burdened by a date transcending its signification, "Huhediblu" refers to a "nevermansday," a date assigned to the poem but exceeding its commemoration, a date that is named by a refusal or/and incapability to name. In "Huhediblu," this date, under which the poet's hands, whether the poet be Celan or the *Feme-Poeten*, "traces" the "on- and by- and slander-script," this date in "September," the date of blooming roses, is allied in the poem with the persecuted: "*on tue* . . . When then?" The date when "one kills" (*on tue*),[8] this date is the date the poem is both questioned by and puts into question.

One needs to be careful in the naming of this date that one does not confuse an insistence that no date can be adequately signified, that the very structure of dating leads to an ambivalence of the date, with a further impossibility introduced by the naming of a particular date, the date of the *Shoah*. Derrida's refusal to name the *Shoah* can be given several readings in this regard. On the one hand, the inability to name any date already consigns it to a sort of holocaust, a sacrifice through which what is assigned in the date remains outside of any possible discourse. In this sense of impossibility, any date instigates a mourning beyond any capacity on the part of the mourner for the recovery or expression of what has been lost in that date. Thus, one mourns that one cannot mourn, that what is signified in the date exceeds not only one's capacity to reverse the actual flow of time but also to remember what time once held. In naming the date one finds oneself always already under the influence of what Levinas calls the immemorial—one is assigned to a past that could never have been a present. Here Derrida's refusal to name the date is in a sense generic—all dates are holocausts, all dates exceed their naming, all dates assign one to a past that transcends one's present.

On the other hand, the refusal to name the holocaust assigns a particular act of refusal to a particular date. Not just any date exceeds my capacity to memorialize it but this precise date, *this* holocaust. Yet this expression of impossibility does not go far enough. For one could then argue that each date is its particular holocaust, *as if* Hitler's fantasies about the Jewish undermining of the German war effort during World War I were somehow equivalent to Celan's traumatized memory of the *Shoah*. Or, in an other mode of differentiation, *as if* the wide-ranging slaughter of German nationals by Allied forces at the end of World War II is somehow in the same key or tone as the mass extermination of Jewish persons during the years of the *Endlösung*. There are dates whose difference from the Holocaust or the *Shoah* are qualitative and/or quantitative. Precisely the particularity of this particular Holocaust, this particular immolation of the date, is revealed in that moral command of Levi to provide the date with a particular and appropriate naming. That this naming of a particular event as utterly singular is ultimately impossible, that one's naming is always subjected to a hermeneutic indecision, does not defeat nor lessen the obligation to so name it.

For there are other dates arguably not as threatened as the particular Holocaust to which Celan would refer his readers. One's paradoxical capacity not to name the date, to resist a straightforward accounting of the date, varies from date to date. At a certain threshold the issue of the quantity and fragility of memory emerges. As chapters 1 and 2 have argued, the *Shoah* (or Holocaust) registers the collapse of the passing from one generation to the next of a heritage. This collapse is due to not only the deaths of individuals but also the massiveness and brutality of these deaths. In the *Shoah*, not only has a date occurred but it has also been subject to a determined and ongoing betrayal of its naming. In the light of the considerations raised in those chapters, could not the following question be posed: in a world of dates, all of which exceed mourning, are there not dates that exceed even this excession? These dates exceed precisely by means of their "decession," their collapsing of temporality. In this regard, Derrida's petition for forgiveness that he not name the Holocaust could be a recognition that this date in particular both is and is not yet another date with another poem that would name it (*"The poem is mindful of its dates"*). This date leaves one begging for forgiveness in a manner that other dates do not. This date is a date in which persecution overwhelms one's naming of the date, in which the disruption of lineage is so severe that one is left speechless, in ethical silence, in the dysfunction of a quandary that ridicules all attempts to play or work with its meaning or to give it a sense. All dates might ridicule this attempt, but forgive me when I am commanded to remember that this is particularly true for this Holocaust, which is also *Shoah*, this date which both obsesses and threatens my very mention of "the date."

"When then?" In the German, a pun repetitively persecutes the signification of this sentence literally into madness: *Wann* (when) becomes *Wahn* (madness): between the saying of *Wannwann* and *Wannwahn* in the fourth verse of the poem no phonemic distinction intervenes. The very collapse of the differences between dates, as well as of the differences between the addresses associated with their respective dates, is itself subjected to the madness of a pun that refuses to distinguish in its saying, in its address, between even madness and the sensible question of "When?" Further, insofar as an answer is suggested to the question of "When?," it is named as "the nevermansday in September." Colin points out how Celan plays with a German locution, "*St. Nimmerleinstag*," that is, "a day that no calender contains" (*HD*, 122), in order to suggest in this naming of the date a collapse of the possibility of naming the date.

But Celan also alters the locution to *Nimmermenschtags*, from a "nevermore" or "never-once day" to a "never-human's day." This alteration of his citation is itself foreboding, or prophetic. Celan's naming would be addressed by that day when no more humans would exist, or alternatively, that day when the humanity of human beings would be no longer possible. The possible meaning, as well as the possible dating, of this day is at best indeterminate. The day could refer to a transcendence of the human, the epiphany of the divine. For instance, the Jewish *Shabbat* belongs to G-d and not to man, although its institution is for the sake of man's, as well as the entirety of creation's relationship with G-d. But the day could also refer to *Yom haShoah*, a day of "total destruction," of an "extermination without justice," registering a collapse of the human and a betrayal of G-d. *Nimmermenschtags* could also refer to the day on which Jews were denied citizenship by the German government within any country, a day in which they were made pariahs in the eyes of the nation states. Or the day could refer to Celan's own particular moment of betrayal when his father's hand slipped away from him and he ceased to feel as if he were fully human. The day could also refer to the persecutor, the annihilator, who by his or her very decision to exclude humans from moral consideration no longer acted as a human. Given the first verse of the poem (in which unidentified beings find "hard, hard, hard / going / on wordways and paths"), the date could also refer to the moment when *the Nameless* in the death camps are lined up to march off to another day of forced labor (or to the gas chambers). In this reading, every day of "existence" within the camps would be rendered *Nimmermenschtags*.

Yet the nevermansday is also the day when roses would bloom again. Does not this figure suggest, however tentatively, a recuperation of loss, a moment in which one's hope for consolation can find an at least vaguely positive answer? But the entrance of this figure into the poem, of September roses again blooming, is mediated by a poem written·by Verlaine that records his conversion to Christianity, as well as his yearning for Rimbaud. Not incidentally, the poem is also associated with Verlaine's later encounter with Rimbaud mentioned above in which Verlaine ends up (reportedly) knocked unconscious on the floor after trying to convert Rimbaud to Christianity. Was Verlaine persecuted for Christ by Rimbaud's own violent reaction to his entreaties? Or was his very insistence on Rimbaud's conversion already a persecution, one that merely mirrored the earlier persecution of Rimbaud when he is shot in the wrist? Further, what would either of these questions have to do with the persecution of Jews, not only by the National Socialists, but also by Christians? By the laterality of his citations, Celan introduces a maze of implications and questions that threaten to dissolve the figures of his poem in a mania of signification.[9]

Further, by his association of Verlaine's tortured passions for Rimbaud with the Jewish victims who undergo the Nazi genocide, Celan angles his citation toward the ludicrous, as well as the indecorous. Colin sees in Celan's citation an implicit criticism of the very manner in which poetry is given a significance within the romantic tradition.[10] This criticism would be allied with Lang's own fears about poetry, namely, that the intensely lyrical voice cultivated by poets such as Verlaine and Rimbaud, while it is a complexly emotional, deeply personal, and self-consciously imaginative, too easily becomes enamored with its own artfulness and pathos. Not unexpectedly, the modern lyric shows a tendency to adopt an attitude of diffidence or even hermetic indifference toward the forces at play within the historical world lying outside the imaginative world of the poem. Celan's poetics of citation counters this tendency by invoking a lyricism reminiscent of Biblical prophecy, in which the victimization of actual, historical persons is registered in the affect of the poem's saying. As Celan himself expressed it, his poems would give a "*Gegenwort*," a "word of resistance," which "rends the wire," which "no longer bows down before the 'do-nothings and show-horses' of history."[11] This word resists those who would use their power to grasp the world for themselves, even as they forget the suffering of those who succumb to violence in the wake of their domination. Celan's citation of Verlaine at this level would be a political act—he wants to resituate what is significant in poetry by focusing poetry's attention upon the persecuted. In the wake of this attentiveness, the nostalgia for roses is revealed to be a ludicrous gesture, but one given in a revolutionary tone of address, a *Gegenwort*.

Christian Typology

But one must also read the citation of Verlaine's poem in regard to Verlaine's own citation of Christian texts. Verlaine's poem begins with an allusion to the Gospel account of Jesus born in Bethlehem:

Hope shines—as in a stable a wisp of straw.[12]

The remainder of the poem develops this allusion in regard to a variety Christian themes and images.[13] Further, in its original publication, this line was immediately proceeded by a poem ending with the question: "Is it you, JESUS?"[14] Celan's citation of the poem, then, introduces multiple dates, the dates not only of Verlaine's own erring and persecution but also, in a more surreptitious manner, the dates of the Christian Jesus's birth, persecution, death and resurrection. This citation of a Christian type by Celan is not unique to "Huhediblu" but recurs throughout the entirety of *Die Niemandsrose*.

The line, "When the roses bloom again," can refer within a Christian interpretive praxis to the resurrection, to the overcoming of persecution to the point of torture and death by a glorious and salvific restoration to life of the one persecuted. While "Huhediblu" is not as replete with Christian imagery as several other poems within *Die Niemandsrose*, it does refer to Christian motifs at crucial moments in its text. Perhaps the most telling moment of Christian typology occurring earlier in the poem, a moment that resonates both with and against that blooming of roses with which the poem ends, is its citation of the Greek letters alpha and omega:

> The note, oh
> the Oh-note, ah,
> the Alpha and Omega,
> the Oh-not-these-gallows again, the Ah-it-prospers,
> (*HD*, 119)

The Alpha and Omega refer in Christian typology to G-d as both beginning and end of the created world. The precise reference to G-d as "the alpha and the omega, the first and the last, the beginning and the end," as well as to "the Lord, who is and who was and who comes," stems from Revelations, in which that tone is to be sounded out by the seventh and final trumpet that brings the world to a final, absolutely decisive judgment.[15] In this apocalyptic tone is given yet another possible meaning to the date of *Nimmermenschtag*, as well as to the blooming again of September roses. The day named in these two figures occurs in that final articulation of the resurrection of the Christ when his return, his "second coming," marks the end of history and the final judgment of all that exists.

Christian typology, particularly as it is developed within the rhetorical and philosophical thought of Europe after the fall of the Roman Empire, assumed that history conformed to a certain pattern of development, in which the time of the Torah, appropriated by Christianity as the Pentateuch (the first five books of the Christian Old Testament), is read as the prefiguring of the coming of Christ and the announcement of the New Covenant.[16] Christ's arrival is in turn read as prefiguring his second coming in which the living and the dead will be submitted to a final judgment and history will perfected. In the words of Revelations: "I am . . . the Lord who is, who was and who comes." While this Christian typology strives to give the historical, incarnate figuration of such a history (the Latin word for the type is *figura*), its meaning, as well as its fulfillment, comes from the presence and intervention of a super-historical reality, the governance of G-d over the domain of history from the "perspective" of eternity. In the traditional Christian context, the horizontally temporal dimension of typology, that is, history, implies the vertically temporal dimension of allegory, that is, eternity, whose interaction in history is to be figured in a narrative textual structure consisting of a beginning (a fall to imperfection), a middle (the granting of a means to perfection), and an end (the achievement of perfection). For this reason, most Christian typologies tended to consist of a threefold figuration (e.g., the paschal lamb that prefigures Christ, Christ as the shepherd of humans on earth, Christ as the lamb of Revelations who delivers the anointed from the fallen earth [14:1–5]). Each of these figures mark a particular mode and stage of intervention on the part of the eternal within history. The first of these three figures is inevitably derived from the Jewish tradition and serves as the prototype for the two others following it and perfecting its meaning.

In this mode of citation, Christianity traditionally has set itself up as both the fulfillment of and replacement for Judaism. In the words of Arthur Cohen:

> Christianity, despite its rejection of Marcion's heresy, had nonetheless introduced into its reading of Hebrew scriptures a mode of differentiation that—even if it did not deny the Jewish G-d of Creation—made him into what Judaism could only consider a duplicitous and ambiguous revealer. To imagine, as Christian figurative exegesis of scripture insists, that the revelation of G-d contained a subterranean course of prophetic adumbration (that G-d used the

kings and prophets as means of announcing the coming of Jesus Christ) not only had the effect of making G-d's revelation to Israel a complexity requiring an uncongenial typological analysis but cast doubt upon the conviction of the ongoing and continuing revelation of G-d to the community that survived the destruction of its Temple and now prayed and learned in order to express its covenant with G-d.[17]

In other words, Christianity's citation of Judaism authenticated Judaism in Christian eyes but only at the cost of submitting Judaism to a mode of citation in which Jews could no longer remain distinct from Christians.[18] In the wake of this rereading of Hebrew texts, Christians insisted on speaking to Jews *as if* they knew better than Jews what Jews themselves expressed in their own tradition.

Here is established a *tone of address* that Levinas would liken to war: one sees the other as a mode of resistance to one's own ideas about her or him, ideas that the other must be pressed to embrace. One is not submitted to the other in an irenic saying but competes with her or him in a polemic discourse. In this mode of citation, one reaches out to the other only to insist the other reflects in her or his demeanor and words what one has already decided the other must already signify. In this tone of address, one prays for the "perfidious Jews,"[19] the Jews who in their very being Jewish have purportedly lost the truth of Judaism, the Jews who really are after all just another, although now lapsed, mode of being Christian.

The rhetorical structure of Christian typology provides yet another instance[20] of how a Christian tradition of reading texts and of writing history serves to blot out the address of those who do not speak in the name of that tradition. In the practice of typological citation, one encounters what Levinas calls historiography, a mode of writing in which those who inherit across the generations the works of others see nothing more in those works than a mode of justifying the lives of those who have inherited them.[21] In their inheritance of the Hebrew Torah, Christians were anxious to make it their own. In making it their own, they adopted a mode of reading Jewish writing that became oblivious to its other unique mode(s) of address.

Widerruf: The Repudiation of the Victimizer's Address

To this manner of textual usurpation, Celan now responds with a *Gegenwort*, that word of resistance mentioned above that "goes against the grain" (*CPr*, 40). Celan's response begins with his own citation of the Christian citation of

Judaism, in his introduction of *the Alpha and Omega* into the poem "Huhedi-blu." In the Christian reading of this figure, the Jewish revelation of G-d as creator becomes the prototype for the coming of the Christian Jesus who as savior and mediator now also promises his second coming, in which the injustices still at play in history finally will be rectified. But in Celan's (re)citation of this Christian figure, its meaning is altered so that the figure within Celan's poem seemingly mocks and repudiates the meaning it was originally intended to have.

First, the Alpha and Omega are cited but only to be reversed in their order. "The Alpha and Omega" become the "*Oh*-not-these-gallows-again" and the "*Ah*-it-prospers."[22] Second, the translation of an alphabetical type into an exclamation of surprise or outrage gives the figure a distinctly human and off-handed tone that is lacking in its original rendition. In this transformation, the type no longer involves a statement on the part of divinity that speaks in the inflection of *mysterium tremendum* about its own distinguishing characteristic but becomes an interjection of everyday affect in one human's speaking to another. Finally, the citation, rather than offering the means for a release from historical injustice in the coming of the judge of all history, cynically pictures a repetition of injustice and its horrors that seem never to be resolved. The gallows (another allusion to a Christian type, the Crucifix, but one that is displaced by the Nazi instrument of capital punishment and that carries resonances of Schinderhannes' persecution of Jews) is employed yet once more in history even as anonymous others prosper. The narrative strategy constituting the structure of Christian typology—cloudy beginnings, revelatory developments, and triumphant ending—is broken open.[23]

What exactly is the tone of the "Ah" and the "Oh" in this citation? Here the very expression of what is said, that voicing with a face that would address its words to another, breaks through the rather abstract surface of the alphabetical figure, even as the history it responds to is revealed to be more like an aimless repetition of disaster than an epic journey through time.

But do the words resonate in the mouth of one who speaks in a tone of genuine outrage at or being overwhelmed by the cruelty of what she or he sees? Or do these exclamations express a jaded indifference, an inevitable resignation to an ongoing injustice that is never resolved? One can even imagine a ludicrous scene in which G-d, *the Alpha and Omega*, the Lord of all creation, responds in trivial interjections expressing either helplessness or indifference concerning the matters at hand. This particular siting of Celan's hologramatic text would be blasphemously comic, a ridiculing of G-d with the precise terms G-d is said (by Christianity) to have used in the characterization of divine majesty. Consistent with the use of citation in the rest of the poem, the line seems to allow and demand all these possible interpretations. And in being submitted to these multiple interpretations, the poem puts to trial how each mode of saying uncovered by each mode of interpretation would offer a witness of the *Häftling*.

Celan's *Widerruf*: Submitting One's Words to Persecution

Given the manner in which *the Alpha and Omega* is cited within the poem, one might be tempted to charge Celan with having engaged in the very polemic against Christianity that Christianity had employed against Judaism. In his doing so, one would be hard pressed to interpret this mode of citation as a hand proffered to another, as an irenic saying in which one is commanded by the priority of the other. Celan's tone seems prima facie more interested in mocking or getting even with the Christian citation of Judaism than in being commanded by its saying.[24] Thus, Celan's response to the Christian citation of Judaism seems to involve precisely that logic of inversion that Derrida continually warns will only end up in reinscribing the very structure of repression that one has sought to avoid. But Celan's reading goes even further than an inversion: for the Christian reading of Judaism never read the Jewish prototype as being blasphemous but only as articulating an imperfect grasp of the sacred; Christian motifs, however, become ludicrous and even blasphemous in Celan's reading. One might be tempted to conclude that Celan's inversion of Christian citation actually worsens the polemic already initiated in the Christian rereading of Judaism.

Yet Celan's citation of almost any figure from any tradition, including that of Judaism, is articulated in terms of a repudiation. For example, the discussion above has already suggested how the Hebraic figure of the prophet in "Huhediblu" is also blasphemous in its implications: as the poem progresses, a prophetic saying that should inspire its listeners continually degenerates into malice and invective. Further, Celan's quotation of Verlaine involves not only a repudiation of the Christian tradition but also of the tradition of romantic poetry. Citing Jerry Glenn's studies of Celan, Alvin Rosenfeld claims this degeneration into blasphemy or a countermeaning is "everywhere" in Celan's poems—"in the ironically destructive allusions to the *Song of Songs* and Goethe's *Faust* in 'Todesfuge'; in the radical undoing of Hölderlin's famous hymn 'Patmos' in '*Tenebrae*'; in denial of the *Genesis* account of G-d's creation of man in 'Psalm.'"[25] Rosenfeld notes that the German critic Götz Wienold employs the

German term "*Widerruf*" or "repudiation"[26] for this structure of paradoxical and seemingly perverse signification, in which the poem's figures are "demoralized, destabilized and subverted" (*DD*, 31) by their manner of presentation.

Key to an understanding of Celan's articulation of *Widerruf* is the realization that the repudiation or countering of any figure cited in Celan's poem does not involve a hostile intention on the part of Celan but is the outcome of submitting the figure to the date to which it has been called in sincerity to respond. As discussed above, Celan's repudiation is in actuality a *Gegenwort* that would resist "the show-horses of history." This resistence is no easy matter and involves far more than a self-righteous moral outrage at the so-called barbarity of any perpetrator or of his or her act of victimization. Such outrage can all too easily forget the real ethical issue, namely that some particular human or group of humans has suffered at the hands of their persecutors and in this suffering have been deprived of a voice with which to address the persecutor, as well as all the other others. The more extreme this suffering, the more extreme is the muffling of the victim's voice, and the more difficult it is for those who lie outside the scene of this suffering to attend to its address. But Celan's *Gegenwort* would be addressed by precisely this suffering. As in the case of Levinas's notion of persecution, Celan effects this address not by magically restoring words to the victim's mouth or power to her or his hands but by listening to how the very suffering of the victim is already an address, an address otherwise than the meeting of force with force.

Thus, the citation of *the Alpha and Omega* in "Huhediblu" occurs "under the / date of the nevermansday in September," which is to say, among other dates under that date in September in which Hitler's armies invade Poland and begin (or continue) the process culminating in the *Shoah*, in the institutionalization of a death world, along with the "creation" of the *Häftling*. In being submitted to this particular date, the poem's figures are submitted to the suffering of particular others. In being so submitted, no figure, no mode of address seeking out the persecuted other seems capable of retaining its former significance. The very capability of one's language to bear its meaning is put into crisis. One's confidence in one's speaking is denucleated. For instance, the very naming of the poem as "Huhediblu," a word emphasizing its vowels and how they articulate the fluidity of one's breath, purposefully omits those two vowels, the *Alpha* and the *Omega* cited in Revelations, the two vowels in which breath is given a Christian articulation and in which an absolute *archē* and *closure* to one's saying are intoned. It is as if Celan is saying that word that continually brings to voice all the voices other than the voice of the G-d of the Christian Revelations, other than the two ends of an absolute principle outside of history by which history might find its measure. The absolute, if it is to be articulated at all, will be articulated in human breath and in regard to the suffering of other human beings—"*Huhediblu.*"

Thus, *Widerruf* names not so much the repudiation or betrayal of a figure's original meaning as its sacrifice,[27] its being submitted to the extremity of betrayal, the persecution undergone by the *Häftling*. In an oft-quoted speech Celan describes how after the *Shoah* the language found in his poems

> had to go through its own lack of answers, through terrifying silence, through the thousand darknesses of murderous speech. It went through. It gave me no words for what was happening, but went through it. (*CPr*, 34)

In Celan's poetry all language, whether it be found in the Christian Gospel or Jewish Torah, in romantic poetry or Greek tragedy, is subjected in his poems to the ordeal of suffering in the place of *the Nameless*. In this subjection, one's language is proffered to *the Nameless*, not in order to empathize with *the Nameless*, to suffer *as if* one were *the Nameless*, but in order to be humbled by one's helplessness before *the Nameless*, by the incapacity of one's language to actively be in the place of *the Nameless*. One takes one's words where no words can be given "for what was happening." This ordeal is not a trial of combat seeking one's heroic response but a submission to suffering eliciting one's attention and one's shame.[28] This ordeal occurs as each figure of what can be said in a particular mode of language is called upon to carry the burden of, in the sense of finding itself responsible for, that particular mode or modes of betrayal to which *the Nameless* were submitted.

In being submitted to this burden of responsibility, one finds oneself accused and in that accusation called to answer at least two questions:

1. Has the manner in which a particular mode of language engaged in an address of the other left it in an uncomfortable alliance with the persecutor, the Nazi?
2. Is the manner in which this particular mode of language responds to the suffering of *the Nameless* attentive enough to the actual dimensions of his or her persecution?

One answers these questions not by justifying one's language, by seeking a manner of extricating oneself from one's own guilt, but by taking to heart how one is never responsible enough in one's saying, in one's response to the persecuted, in one's approach to *the Nameless*. Only language that undergoes this interrogation of not only its capability but also its commitment to signifying *the Nameless* can command one's attention after the *Shoah*.

Differing Versions of Inversion

"Oh roses, when will your septembers flower again?" At the beginning of this chapter it was claimed that these lines pose a turning in the address of "Huhediblu." What then is the relationship of *Widerruf*, which also suggests a turning, a paradoxical re-inversion of the perversion of goodness enacted by the Nazis—to the turning of the poem's ultimate question? The answer to this question must take into account that the turning held in the *Gegenwort* of *Widerruf* is not without its own darkness, its own troubling derangement of conscience and consciousness, in its submission of the witness to the victimization of *the Nameless*. In this submission, the reader cannot become humble before the other without also attending to the humiliation of the other. Humility is infected by atrocity.

If the question ending "Huhediblu" is given a superficial reading neglecting the multiplicity of its tones, then it could be concluded the poem closes in a restoring and consoling inversion of the Nazi's blasphemous inversion of the victim. The line would revivify the Septembers lost to time by means of an evocation that transcends their withdrawing. What was taken away can be renewed in the future—the *Alpha* will lead to its *Omega*. Asked in this tone, the question is also the tentative assertion of a hint of an expectation—one hopes for a release from or resolution of the unbearable suffering to which the poem has attended. Of course, the thought that at least one of the Septembers implied in the restoration of time dreamed of by the poem is the Nazi invasion of Poland should warn the reader of the danger of this tone.

As Hammacher points out in his highly regarded essay on the poetry of Paul Celan, the lyric has generally been engaged in a recuperation of language by means of "an overturning and transformation" of the negative.[29] Rather than signifying the absolute limit of one's capabilities, death's entrance into the poet's thought marks the beginning of "reflection and speculation" (SI, 220). In this mode of consciousness, even the collapse of the real into the unreal, of life into death, *paradoxically*, is transformed into new and more complex modes of presence and significance. In this mode of thought, the inversion of the normal world given in the figure of the *Häftling* would be followed by a second inversion, the inversion of its inversion, in which the meaning of the *Häftling's* degradation would be rewritten as an initiation into a more encompassing insight.[30] Hammacher reports how Hegel characterizes Spirit, for whom and through whom the poet would speak, as that power in the subject "in which absolute dismemberment finds itself again."[31] The power given to Spirit is not one of domination but of an appropriation through a paradoxical mode of capitulation—the Spirit appropriates death "only when it looks the negative in the face and dwells there." Hegel speaks of this act of dwelling in the negative as itself "a magical force that turns the negative into being."

Celan, Hammacher argues, develops a strikingly different notion of paradox than that found in the Hegelian lyric. Celan's "second of inversion," in which the other's absence from the text is addressed by the text, remains "a disfiguration of figures." In Hammacher's version of the paradox, one does not "overturn and transform" the negative but attends to the coming of the other to the point of selflessness. This turn "toward another" is one in which "the most hardened and petrified self" is, in a locution Hammacher takes from a poem of Celan, "turned to heart" (*Herzgewordenes*). Rather than sublation the poem bespeaks humility—the very attending upon the other's coming is articulated as the poem's sacrifice of its *own* voice: "In the ellipsis of Celan's inversion, they [linguistic signs] are only the barren space opened by a muteness lost in itself" (SI, 225). Overcome by its muteness, the poem does not *re*member the *dis*membered body of the other, does not subsume the suffering already suffered by the other under a greater good, but articulates the trace of the "unrepeatable," of that date, that "second" (both in its temporal and hierarchical meaning), whose citation is itself also secondary, that rose of September.

As in Hammacher's "second of inversion," Rosenfeld's *Widerruf* also refuses to approach *the Nameless, as if* he or she were involved in "a magical force that turns the negative into being." Like Hammacher, Rosenfeld insists that what he terms the Holocaust involves an inversion of the world that is not capable of being righted, that leaves the poem's figures inevitably disfigured. But unlike Hammacher, Rosenfeld emphasizes the burden of humiliation, of a wounding that debilitates, in one's confrontation of the *Häftling*. *Rosenfeld is anxious to remind us that the "negative" in the matter of* Häftling *is due not simply to his or her suffering death but also to his or her subjection to cruelty.* In the previous chapter, it was argued that the persecuted not only suffers due to a harm undergone but also due to her or his betrayal by the perpetrator. Thus, the humility one comes to in the wake of the *Häftling's* persecution is not shorn of its humiliation but continues to be troubled by it. Humility without the witness of humiliation would be a humility that refuses to attend to the *Häftling's* address.

Burdened by the witnessing of cruelty, Celan's poems continually suggest in their tone of *Widerruf* or repudiation that a residue of demoralization and perversion remains no matter how artfully one poeticizes the "negative," or how committedly one looks it "in the face." For example, lines from a poem already discussed in the previous chapter—"Whichever word you speak—/ you owe / to destruction"—raise the issue of how Celan's poetry is a confrontation with this negative. The German word translated as 'destruction' in these lines is *Verderben*, which also implies a spoiling, depraving, corrupting, or demoralizing. Celan's use of this particular word suggests the shamefulness of destruction rather than its power to inflict harm. The connotations of *Verderben* fit quite well with Rosenfeld's own characterization cited above of Celan's poeticizing as having been infected by "demoralization, depravity, destabilization."

According to Rosenfeld, in *Widerruf* one continues to find both "preposterous and obscene" that the "gross evil" of the Holocaust becomes "simultaneously searing and illuminating" (*DD*, 31). By "gross evil" could not Rosenfeld be referring at least in part to the perpetrator's insistent and cunning disregard of the other's voice, which in turn allowed a cold-hearted exploitation of the other's vulnerability to the suffering that her or his voice expresses? When one turns to the perpetrator's treatment of the victim, one looks *"into* the face" of an unmitigated attack *upon* the human face that left many victims in the state of the *Häftling* before their generations disappeared in mass annihilation.

For Rosenfeld, the task of Holocaust literature, a vocation that is "inflicted" upon its writers, involves one in a crime, of which simply to be aware is "impairing" and yet also "powerfully vivifying, exposing the world as never before in all of its most frightful detail. . . . It is as if the fires that consumed so many also carried with them a kind of wicked illumination" (*DD*, 32). In this characterization of the witnessing of the *Shoah*, one finds an inversion of everyday life whose very illumination lies in how its perversion of that life cannot be reversed, cannot be given a better reading retrospectively. In this manner, the suffering of the *Häftling* is a revelation, but one inevitably burdened by the malice it suffers. Rather than being lifted up in a saving inversion, one is mired in an tormenting ambivalence. Humility cannot be entirely rid of its being touched by *the other's* humiliation. The poem is obsessed by its shame before the other. Yet this shame resists the humiliation of the other's suffering even as it is obsessed by it. The *Gegenwort* of Celan's poems both succumbs to and yet resists the crushing assault of the perpetrator upon *the Nameless*.

"HINAUSGEKRÖNT": Shame before the Persecuted

Given this altered sense of paradox in Celan, the reading of Huhediblu's ultimate question—*Oh roses, when will your septembers flower again?*—leads not to a resolution of the poem's address, or to a recovery of the voice of *the Nameless*, but to an even greater entanglement in the quandaries of witnessing her or his violation. The question's seeming fluidity, its effortless grace, are undermined by a vertiginous welling up of the possible tones of its address to the other as they would be articulated by the various traditions whose demeaning citation of the victim has been put under accusation within the poem. As the discussion above has already suggested, in attending to the poem's turning one is brought into accusation. If one is to respond to the poem's question, one is submitted to a series of questions about the sincerity and sensitivity of any number of different manners in which even a given tradition, let alone these several traditions, might come to respond to how the poem would speak to its other.

Crucial in this becoming burdened by the address of the victim is the manner in which the poem's ultimate question is weighted down by shame in spite of its ongoing resistance of the other's humiliation. One's helplessness before the other who suffers is not wondrous but burdensome. Although Celan himself never speaks directly of the pathos of shame in his critical writings, others have made much of it. Adorno, for example, argues that Celan's poems are "permeated by a sense of shame stemming from the fact that art is unable either to experience or to sublimate suffering."[32] Caught in the net of its own helplessness, the poet's saying registers in its shame a denucleation of the aesthetic impulse, an undoing or humbling of any delight in the playfulness of the poem's language.[33]

That this tone of shame is registered in the reader's encounter with the poem is crucial, for instance, in Celan's "*HINAUSGEKRÖNT*" ("Crowned Out"). The analysis that follows takes up with three particular ways in which this poem's figures are submitted to the *Häftling* in the mood of shame and how accusation is registered in the wake of this submission. By way of the poem's first verse, the issue of a particular tone of the Christian reading of Judaism is given renewed attention. By way of the second verse, the issue of the witness's demoralization by her or his witness of the persecuted, of the *Häftling*, will be addressed. By way of the poem's final verses, the issue of blasphemy both against G-d and the human is focused upon.

Witnessing Christians Witnessing Jews

Felstiner points out how, in a poem addressed to his mother, Celan writes: "I speak you free / of the Amen that deafens us."[34] The "Amen" here alludes to Jesus's last words on the cross ("So be it") translated into ecclesiastical Latin, as well as to two millennia of Christian "Amens" in affirmation of Christ's death and resurrection. On one level, the poet relieves his mother of the Christian accusation that Jews murdered Jesus. On another level, the lines imply a rejection of Christianity, or at the very least, an abandoning of it as a mode of articulating Jewish suffering in the *Shoah*.

Yet in "*HINAUSGEKRÖNT*," as well as in "Huhediblu" and other poems of *Die Niemandsrose*, Celan engages in an ongoing citation of Christian types. The particular citation found in "*HINAUSGEKRÖNT*" is that of the humiliated king who is crowned in thorns and spat upon, of an incarnated G-d's majesty subjected to humiliation. If Celan is obsessed with speaking the persecuted Jew free of Christ, why then does he continue to call upon (and be called by) Christian modes of language?

"*HINAUSGEKRÖNT*" begins by referring to those who have been "CROWNED OUT, / spewed out into night" (*PPC*, 209). In this figure is found an elliptical allusion to the smoke of the burning corpses of *the Nameless* as it rises at night from the chimneys of the crematoria to the stars overhead. As in those lines discussed above concerning the scene of the *Häftling* in other Celan poems, the allusion here is gruesome in its tone. But the figure also suggests: (a) the Davidic kingship and the establishment of the Temple in which incense would be burnt whose smoke would rise up in an offering of prayer to G-d; and (b) the Christian type of the suffering Christ, which in turn is based upon the Old Testament "prototype" of the suffering servant, as well as the Davidic kingship. Celan's figure of *Hinausgekrönt* implies a crowning that thrusts outward he or she who is crowned. The very identity of he or she who is to be so crowned is left anonymous, as if the crowning itself lacked a recipient. Insofar as the crown is to be thought of as a symbol of kingship, the reformulation of its verb, "to be crowned," has transformed it into an oxymoron—he or she who is crowned is thrust away from the center, into the distances. Crowning brings one into exile rather than kingship.

But unlike that mode of citation in which the Jewish figure inevitably serves as the precursor for the Christian, Celan's type complicates this relationship by submitting the suffering Jesus "crowned out" as king to the *Häftling*'s humiliation in order that the *Häftling* now serves as the measure for Jesus' suffering. Jesus has become the precursor for the *Häftling*, just as David (in the Christian view) had been the precursor for Jesus. Yet the poem's subversion of the Christian type of the suffering or exiled king, rather than simply dismissing or mocking Christianity, would transcend its shameful history, its problematic alliance with the persecutors of the *Häftling*,[35] by rendering the figure of Jesus vulnerable to the address of the *Häftling*. The Davidic type, which stems from the Jewish tradition, is given similar treatment.

What Celan would free his mother from is not the Christian *Amen* in itself but that tone of the *Amen* "that deafens us." In doing so, Celan would continue to take seriously that manner in which the Christian type would be addressed by a suffering for the sake of the persecuted. Celan's *tone of address* implies a prophetic exhortation of Christianity, in which that religious tradition is challenged to give up a reading of Judaism that allows, if not cultivates, condescension and scapegoating. Celan's address would ask of the Christian the particular sacrifice of no longer using the figures of the crucified Jesus or the risen Christ in order to appropriate the other's suffering, particularly the Jew's suffering, as a mere justification for or illustration of Christian belief.

For example, Felstiner points out that Celan explicitly warns "against fixing on Christian resonance in 'Psalm'" (*PC*, 169). Notice that Celan's warning does not dismiss the possibility of a "Christian resonance" but is anxious concerning the tendency on the part of his readers to hear it at the expense of all other modes of address in their reading of his poems. As discussed in the previous chapter concerning Levi's figure of the *Häftling*, the witness of the *Shoah* must keep in mind how the very language to which he or she turns is already under Christian occupation. Yet Celan's freeing that language of "the Amen that deafens" is also a gift from Celan to Christianity—for in his poetry, Christian modes of address continue to be significant, even if not predominant, in spite of the history of persecution by which they are tainted.

Thus, rather than turning the *Häftling* into a moment of Christianity's own narrative or historiography, Celan's citation of the Christian figure of Christ now becomes a call to accusation, to the posing of how one's alliance with the persecutor, as well as one's attentiveness to the *Häftling/the Nameless*, must be reconsidered incessantly. In his response to Christianity, Celan is not so much interested in either upholding or dismissing the particular doctrines of the Christian resurrection or crucifixion, or in the various manners in which theologians and philosophers might render these doctrines, as in the *tone of address* Christianity takes in regard to *the Nameless*. This tone, if it is truly to respond to *the Nameless*, must be sincere, an exposure to the point of one's exposing of one's exposure before the *Häftling*. Without this tone of address, Christian philosophy and theology has been in the past and will become again in the future morally and spiritually outrageous in regard to the persecuted.

Thus, in the figure of *Hinausgekrönt*, of being "crowned out," Celan submits both Jewish and Christian citations of kingship to the address of the *Häftling* and to the degradation she or he has suffered. The submission of both Christian and Jewish traditions and their significant figures to the particular burden of the *Häftling's* suffering empties out their meaning not by initiating a dialectic in which what seemed humbled is now demonstrated to be in reality an even higher form of glory, of *kavod*, of the theophany of G-d's divinity, but by a shaming to the point of blasphemy. For, as was argued in the previous paragraphs, the *Häftling* is crowned out in a manner that leaves the notion of her or his being rendered in majesty, even in a majesty that tarries in the negative, as ludicrous. The issue is not one of an effortless paradox—that what seemed to be humbled is to be exalted and what seemed to be exalted is to be humbled—but of a paradox crippled by perversion—that one resists the other's violation, even as the helpless are crushed by a destruction that cannot be undone, an extermination without justice, an attack upon goodness exceeding any rationally explicable motivation. Kingship has been infected by execration. As has been argued from the first chapter, there is nothing saving or justifiable about cruelty. For precisely this reason suffering cruelty is to be distinguished from the suffering of pain, as well as a suffering that humiliates from a suffering that humbles.

Submitting the figure of the exiled king to a "wicked illumination,"[36] Celan immediately situates his poem in a crisis of significance that leaves both reader and poet shamefully disoriented. The disorientation occurs as the attempt to address *the Nameless* in a tone of reverence is inevitably contaminated or repudiated by the shamefulness of their victimization. Just as in "Huhediblu," in the "Ah" and the "Oh" of one's saying before the *Häftling*, the very articulation of one's address here seems burdened with an unforgivable, wounding ambivalence. The elliptical and condensed references permeating the first line of "*HINAUSGEKRÖNT*" lead to a fragmented series of images and allusions that reflect a mind caught up in unresolvable conflict. Every attempt on the part of the reader "to make sense" of the figures only instigates a shameful quandary, in which one must either admit that the *Häftling*'s humanity has been degraded or attempt to justify retrospectively the ignominy of the *Häftling*'s suffering through an appeal to its place within a process of historical or metaphysical recuperation. Neither alternative, as the discussion in this book has repeatedly argued, is acceptable. One remains within the quandary. One remains obsessed by the persecution of *the Nameless*.

Witnessing the Persecuted

The insistence of this quandary and its attendant tone of ambivalence is elaborated upon in the second verse's figure of the plaiting and unplaiting and plaiting yet again of the strands of "Berenice's head of hair" (*PPC*, 209), a figure that juxtaposes the intimate and tactile gestures of a lover caressing his beloved with that shameful ascent toward the constellation *Comus Berenice* of the beloved's cremated body in columns of smoke that wreathe and unwreathe.[37] Troubling the juxtaposition of these two allusions is an implied reference to the hair shorn from Jewish women before they were gassed and cremated. To remember the annihilated, according to the subliminal association made in this figure, is to submit to fingering this hair, to plaiting and unplaiting it, even after the persons to whom it belonged have been annihilated. As in the case of Celan's relationship with his own parents, loving remembrance here is tormented by its helplessness before the suffering of the beloved.

By remaining subjected to this helplessness, the figure functions like Levinas's description of persecution—one responds to a blow in a manner that transcends one's own forceful resistance to that blow. Yet this response, which here is not articulated in regard to the smiter but to the one smitten, remains infected by the smiter's violence. This infection does not render one's response violent, but it does submit one to the violation of another that is beyond being prevented. *One witnesses that one's powerlessness before the victimizer involves one not only in the victimizer but also in the victims of the victimizer.*

The transcendence of the other is doubled in the case of the victim who is rendered servile or who is annihilated. On the one hand, the other has always already submitted one to a time beyond one's own in the very vulnerability of the other to suffering. The other's succumbing to death occurs beyond my own capability to assume this suffering, or to enter into the other's time, *as if* it were mine. Given the transcendence of the other's suffering, the gesture of substitution, in which I would take the place of the other in his or her suffering, is not to be confused with that of appropriation. Precisely because one cannot appropriate the other's suffering as one's own, one offers one's suffering in the place of the other—one takes the bread from one's mouth for the sake of the hungry, one receives the blows directed toward the other, one stands between the child and those who would slay her or him. In these gestures, one assumes the burden of a submission to the other that is always already at the heart of one's subjectivity. One is always already called upon to dedicate one's capabilities in service to the other. While the authority for that call lies beyond one's capabilities, in one's already having been submitted to the other, the call or command articulated in this submission could have no significance in a world in which people did not have capabilities!

But what is left to offer the victim who has already succumbed to violence, particularly to that extremity of violence to which the Häftling was submitted? Here one is confronted with a mode of transcendence in which what is undergone by the other interrupts any possibility for one's own intervention on his or her behalf. In this mode of transcendence, one finds that precisely because the other suffers uniquely and because the other is vulnerable "even unto death," the other resists my gesture of substitution. The other's capitulation to suffering is final. To revert to speaking of the issue of justice in this extreme instance, *as if* there were yet something one might do to ease the other's suffering, would seemingly be to make light of the degree of injustice to which the other has been submitted.

The poet would touch Berenice and would plait her hair. The gesture of touching alluded to in this figure goes beyond an indexical notion of witness, in which the poet would objectively locate and number the wounds of the persecuted. The poet desires contact with the beloved in a touch that would be open to her proximity, a touch that would be reassured and reassuring of her. But the gesture of plaiting Berenice's hair plays around a temporal lapse. The poet is careful to say: "I plaited, / I unplaited, / I plait, unplait" (*PPC*, 209). Between past and present lies that moment of persecution in which the beloved is stolen away, in which she is annihilated, in which she is transformed into the ash-laden smoke that rises into the night and turns the stars a "grey-beaten, heart-hammer silver."

In the wake of this "alchemical" transformation, the poet's touch is also transformed. No longer capable of proffering a contact that would protect and sustain the other, the poet's hands reach out to ghosts or to those morbid remnants of hair cut away from now incinerated bodies. But to plait the hair of one who has been rendered as smoke is to find the very notion of touching the other to have become defiling and demoralizing. This activity also transforms touch into a mode of delusion—one acts *as if* Berenice were still alive, *as if* her hair could be actually plaited. The poem borders on a psychotic break with reality, as the obsession to be with Berenice continues in spite of her disappearance.

The plaiting and unplaiting of the smoke could also refer to the poet's own voice, to his saying of the poem, to his breath that rises up to the stars in an address darkened by the annihilation of the beloved. As indicated earlier, Celan himself characterizes the poem as a hand proffered to another. Celan's poem also carries his very breath toward the beloved, a breath that would give her life in a gesture reminiscent of G-d's creation of Adam. But this traditional figure becomes defiling and demoralizing as one associates the inbreathing of soul with *churban*, an unmitigated destruction. What should flare into Berenice's nostrils and call her into life must now become the sign of the incinerating of her flesh. The in-breathing of soul is transformed within the *Shoah* to the fire of extermination. The vulnerability of the body of Berenice to betrayal—to her hair being shorn, to her lungs being filled with gas, to her corpse being disposed of through mass cremation—leaves the poet speaking to a phantasm, to his own desire to touch a beloved whose hand has not only slipped away but also has been annihilated. In the wake of this annihilation, even the poet's attempt to be perverse—to fix his attention upon a repetitive touching of the corpse's hair, a gesture bordering on necrophilia—is rendered ludicrous. Not only is the lover absent but the destruction to which she was subjected renders her without a corpse. Further, whatever hair Celan might finger is "no-one's" hair, the hair of tens of thousands of women stored in warehouses by the Nazis for use in the production of various products. The "death" of his beloved has become anonymous, *the Nameless*.

The poet would mourn his beloved. In the act of mourning, particularly as it might be articulated by a Hegelian approach to loss, one tarries in the negative, in the absence left by death, so that one might be given an orientation toward, as well as a mode of contact with, what is past. In this contact one's own life is nurtured and the other who is dead is honored. In this manner, one integrates the memories of those who are dead into the memories of those who are living and the address carried in those memories is articulated through the generations of time.

But in the annihilation of Berenice a loss occurs that is beyond that of death. The repetitive action of doing and undoing and doing yet again the hair of the one annihilated characterizes a disturbed witness, one that both refuses and is incapable of catharsis, one that is distrustful of its own efforts even as it embraces a responsibility to continue its encounter with what cannot in principle be resolved. As in Levinas's notion of a speaking involved in an incessant correction, the discourse here is burdened by the injustices suffered by the other others and the ambivalence this provokes in one's address of one's society. But unlike Levinas's notion of incessant correction, Celan would confront the reader with those others whose annihilation puts them beyond the pale of justice. To speak of justice in this situation is to find oneself obsessed by the failure to render any justice whatsoever. Even the willingness to offer one's life in the place of the other *Häftling*, a possibility that *perhaps* remained for the mother discussed in Borowski's short story in chapter 2, is impossible here. One cannot bring back the moment in which the other succumbed to torture, in which he or she was broken or annihilated. One is incapable of placing one's own body between the blow of the smiter and the one who was smitten, not because one was indifferent to the persecuted in the instance where torture occurred but because the blow had already been struck and its destructive effect has already been registered upon the other. Thus, the figure of Berenice, of the beloved who is violated, obsessively repeats in Celan's memory the singular occurrence of her persecution in actuality.

Elisabeth Weber speaks of Celan's poems as "making mourning, and hence death, again possible" for those who have suffered the trauma of persecution.[38] But Weber's argument also implies that the mourning that is made possible by Celan's poems is a continually interrupted thematization of the impossibility of mourning: one finds the words for one's inability to speak, one remembers that one cannot remember. Memory's lack still finds words for an address that is immemorial, that transcends *what* might be expressed by the other and leads one to the very address of that expression and the vulnerability it reveals in the other. This address will have already addressed one no matter how thoroughly the other's historical presence has been blotted out in one's empirical memory.

But the impact of that address, Weber argues, verges on psychosis. In making this claim, she refers not only to Celan's poems but also to the texts of Emmanuel Levinas from *Otherwise than Being* where he defines the "one-for-the-other" of witness (a witness that is in actuality the very structure of one's soul or subjectivity, the animation of one's psyche) in terms of "possession" and "psychosis" (*OB*, 191n3). When he speaks of this possession, Levinas might have in mind how one's confrontation of the suffering of *the Nameless* leaves one's witness before "a gaping pit" that "nothing has been able to fill or cover over" (*PN*, 120). The address of the *Häftling* is so disorienting, so without precedence, so dangerous that Levinas is moved to ask: "Should we insist on bringing into this vertigo a portion of humanity whose memory is not sick from its own memories? And what of our children, who were born after the Liberation, and who already belong to that group? Will they be able to understand that feeling of chaos and emptiness?" (*PN*, 120).

The psychosis implicit in Celan's address does not instigate the breakdown of the other's significance but its enduring in spite of all odds. As was developed in chapter 3 no matter how abject the other is rendered in her or his persecution, her or his suffering not only continues to matter but matters all the more. *The Nameless* confirms that the very articulation of one's own subjectivity is an exposure to the other that cannot be undone no matter how violently and powerfully the world about one conspires to ignore that exposure, to undo the other's address.

Already exposed to point of exposing its exposure, Celan's voice refuses any easy consolation, any facile resolution of the impossible witness confronting it. The final declaration of the second verse of *"HINAUSGEKRÖNT"*—"I plait"—can be read as giving voice to the poet's commitment to continue to witness the beloved who has been submitted to Nazi persecution no matter how impossible this witness might be. In giving this *Gegenwort*, in refusing to succumb to violence in spite of the impossibility of one's position, the poet offers what might be termed a *Schneetrost*, a snowy consolation.[39] The utter gratuitousness of one's witness transcends whatever powers might be arrayed against it. But paradoxically, this gratuitousness, this grace, does not release one from suffering or from humiliation but intensifies its impact all the more. Yet this impact is not one that leaves one centered in one's own disorientation, *as if* the psychosis of witness were simply a falling away of one's capability to be one's self, *as if* humiliation simply left one without responsibility. Rather, one is all too outside of one's self, which is to say, already traumatized by the other's address, already submitted to the other's suffering in a manner that leaves one uniquely responsible for (even if not capable of preventing) the other's suffering. Weber's thoughts about Levinas's own citation of witnessing as a psychosis fit well with what has been termed above the quandary of witness.

Blaspheming G-d

Perhaps the most startling type of disfigurement in Celan's poetry, one that occurs often in the poems of *Die Niemandsrose*, involves blasphemy. In his troubling of consolation, Celan's voice exceeds the outrage of that prophetic voice which would emphasize the shame of history in order to highlight the righteousness of a G-d transcending history. In counterdistinction to this viewpoint, Celan's voice finds G-d is as much involved in the shamefulness of history as any of G-d's creatures. Thus, *"HINAUSGEKRÖNT"* seemingly deflates the grandeur of G-d in its third verse by provocatively juxtaposing a kabbalistic image for G-d ("Blue Chasm" [*PPC*, 209])[40] with a whore upon whom the poet, weighed down by his remembrance of the victims of the *Shoah*, would then sexually advance with both "curses and prayer." Such a gesture of taking G-d for one's harlot inverts the more traditional gesture of shame that a righteous G-d expresses concerning humans when he commands the prophet Hosea to "take to yourself a wife of Harlotry, for the land commits great harlotry by forsaking the Lord" (Hosea 1:2).[41] In Celan's image, it is as if G-d has taken the "wife of Harlotry" because G-d has forsaken human beings. As in Celan's *"Tenebrae,"*[42] G-d is put into question by the suffering of the *Häftlinge*, by their helplessness before a perverse persecution.

For Celan, the violence of the *Shoah* so threatens all expectations that history might become just, that humans might be treated with compassion, that the poet is left with no other alternative than to let the disturbance of this threat, the restlessness it inspires, become the meaning of the victim's suffering. Mired in a history of injustice, the poem indicates that prayer has become shameful but remains prayer none the less. If prayer indicates a *transcendent* address, then the only prayer that can occur before the annihilated is a prayer infected by the helplessness of the victim, a prayer burdened by its own quandary of witness but a prayer whose commitment to the victim is intensified in its very quandary. One's resistance comes *otherwise* than as a resolution of dissonance, a restoration of integration and harmony. In one's unrelinquishable allegiance to the shame of the victim's suffering is given the *Gegenwort* that would resist the "show-horses" of history, precisely those who would forget such shame in the heralding of their victories. The lips singing such a *Gegenwort*, as suggested in the penultimate verse of *"HINAUSGEKRÖNT,"* would be "reedy," thin with starvation, and would direct their voice into "tundra-ears" (*PPC*, 209), the ears of a history bent upon the repression of the *Gegenwort*.

The allegiance of Celan's voice to the shameful memory of the other's victimization is an absurd or gratuitous gesture, one entirely lacking in the power to erect a civilization, to give orders that will be followed by one's fellow citizens, or even to write the history of one's accomplishments. Yet this voice is obsessed with its responsibility to the other whose address transcends all these considerations. In this transcendence is given the possibility of a judgment of history in which those who inherit its violence resist succumbing to its logic, that is, to a logic in which might makes right, in which only the survivors of history have a voice in its writing. Thus, the final lines of *"HINAUSGEKRÖNT"* state:

> And an earth rises up, ours,
> this one.
> And we'll send
> none of our people down
> to you,
> Babel.
>
> (*PPC*, 211)

Here the dead are given a voice, one held in solidarity with the poet's own voice and one that refuses succumbing to a history of victimization. Finally it seems that Celan moves beyond the troubling of consolation.

Yet this new gesture of resistance is once again announced in the tone of *Widerruf*; the new earth referred to here is "this one," that is, precisely the gesture of the poem itself, its address of the other. This gesture is not the establishment of a heavenly city beyond the boundaries of time, *as if* eternity were simply another place beyond history. The poem can speak the command of eternity only by means of a language enmeshed in history and under the burden of a Nazi occupation. Further, in the place of G-d's address of the builders of Babel's tower in the biblical story, the poet puts his own voice in alliance with the annihilated. Not G-d but the poet renders judgment. This reversal of the roles of G-d and man puts the entire project of these last lines on the very lip of blasphemy. Rather than judgment, a repetition of the very inattention to G-d's transcendence that was the hallmark of the builders of the biblical Babel is seemingly threatened. This blasphemy through implication is in league with the earlier accusation found in *"HINAUSGEKRÖNT"* that the majesty of G-d was shamed by the suffering of the *Häftling*, of *the Nameless*.

Blaspheming G-d to Attend to *the Nameless*

As already discussed in the preceding chapter, the undermining of the prophetic stance, of he or she who would speak for the afflicted *in the name of G-d*, occurs even more insistently in 'Huhediblu" than has been described so far in the analysis of *"HINAUSGEKRÖNT."* Indeed, the figure of prophecy is introduced there only to be subverted by the poet's inability or refusal to give a prophetic condemnation. That poem continues to its very end to record a series of decompositions, of subversions of prophetic, poetic, and religious symbols. In these subversions, one senses the vulnerability of the poet to the very forces he seeks to denounce.

But this vulnerability is not located in the poet's heart, which is the prophetic vulnerability explored, for example, in Psalm 73.[43] The poet does not lack the sincerity to speak the truth, to be true to those who have suffered annihilation in the Nazi genocide. Rather, the poet's sincerity makes him all too aware of how every word he might choose to address the annihilation of human beings in the Nazi genocide has already been mutilated and defamed by that very genocide. The Nazis have not only persecuted Jewish persons but also have violated the poet's language through an appropriation of its words in order to incite the collapse of address, the facelessness of the *Häftling*. For Celan to intone the German words *Prophet* or *G-tt* is to find himself caught up in a saying before the other with words resonant with the tone of the Nazi. In the Nazi genocide, a detonation of the figures of the real, of the words that might be called upon to respond to the other, occurs before the prophet had the time to speak. The poet struggles for a language uncontaminated by the tone of address that characterizes Hitler's announcement that he is the "prophet" and that the Jew is anathema.

In his resistance to the Nazi's purportedly prophetic stance, Celan adopts a prophetic mode of speaking, insofar as he seeks to be addressed by the victims of history in such a manner that the impact of their address destablizes the figurative space established by his poetic praxis. Thus, the metatrope of the prophetic, in which the personal becomes exposure to the other's suffering, in which abstraction becomes commentary,[44] must be given yet another turn in the metatrope of *Widerruf*, of a repudiation by subversion. This turn of the prophetic turning doubles the destabilization already inherent in biblical prophecy. Disfiguration becomes dysfiguration. Not only is the evildoer now suspect, but the figure by which one introduces G-d as speaking directly and with authority within a biblical pronouncement is also under suspicion. One can make a case for such a doubled suspicion beginning as early as the rabbinical rereading of Jeremiah's Lamentations.[45] In Celan's poetry, as in much of the poetry of the Nazi genocide, this suspicion becomes extreme to the point of blasphemy. Celan himself remarks to Nelly Sachs that he "hoped to be able to blaspheme up until the end" (*PC*, 156).

But Celan's blasphemy is not a simple repudiation of G-d or of G-d's prophet. Rather, it is a repudiation of the presumption that the *figure* of a G-d who speaks out in particular words, a particular command, is enough to resist the collapse of address enacted by the Nazis in their depersonalization of the annihilated. One repudiates the figure of G-d for the very sake of remaining true to a concern for the other that is itself its own command. One reaffirms that the name, whether it be of G-d or of the human other, is ultimately a figure, a movement toward as address rather than a producing of the other as a being. Thus, in the figure of G-d, one's address of G-d is at issue, an address that precedes and inevitably disrupts any possible knowledge *of* G-d.

This repudiation of the name of G-d is not unlike Levinas's own notion of *illeity*, discussed in chapter 4, in which "the infinite orders to me the neighbor as a face, without being exposed to me" (*OB*, 150). The figurative language of Celan's poem, in much the same manner as prophetic witness, seeks to be addressed by the victims of history, in this case of the Nazi genocide. One refers to historical others not only through an act of representation but also through a being addressed by how the suffering of actual and particular others exceeds any poetic figure or rational theme that would represent or evoke that suffering. The suffering already has ordered me to attend to it in spite of the very imperfection and frailty that the suffering indicates in the sufferer. The glory of this command, that it effaces its own name in ordering me to the other who suffers, becomes the disruptive revelation of a G-d without theism haunted by the possibility that history might be consumed in an extermination without justice.[46]

This turn to the eternal as *illeity* makes the suffering of history even more problematic, even more shameful, since G-d's transcendence is no longer defined in terms of an omnipotent manipulation of history from outside of its boundaries but in terms of an absolute ethical command articulated from within historical life. This command insists that human beings attend to the other's voice *no matter what power intervenes*. But the command does not guarantee that annihilation will not prevail, that historical powers will not continue to ignore the prophetic call to responsibility. G-d's address is not to be thought in terms of a power arrayed against another power, *as if* the *polemos* of the evil-doer now makes necessary that goodness itself become warlike.

For instance, in speaking of that coming to oneself constituting Abraham's *teshuvah*, his turning from the culture of Idolatry to that of Judaism, Avivah Zornberg refers to a midrash in which G-d in G-d's glory is revealed to a man "traveling from place to place," who "saw a castle on fire."[47] According to Zornberg in this midrash the revelation of G-d involves "a moment of self-awareness [on the part of Abraham], of the extent of his protest and his terror/wonder at the Masterless world" (*BD*, 87). The distress of this mode of revelation, in which the world is consumed by a fire not unlike Celan's *Verderben*, "generates an intense receptivity to every shred of communication that comes from G-d" (*BD*, 89). But that very communication is itself that humans are to be torn, to live in *teruf ha-da'at*, the "rending of the mind" (*BD*, 90). This in turn, Zornberg argues, leaves one knowing oneself as bereft, as undergoing wounds "that can never be sewn together" (*BD*, 92). One is burdened by "irreparable losses" that complicate forever the process of mourning. Yet in undergoing these losses, one must "seek for ways of magnifying the breakdown" (*BD*, 95).

One mode of this breakdown comes in the consuming of language by National Socialism. This consumption was not simply a pollution of what words indicated, *as if* language were only a mode of speaking *about* the world. The very address of the other was consumed in the Nazi tone of speaking. This tone of indifference, in which the very tonality of one's saying before the other was denied, feigned an invulnerability to the other's vulnerability. In confronting this tone, Celan is neither in the wonder or terror referred to by

Zornberg but in shame. Still, the very shamefulness of this shame is an indication that G-d is revealed not through a figure proclaiming Its own authority, showing Itself as Its own *archē*—"I am the *Alpha* and the *Omega*"—but as a *kenosis*, as an emptying out before the other who suffers. Not the figure of G-d but the suffering of the *Häftling, the Nameless*, is to be attended to.

Celan, unlike Levinas, takes this principle to the point of blasphemy. But Celan's blasphemy of G-d is also a rendering of G-d as kenosis. G-d, like the poet, is submitted to execration, to that tone of betraying address which has been undergone by *the Nameless*! In this manner, one's blasphemy of "G-d" does not indicate the eternal but is itself the very expression of the eternal, of a prior orientation to goodness that even the Nazi tone of address cannot undo. Celan's blaspheming of G-d differentiates a transcendent G-d from the G-d who is used by the persecutor to blaspheme the human. The true G-d, the G-d beyond G-d, *En Sof*, does not insist on G-d's divinity but is utterly given over to the revelation of the height of the other's address. In Levinas's words: "Auschwitz did not interrupt the history of holiness. G-d did not reply, but he has taught that love of the other person, without reciprocity, is a perfection in itself" (RM, 21).

As in Zornberg, one proclaims in one's suffering of the *Häftling*'s address that to be infected by atrocity does not mean that one has succumbed to it. As Celan's own poetry shows, the very infection to which one is submitted by the perpetrator can in turn becomes a mode of resistance to the perpetrator's malice. Unlike the perpetrator, Celan's voice will assume the shamefulness of the *Häftling*'s suffering as one that cannot be thrust out. In this way he magnifies the distress of the *Häftling*. Magnification is itself the submission to the impossibility that one's own suffering of the *Häftling*'s suffering could ever become that suffering. One magnifies the other's suffering by suffering one's inability to magnify in one's own suffering what the other has suffered. Magnification is a rendering acute rather than an aggrandizement. What is intensified here is a commitment to the other that does not end up in appropriation but shudders in a paroxysm of shame.

The ending of *"HINAUSGEKRÖNT"* confronts a turning in which the distress of one's shame for the other is magnified, even as one articulates this distress as a mode of resistance to the other's shame. In turning to Babel, Celan confronts that mode of address which would render the other faceless, a mode of address that has already infected his own witness of *the Nameless*. For Celan Babel signifies not only the babbling of tongues that followed upon the building of the fabled tower but also the initial commitment of its builders to ignore their creatureliness and to challenge the address of a transcendent G-d

with their own artefact, their own historical regime. In this way of interpreting the figure, Babel becomes in *"HINAUSGEKRÖNT"* that tone of address
articulated in Hitler's dream of a thousand-year Reich. In refusing to send
"any of ours" to Babel, Celan expresses his resolve to write in such a manner
that the *Häftling* does not remain faceless and is no longer consumed by the re-
verberations of the Nazi address within the German tongue.

Babel signifies a voice that would own itself, that would be its own *archē*,
its own creator. But Celan's poems witness that the monomaniacal voice of
Babel had always already been commanded to an attentiveness to the other's
address. G-d's punishment of the builders in the biblical story, that they suddenly find themselves speaking in different tongues so that their voices become incomprehensible to one another, does nothing more than make clear
what was already the case. Human address that demeans or ignores the other
is a delusion—the founders of Babel seek a single voice that is its own, that
authorizes for itself from itself what is to be intended, what is to be accomplished. Yet Babel's voice was already speaking in many other tongues, was already obsessed by the laterality of the other's address, was already beyond its
own understanding of its saying. In his response to Celan's citation of Babel in
"HINAUSGEKRÖNT," Derrida finds something similar: "Multiplicity and
migration of languages, certainly, and within language. Your country, it says,
migrates all over, like language" (S, 30).

In refusing to hand over his witnessing of the annihilated to Babel, Celan
places his own hand, the work of his poem, between himself and those who
would continue the *Shoah* in the precincts of Babel. Celan offers his words in
place of the annihilated who no longer can speak for themselves. This sacrificial saying begins from the very first lines of his poem, in which its figures are
burdened down by the *Häftling*'s suffering, by her or his submission to becoming faceless before the Nazi regime. Celan's sacrifice brings a voice to the
Häftling, although one that must inevitably bear witness to the crushing of
the *Häftling*'s voice. In this most tentative of turnings, the poem refuses to let
the annihilated become yet again consumed by a tone of speaking that would
speak without a tone, without deference to the other. Yet in doing so, the
poem finds itself resubmitted to the very address of the regime. To recall a locution of Frieda Aaron, *the Nameless* cannot be "mourned restoratively." In
mourning its own impotence, the poem suffers the toneless, demeaning address of Babel precisely as its mode of resisting Babel's project to render humans without a voice, or to consume all the other voices in its own voice.
Celan does not hand over the annihilated to Babel, but this does not keep
Babel from being intoned in that very refusal.

Yet paradoxically, the babbling of the tongues in Babel is heard in Celan's tongue as the transcendence of the other's address, as a disruption of Babel on the part of *the Nameless* for which Babel itself could never have accounted. Not G-d but *the Nameless* provides the inspiration by which Celan's prophetic tone humbles the arrogance of the regime. And here even G-d assumes the execration, that blasphemy of the human, invoked in the Nazi tone of speaking. In this humbling, in the submitting of the regime to the prophet's exhortation, the multiplicities and migrations of Babel's tongues need not be seen as the onset of chaos but as the affirmation of an impossible and anarchical responsibility to others without which language itself would not be possible. In this manner, Celan's poem witnesses that listening has already placed the listener beyond the bounds of his or her own power. If Babel would listen to the listening already commanded of it, it would acknowledge that it was already responsible for the other before it could have decided otherwise.

Celan's exhortation that Babel listen to the commandment to listen to the *Häftling* is helpless before Babel in the sense that the regime may or may not choose to acknowledge its submission to the command. Yet the command continues to be commanding regardless of what the regime seemingly has chosen to have heard. Thus, the danger of history's succumbing to the forces that drive victimization is real, even if the resistance to those forces remains eternal. The logic of victimization that strives to become the final law of history must be resisted here and now—one is commanded to speak in regard to the other's suffering. But there is no guarantee that eternity will undo the shame of history, even as it commands a resistance to violence that transcends the crude or artful manipulations of the perpetrator. As Celan has stated, one must raise "the claim of infinity" but "grasped through time, through time to the end (*durch sie hindurch*), not over it and away (*über sie hinweg*)."[48]

Given the vulnerability of the *Häftling* to the machinations of the regime, Marlies Janz can argue with reason that in the last lines of "*HIN-AUSGEKRÖNT*," "the metaphor [of an earth rising up] expresses a wish but hardly a confidence."[49] The new earth that rises up in this verse exists only in the "light" of what Celan would have termed "u-topian" (*CPr*, 51), that is, in the impossible expectation of a gratuitous messianism by which one is commanded to act *as if* historical shame might be overcome. The implied threat of the poem's last four lines, namely, that the persecuted might be handed over (for which reason the poet must reiterate his commitment not to do so), emphasizes the historical crisis figured in the *Shoah*, a crisis in which history itself, as well as the transcendence at work in it, threatens to succumb to the regime's indifference to suffering. In such a world, history will be written *as if* its victims had never mattered.[50] This crisis awakens the poetic voice both to a shame that will not be stilled and to a solidarity with those whose victimization remains beyond consolation. The poem becomes the articulation of a "cellular irritability," of an affirmation of the persecuted that refuses to edge into wonder but inevitably recurs to one's shame before the other.

Impossible Memory/Impossible Address

The discussion of Celan's poetry in regard to its witnessing of the *Shoah* was in part initiated by a consideration of Lang's misgivings about its suitability for this task. As the intervening discussion has indicated, the highly allusive quality of Celan's poetics, in which only the vaguest trace of the historical victims of Nazi genocide lies hidden within a maze of word plays and historical references, forces one to incessantly reevaluate in a mode of deliberative witness how one comes to have any sense at all of the historical other and in particular of the historical other of the *Shoah*. Celan's response to Lang's complaint that poetry too quickly moves to the literary abstract is to confront the reader with a text that is an implosion, a radical condensation and displacement of all sorts of poetic figures and tropes. He thus intensifies the imaginative space of the poem even as he destabilizes it. In the mania of signification welling up within the poem is given a poetic space in which something other than a move toward universalization takes place. This "something other" involves an appeal to one's affectivity but in a manner that exposes one to the collapse of feeling, to the failure of an appeal. But that very failure becomes at the very last moment the only appeal that might be made. That the poet continues to write in the face of this dissolution, that the poem continues to mean in spite of its tortured address, its twisted rhythms and fragmented syntactical structure, gives the resistance of a prophetic writing that would "travel through its own inability to answer."

One might also caution Lang that his devaluation of poetic responses to the Nazi genocide as lacking a specifically historical import is itself in danger of functioning as a repression of the traumatic dimensions of genocide. What is most distinctive about historical catastrophes is that they resist being experienced, being remembered, precisely because they so viciously obliterate the normally given contexts of human experience.[51] In the wake of this obliteration, those who strive to remember precisely what made the event a catastrophe, namely, the depth and cruelty of the victim's suffering, inevitably must have recourse to a writing in which one encounters the limits of one's grasp upon that event, even as one is drawn into an encounter with those who underwent that event. In insisting that one's writing about the *Shoah* become obsessively empirical and antifigurative, Lang ignores the special role a prophetic use of figurative language (accompanied by the dysfiguration of *Widerruf*) assumes in registering traumatic events, that is, events in which the very eventfulness of the event is obliterated in an overwhelming loss of memory or experience. On the other hand, the very manner in which *Widerruf* is articulated in Celan's poems offers a writing that is paradoxically as antifigurative as the historiographical writing Lang supports.

Finally, one must admit that the citing and siting of the all the scenes occurring in this book's discussion of the *Shoah* are open to interminable critique, to their reciting and resiting in displacement. This is true whether the scene referred to be that of prophecy, the German language, poetry, the victim whose wounds are empirically indexed, or even of the *Häftling* or the *Shoah* itself. In the witnessing of the other's suffering, no scene can *ultimately* predominate in the writing of that witness, no recorded word can *ultimately* take the place of what is not a word that has been said but a tone of address, a saying. In *Widerruf* is given the trope of a citing and siting that cannot hold itself still, that is caught up in a cellular irritability about anything it might say, that always already has refused the facile gesture of a mere reinversion of an inversion. One moves in *Widerruf* to the citation of the irreparable loss of citation, as well as a siting of the irreparable loss of site.

In following out the instability of Celan's *Widerruf*, one should keep in mind that the breakdown in language in which one is caught up is twofold:

1. The very confrontation of or address by the other has always already exceeded what can be said of it or about it. As chapters 3 and 4 suggest, one is traumatized by the other before one could have evaluated what this was to mean.
2. But there is also a secondary trauma, in which the other is betrayed historically and also for which no mourning can be restorative. The breakdown of speaking suffered in the *Vernichtungslager* is in addition to the breakdown of speaking suffered in the other's address.

With this secondary breakdown of language came as well a breakdown of feeling. Like the prophet, Celan's poems struggle to reinstitute a space for feeling, in particular that ethical dimension of feeling in which one is no longer caught up in one's own interests but finds oneself claimed by the plight of the other. But the plight of the other in the Nazi genocide was to be caught in a world in which feeling for the other was so systematically undermined that the other was not even capable of being devoured *as if* he or she were bread. The other was treated *as if* her or she were refuse.

Ultimately, Celan's poetics seeks the impossible: to remember affectively how affectivity itself collapsed in the Nazi genocide. To witness this collapse of affectivity, one must have more than a detailed chronology of the various empirical events comprising the Nazi genocide. One must also assume the burden of how the very events comprising the death world utterly overwhelmed any *Häftling's* capability to feel their impact. The Nazi genocide is also the *Shoah*, which is to say, that event in which the very eventfulness of the event disintegrated. Thus, it becomes clear that the naming of "nevermansday" does not belong only to the *Feme-Poeten*, the false poet-prophets, but also to Celan himself, whose own naming of "nevermansday" in the poem "Huhediblu" becomes an effort to name the day of annihilation with a prophetic voice, although one under the disruption of its own *Widerruf*, of its overwhelming shame before the persecuted, *the Nameless*. To refer to these victims calls, as Lang himself argues, for extreme circumspection and moral caution. To remember their suffering by importing our own need for catharsis and reassurance into that memory would be to forget them altogether.

Perhaps in this mode of listening burdened by the shame and instability of its own saying, by the impossibility of its own address of the humiliated other, one now hears the tone of a turning, as well as the turning of a tone, in Celan's ultimate line of "Huhediblu." And in that tone one hears again the words of Levi's own address, injunction, malediction, and prayer:

I commend these words to you.
Carve them into your hearts . . .

Notes

Introduction

The epigraph is from a symposium edited by Harry Cargas and Bonny Fetterman and included in Simon Wiesenthal's *The Sunflower: On the Possibilities and Limits of Forgiveness* (New York: Schocken Books, 1997), pp. 181–82. Henceforth *S*.

1. The claim that ethical responsibility precedes epistemological clarification in the matter of one's relation to the victim does not counsel one's neglect of the exact structure or shape of the victim's plight. In fact, the very urgency of one's ethical involvement in the victim demands this clarification. And one must allow that at a certain level of discourse, a determination of the specific characteristics of an instance of violence leads to the possibility and even the moral necessity of comparing and contrasting it with other instances. The discussion in the first two chapters of this text, for example, makes much of the notion of a doubled betrayal as an essential element in the suffering of those who were consigned to the Nazi death camps. But any finding made in relation to the shape of the other's suffering must always be considered in light of the prior revelation of the other's vulnerability to that suffering. The most important question before the witness is not the determination of facts about the other but of whether one has fully been submitted to one's responsibility for the other. All epistemological discussions of the victim's plight take place in the aftermath of this submission. (See chapter 4 for an expansion of this point.) Any determination about the particular plight of those who suffered the *Shoah* can be ethically significant only if the suffering of those very same persons matters to those who witness. Put otherwise, the epistemological determination of the *Shoah* will be continually disrupted by the urgency of one's address by those who suffered in the *Shoah*.

2. Saul Friedlander's remarks upon the diverse names of this event in his keynote address delivered to participants of the International Scholars' Conference, "Remembering for the Future," (Oxford, England; July 10–13, 1989) were helpful in the development of the following analysis, as was the essay by Emil Fackenheim titled "The Holocaust: A Summing up after Two Decades of Reflection" (in *Argumentum e Silentio*, ed. Amy Colin [Berlin: Walter de Gruyter, 1987], henceforth TH). At least some part of Friedlander's remarks then found their way into his essay, "The *Shoah* in Present Historical Consciousness," in *Memory, History and the Extermination of the Jews of Europe* (Bloomington: Indiana University Press, 1993), p. 42ff.

3. This claim, which is itself made in the form of an argument, need not imply that making an argument is trivial or senseless. But arguments can only make sense insofar as they are already addressed to a transcendent other for whom one is already responsible. Otherwise one's argument would not be given toward the other but only made about the other. In the second case, the address of the other as other would utterly fall outside of one's discourse, and the other would be absorbed into a system of rationality committed to the maintenance of its own *archē*, its own self-consistency. Levinas considers this mode of rationality to be a state of war—one insists that the other can only be significant in terms of how one can characterize or represent the other in one's structure of reasoning. This forces the other to find her or his voice already articulated by the anonymous voice of reason. This issue receives a more explicit discussion at the beginning of chapter 3.

4. See the discussion in chapter 5. Also see *OB*, 111ff.

1. The Imperative to Witness the *Häftling*

1. While this point is not specifically addressed in the analysis that follows, it is important to note that Levi's prologue is also a parody of the prayer in the Jewish liturgy immediately following the reciting of the *Shema*, the unequivocal affirmation by Israel of G-d's lordship and oneness (Deuteronomy/Devarim 6:4–9). In the words following upon that declaration, one considers one's responsibility to love G-d with one's whole heart, soul and being, as well as to be dutiful in passing down to one's children the words by which G-d engages Israel in the Covenant. Obviously much can and should be made of this allusion by Levi. By rewriting the *Shema* in the context of the *Häftling*, Levi suggests much about what Judaism in the wake of the *Shoah* might signify. But that particular issue lies outside the

theme of this book. Perhaps within the context of the argument that follows it can be suggested that Levi's rereading of the *Shema* (which leaves out its decisive first words affirming G-d's reality) functions somewhat under the metatrope of *Widerruf* (see chapter 6) and places the *Shema* in a mode of persecution for the sake of the *Häftling*. Certainly, the discussion of Celan's use of blasphemy in chapter 6 also is related to Levi's gesture. But the *Shema*, being so explicitly a Jewish prayer of worship, leaves the author unwilling to comment too far on its meaning in the context of the argument being elaborated here.

The Prologue, although not found in the first American edition of Stuart Wolf's translation (*If This Is a Man* [New York: The Orion Press, 1959]), was included in the first Italian edition published in 1947.

2 This citation is taken from a special edition of Bill Moyers' *World of Ideas* titled "Facing Evil: With Bill Moyers" (Produced and Directed by David Grubin, WNET NY) in which Philip Hallie spoke on his experiences of living through World War II, as well as his attempts to make sense of its violence during the remainder of his life.

3 See Lawrence Langer's *Holocaust Testimonies: The Ruins of Memory* ([New Haven: Yale University Press, 1991], henceforth *HT*) for his distinction—borrowed from Charlotte Delbo and applied to the oral testimonies of survivors—of "common memory," which finds its orientation in regard to the everyday life world, and "deep memory," which is traumatized, a memory of deprivation rather than of survival. Deep memory "tries to recall the Auschwitz self as it was then" (p. 6), even as it is dependent upon common memory to provide deep memory's account of the past with the rational perspective that can only occur beyond the moment of one's suffering. Yet deep memory exceeds the capability of common memory to make sense of the inmate's suffering and so continually disrupts it. One could read Levi's prologue as the command to attend to this excess and disruption, this other form of memory, even if one cannot directly enter into it. Insofar as the reader is shamed before the memory of the *Häftling*, the excess of this other memory disturbs the reader's own articulation of memory in its common mode.

4. Alan Udoff ("On Poetic Dwelling: Situating Clean and the Holocaust," in *Argumentum e Silentio*, ed. Amy Colin [New York: de Gruyter, 1987], henceforth PD) points out that the shamefulness of one's memory of the *Häftling* dominates Levi's account of Auschwitz. In doing so, he argues that Levi asks that we distinguish between our own feeling of shame and the *Häftling*'s state of shame, in which he or she is "driven into the muteness of defilement" (p. 330). The shame of the *Häftling* no longer illuminates experience

but disfigures it. This shame also signifies a change in reality that leaves the normal notion of shame in crisis.

5. The term Auschwitz is used equivocally in this text, at times standing for the series of death camps (*Vernichtungslager*) built by the Nazis specifically for the carrying out of genocide, and at other times signifying the actual camp of this name. In regard to the actual camp of Auschwitz, the facilities for mass annihilation were constructed near the main camp at Birkenau. See Lucy Dawidowicz's discussion of this arrangement in her *The War Against the Jews* (New York: Bantam, 1986), p. 135. In addition to Birkenau, work camps (*Arbeitslager*) were also located in the neighborhood of Auschwitz to which its inmates could be consigned. Primo Levi, for instance, was interned at Monowitz in such a work camp.

6. As Levi's own text, as well as the glossary found in Wolfgang Sofsky's *The Order of Terror: The Concentration Camp* ([Princeton: Princeton University Press, 1997], p. 284), reports, another term existed within the camps for the inmate whose autonomy was utterly crushed, the *Müselmann*, literally "the Moslem," but figuratively "the walking dead." The term *Häftling* is used in the text above, because it suggests the universal nature of the attack upon human autonomy occurring in the camp. But this term includes the notion of "the walking dead."

7. See Edith Wyschograd's discussion of this issue in regard to the philosophy of Emmanuel Levinas in her *Emmanuel Levinas: The Problem of Ethical Metaphysics* (The Hague: Martinus Nijhoff, 1974), p. 86. The phenomenological account of Levi's command in this chapter was inspired in part by Levinas's own discussion of the face in *TA*. Levinas's more abstract account of the other's command of me in the face-to-face relation is treated in chapter 3.

8. This mode of forgetting is not ontological but moral, which is to say, that form of anamnesis that involves a denial shadowed by shame rather than a mystery haloed by wonder. One needs to distinguish a forgetting with which one is in complicity from a forgetting by which one's very consciousness of the world and of oneself is sustained and enriched.

9. For a more detailed account of this issue, see chapter 2, p. 64–67.

10. See Shoshana Felman and Dori Laub, *Testimony: Crises of Witnessing in Literature, Psychoanalysis and History* (New York: Routledge, 1992), especially chapter 1: "Education and Crisis, or the Vicissitudes of Teaching."

11. The argument of this paragraph does not entail accepting the victimization of other persons as a necessary evil, or as a distressing fact of life that evades my responsibility. In the face of the victim, one is always obligated

to do whatever is possible to heal the victim. Certainly, in many cases of victimization one is obliged and desires to encourage both oneself and the victim in the imagining of her or his restoration to a flourishing existence. But this does not alter the fact that there are victims who remain victimized no matter what one's response might be. This subcategory is the focal point of the discussion of this chapter and of this book.

12. This camp was located near Auschwitz.

13. See Hamida Bosmajian, *Metaphors of Evil* (Iowa City: University of Iowa Press, 1979), p. 19, where the author argues that although "in Dante's Hell the damned are locked rigidly in their egocentric individuality, no corresponding human eidos exists in the Camps." What gives Dante's Hell its justice is that the suffering of the damned does not deprive them of their individual personalities, whereas in Auschwitz the very personhood of the person is etched away in the moment of suffering.

14. See Emil Fackenheim's discussion of this point in his *God's Presence in History* (New York: Harper & Row, 1972).

15. In this passage, Udoff is quoting Hannah Arendt. Udoff's reflections upon the collapse of death and of mourning within the space of dehabitation instituted in the death camps have been crucial in orienting my own claims concerning the attack upon the *Häftling's* autonomy.

16. To term genocide "aggressive," as if there were a genocide that is not so, seems unnecessary. But "aggressive" denotes that form of genocide that not only attacks a nation, culture, or society of human beings *but also their very bodies*. One cannot opt to be assimilated in order to escape the Nazi form of genocide, nor were there to be any exceptions made for what Himmler once derisively called "good Jews." Not only the form of life was to be destroyed, but also every particular human being who had ever lived that form of life or was even related to someone who had lived that form of life.

17. See Udoff's explication of a passage from Adorno: "Death *happens* to *that which* lives, but it is the *possession* only of *one who* lives self-consciously. The consciousness of death, however, belongs to one mediately and in anticipation—it is, in effect, one's own by virtue of being a common possession. . . . To possess death then, is to *have* the traditions, usages, examples, the *publicness* through which death comes into the possession of one who lives humanly" (PD, 341). Udoff goes on to argue provocatively that a merely phenomenological appreciation of one's death in terms of a "temporal mode" reduces it to a "biological facticity." Without a cultural narrative, one's death loses its dignity. The mode of this narrative could be, I think, rather loosely interpreted to include introjection of the other's gestures into one's own, living out one's own

thoughts with the echo of the other's voice within them, etc. (See Edward Casey's insightful discussion of this point in the chapter titled "Commemoration" in his *Remembering: A Phenomenological Study* [Bloomington: Indiana University Press, 1987].) What is important about a death narration is that one's own passing away becomes a gift for those who follow, as well as an address to them. Death narratives are vocative; they call to one's survivors for some mode of response.

18. Edith Wyschogrod, *Spirit in Ashes* (New Haven: Yale University Press, 1985), p. 11. Henceforth *SpA*.

19. Hannah Arendt, *The Origins of Totalitarianism* (New York: Harcourt Brace Javanovich, 1973), p. 452.

20. This claim is equivocal but not, to my mind, deceptive. On the one hand, it should be claimed (and will be claimed in the following chapters) that no matter what may occur, no matter how deep is the amnesia that follows in the wake of the *Shoah*, the other's victimization still commands one to its resistance. The other transcends one's forgetfulness of the other. On the other hand, history can only be as accurate as the documents and memories it has been given to respond to and analyze. The annihilation of the victim intentionally leaves history shorn of the other's story, of his or her memories and perspectives and, in the most extreme cases, even of the record of the other's existence. This mode of history written in the wake of the victim's erasure becomes what Levinas calls "historiography," the self-justifying account of the survivors.

Given this second perspective, one ends up arguing that the *Shoah*, insofar as it is carried out, erases the very text Levi is writing. This erasure leaves the victim shorn of any voice or witness whatsoever within history. And yet, from the viewpoint of the first perspective, the victim's plight would still command one transcendently from beyond the confines of historical or personal memory. One encounters here a command to remember that is dependent upon finite, ontical texts in order to bear its voice into the future and yet continually interrupts these texts and puts their very claim for a complete authority into utter question. This issue will be discussed more thoroughly in chapter 4.

21. Emmanuel Levinas, *Autrement que savoir*, ed. unknown (Paris: Editions Osiris, 1988), p. 61 (henceforth, *AS*).

22. Emil Fackenheim, *God's Presence in History* (New York: Harper, 1972), pp. 74–76.

23. As Langer sums up the testimony of Zoltan G., a survivor and witness of the death camps: "You're not 'going to nowhere,' . . . they're '*taking*' you to 'nowhere'" (*HT*, 47).

24. See *HT*, pp. 44ff.

25. Odysseus's story is found in canto **XXVI** of *The Divine Comedy*. The translation of Dante's lines is provided by Stuart Woolf, translator of Levi's *Survival in Auschwitz*.

26. The issue of theodicy receives a more extended consideration in the concluding section of chapter 3.

27. Georg Wilhelm Friedrich Hegel, *Lectures on the Philosophy of World History: Reason in History*, trans. N. B. Nisbet (London: Cambridge University Press, 1975), pp. 42–43.

28. Emmanuel Levinas, *De la signifiance du sens*, in *Heidegger et la question de Dieu*, ed. Richard Kearney and Joseph O'Leary (Paris: Bernard Grasset, 1980), p. 242.

29. One must question whether the very notion of interpreting the infinite as a quantity is not only deceptive, as Kant establishes in his essay on *The End of Time*, but also ethically suspect. As the discussion will show in chapter 3, the infinite interrupts the finite rather than supplying it an infinite extension. This interruption involves one's being claimed by the face of another whose very alterity is impossible for one to seize. To be obsessed with a notion of infinity that is quantitative (as occurs in our culture) covers over the uncanny manner in which the infinitude of the other seizes hold of my intentions before they could ever have been solely my own. To confront infinity is to be initiated into humility before the other rather than to be granted an inexhaustible field of possibilities for the actualizing of one's own self.

30. Jonathan Schell, *The Fate of the Earth* (New York: Alfred Knopf, 1982), p. 116.

2. The Scene of Annihilation

1. Hannah Arendt, *The Origins of Totalitarianism*, p. 441.

2. The use of this term here is meant to suggest not the affect of wonder but of righteousness.

3. See Emil Fackenheim, *God's Presence in History* (New York: Harper & Row, 1970), p. 70ff.

4. See Edith Wyschogrod's discussion of the poetry of Rilke in the first chapter ("Kingdoms of Death") of her *Spirit in Ashes* for further reflections upon modern attempts to celebrate death as a heroic gesture.

5. Saul Friedlander, "On the Unease of Historical Interpretation," in *Memory, History and the Extermination of the Jews of Europe* (Bloomington: Indiana University Press, 1993), p. 111. Henceforth, *MHE*.

6. It can be argued that because the narrative of Borowski remembers this child, as well as the woman who denies him maternal comfort, their lives remain to be mourned by those who read the account of their annihilation. Their memory, indeed, has been magnified by the very fact that Borowski has chosen them as exemplars of Auschwitz. This assumes the two figures are actual persons and not fictive characters, something of which the reader cannot be totally assured.

Nevertheless, the two figures are only remembered insofar as they have become evidence for the shamefulness of their victimization. Their memory, which is to say, their provenance for those who inherit their lives across a generation, is reduced to this account of the collapse of their autonomy as they are being submitted to the annihilation of their succeeding generations. To read this passage is to remember one's inability to mourn these annihilated existences.

7. Immanuel Kant, "Grounding for the Metaphysics of Morals," in *Immanuel Kant: Ethical Philosophy*, trans. James Ellington (Indianapolis: Hackett, 1983), p. 49: "The proposition that the will is in every action a law to itself expresses, however, nothing but the principle of acting according to no other maxim than that which can at the same time have itself as a universal law for its object." Also see Hans Jonas, *The Imperative of Responsibility*, trans. Hans Jonas and David Herr (Chicago: University of Chicago Press, 1984), p. 11. In regard to Kant's categorical imperative, Jonas states: "Mark that the basic reflection of morals here is not itself a moral one but a logical one: The 'I can will' or 'I cannot will' expresses logical compatibility or incompatibility, not moral approbation or revulsion."

8. Frieda Aaron, *Bearing the Unbearable* (Albany: State University of New York Press, 1990), p. 194.

9. Hannah Arendt, *The Origins of Totalitarianism* (New York: Harcourt Brace Javanovich, 1973), p. 452.

10. See Lawrence Langer's discussion of oral testimonies of the *Shoah* in his *Holocaust Testimonies: The Ruins of Memory* (New Haven: Yale University Press, 1991), p. 11: "Choosing moral duty over self-preservation suddenly appears as an *outmoded* ideal, overridden by a situation that makes *either* of these options irrelevant. . . . Witnesses themselves, prompted by common memory, sometimes . . . judge themselves harshly; fortunately, their deep memory knows better, intuitively perceiving the almost droll understatement of a formula like 'a situation that does not contain a good choice.'" Henceforth, *HT*.

11. Zygmut Bauman, *Modernity and the Holocaust* (Ithaca: Cornell University Press, 1989), p. 206. Also: *RM*, 11.

12. See Michael Morgan, "Jewish Ethics after the Holocaust," in *Contemporary Jewish Morality*, ed. Elliot Dorf and Louis Newman (Oxford: Oxford University Press, 1995), p. 201. There he discusses the injunction of Rabbi Yizhak Nissenbaum in regard to the practice of martyrdom: "'In former times,' he [Nissenbaum] said, 'when the enemy demanded the soul of the Jew, the Jews sacrificed their bodies for the sanctification of G-d's name; now however, the oppressor wants the body of the Jew; it is therefore one's duty to protect it, to guard one's life.'" While this decision is not directly applicable to the situation between the mother and the child, it does suggest how the preservation of one's bodily life became an overriding moral command before the extremity of genocidal violence.

13. See Hans Jonas, *The Imperative of Responsibility* (Chicago: University of Chicago Press, 1984), especially p. 46, where he finds the preeminent question of contemporary ethics to be: "Ought there to be man?" As in the above discussion, Jonas also finds Kant's derivation of ethical imperatives to be blind to the vulnerability of human existence to being annihilated. See pp. 10–11: "Kant's categorical imperative said: 'Act so that you *can* will that the maxim of your action be made the principle of a universal law.' The 'can' here involved is that of reason and its consistency with itself. *Given* the existence of a community of human agents . . . the action must be such that it can without self-contradiction be imagined as a general practice of the community. . . . But there is no self-contradiction in the thought that humanity would once come to an end."

Jonas also mentions in this passage how Kantian ethics is based upon a *logical rather than moral* reflection concerning the self-consistency of statements. The distance this puts between oneself and the other for whom one acts is already distressing. As Jonas argues on p. 85, one's actions should be true to the other for whom one acts rather than to an anonymous principle for which the other serves as an instance or example. But those inconsistencies that arise when one tries to act rationally within a death world also show by means of reason itself the difficulty of Kant's position. It could be argued that one imperative coming out of the *Shoah* is to articulate ethical commands through insights that are more immediately ethical themselves. This issue is addressed more directly in the next chapter in the discussion of Levinas's derivation of ethics from the face-to-face encounter that commands one from beyond the mere necessity of reason.

14. See Roger Manvel and Heinrich Fraenkel's *Himmler* (New York: G.P. Putnam's Sons, 1965), pp. 121 and 147. The authors' rendition of Himmler's comportment in regard to Auschwitz makes clear that he was un-

concerned about the treatment of the prisoners before they were escorted to the gas chambers. From his viewpoint, the purpose of Auschwitz was not so much to torture the inmates who were temporarily allowed to survive as to exterminate them. At one point early on in the development of Auschwitz, Himmler simply told Höss to "improvise" when it came to the treatment of prisoners (121). During his second visit to Auschwitz in the summer 1942, Himmler was impatient with Höss's complaints about (in the author's words) "the fearful living conditions of the prisoners and their subjection to disease and overcrowding" (147). Again his reaction was simply to order Höss to take whatever measures were necessary. Nevertheless, the crushing of the *Häftling's* autonomy is already implicitly a part of the process of annihilation, as Höss's "improvisations" were soon to show.

In order to understand the level of cruelty practiced on individual inmates, one must understand how this cruelty in turn found its measure or standard in the annihilation of an entire people. Arendt argues that the death camps were the ultimate laboratories for the institution of a social order of terror, which included the verification of totalitarianism's belief that "everything is possible" (*OT*, 437). In carrying the effects of a *force majeure* to its ultimate possibilities, one became caught up in the destruction of every aspect of another human's dignity. Thus, one found it necessary to *both* crush the *Häftling's* individual autonomy *and* to submit her or his *genos* to annihilation.

The following discussion above, as well as that of the next chapter, focuses in more detail on how the rendering faceless of the individual victim was already the symptom of the Nazi desire to annihilate a *genos*. Annihilation of *a genos* implicitly includes the dehumanization, the crushing of the autonomy, of all members of that *genos*. What both prongs of this attack upon the other would secretly accomplish is to deny that the perpetrator had ever been responsible for this other human being in the first place, or that the victim's suffering could ever have mattered to the perpetrator.

15. From Joachim Fest, *Hitler*, trans. Richard and Clara Winston (New York: Harcourt Brace Jovanovich, 1974), p. 212. Quoted by Berel Lang, *Act and Idea in the Nazi Genocide* (Chicago: University of Chicago Press, 1990), p. 16. Lang's discussion of the process of genocide in chapter 1 of this book is highly instructive.

16. Kant's intonation of this other "kind" in the masculine voice—his naming of the reasoning entity as "he"—belies his very claim of "its" transcendence of embodied category or kind. Yet Kant's "he" thankfully reminds us that no reasoning entity, at least of the human kind, can come to "his" autonomy without having been born of male and female. The reasoning entity

bears the imprint of a sexuality, a *Geschlecht*, that both bears "him" into existence and then calls upon "him" to bear the next generation into existence, an act that remains impossible as long as "he" is uttered without distinction from a "she." Kant's splitting of the grounding of morality from the specifically embodied subject leads to all sorts of peculiarities in this fashion. Further, the very structure of the generations of reasoning entities, both male and female, both he and she, in which reason finds "itself" in a diachronous rather than synchronous relationship with its "fellows" (and in which its fellows turn out to be also its children and the children of its fellows, as well as its parents and the parents of its fellows), suggests another sort of kind than either the kind of a determinate body or the kind of a capacity to reason. This third other kind is a being who is a translation of responsibility across the generations. More will be said about this in the following section.

17. Berel Lang, *Act and Idea in the Nazi Genocide* (Chicago: University of Chicago Press, 1990), p. 18. Henceforth, *AI*.

18. In this suffering is given another sort of commanding singularity in regard to the other than that given in Kantian autonomy. This other sort of singularity is not capable of being thought as an abstract universal or of being confronted as an example that is synchronous with all other examples of its kind. The significance of the other's suffering actually interrupts any determination of what sort of kind it is in the command that one was already commanded to have responded to it. One determines its kind, its *genos*, only retrospectively and in the wake of the command to respond to the *Häftling*.

When compared to the urgency of the other's face, the categoricality of Kant's imperative is after all not so thoroughly categorical. It really reads in this manner: "Insofar as the other is a reasoning being, treat her or him as an autonomous being." But what then should one's response be to the other who is overcome by her or his suffering and who has been rendered incapable by means of that suffering of addressing one reasonably? To respond to this question by saying that one is obligated in this instance to alleviate this suffering to the point that the other can then again begin to reason autonomously forgets that one then is acting in place of the other, literally substituting one's autonomy for the autonomy of the other. In forgetting this, one forgets the fragility of the other's autonomy, the vulnerability exposed in her or his address of one through the face. One must act in place of the other to bring the other back to her or his autonomy. In this acting one is transcending a call to merely respect the autonomy of the other.

Further, there will be instances, such as those found in Auschwitz, where no amount of intervention by one on the behalf of the other will alleviate her or his suffering to the extent that the other's autonomy can be restored. What then is one to make of the categorical imperative in the instance of the irreparable? As the discussion above has demonstrated, reason itself falls into quandary before the irreparable. One cannot fault the command to bring human life to a universal end for its lack of self-consistency. (See note 13.)

19. The infinition of responsibility in the vulnerability of the other to suffering does not excuse one from respecting the other's autonomy as a capacity to reason, or of one's being called to be attentive to the reasonableness of one's own reason. That the measure of reason is disrupted does not mean that the measure of reason becomes irrelevant. But the capacity to reason is transcended in another sort of call to responsibility whose urgency exceeds the reflexivity of reason, which is to say, the assumption of reason that it will find its own reason to conclude as it does. As pointed out in the previous chapter, it makes no sense to say we are only obligated because we found it reasonable to be obligated. The very obligation of obligation is forgotten in this gesture of reason's self-justification. The urgency of obligation is what calls reason to sincerity in the first place. Only in the wake of a being exposed before the other, so that the very sincerity of sincerity is exposed as the exposure of exposure, can reason in turn find itself sincere in its reasoning.

20. Jean-François Lyotard, *The Differend: Phrases in Dispute*, trans. Georges van den Abbeele (Minneapolis: University of Minnesota Press, 1983), p. 9.

21. This doubled intention of the perpetrator, namely, to inflict a suffering upon an individual who is then not to be acknowledged as having suffered, characterizes the contradictory state of mind of the victimizer. The perpetrator lives in the *delusion* of having turned away from a suffering it is impossible to ignore. This doubled intentionality is not a splitting off of goodness from evil (as Lang discusses and rightly criticizes [*AI*, ch. 2]), but, as the following chapter's discussion will argue, the impotent gesture of an intention attempting to escape the priority of its command to goodness, its inescapable responsibility to the other. Or to anticipate Levinas's phrase quoted below, the other resists my violence toward her or him with "an opposition prior to my freedom" (FC, 19).

22. Jacques Derrida, in his essay "*Geschlecht* II" (see *Deconstruction and Philosophy*, ed. John Sallis [Chicago: University of Chicago Press, 1987]), questions any univocity in the use of the term *Geschlecht*, which he refuses to translate as "race" or "sex" or "people" or in any other specific, determinate manner. Derrida also makes problematic Fichte's use of the term, in which *Geschlecht* defines a "we" transcending any specific determination of qualities

or category but who nevertheless remains empowered to speak for its own *"Geschlecht,"* its own "We." Finally Derrida comments: "Perhaps it (*Geschlecht*) is no longer a word. Perhaps one must begin by gaining access to it from its disarticulation or its decomposition, in other words, its formation, it information, its deformations or transformations, its translations, the genealogy of its body unified starting from or according to the dividing and the sharing of the words' morsels" (189). Refusing even the gesture of Heidegger toward "polysemy," Derrida would argue for a "dissemination" of *Geschlecht*, in which the site by which a people might find itself as a people is denied any originary claim.

In the analysis of *genos* being developed here, *Geschlecht* is given a particular etymology and orientation, although one that is articulated through responsibility rather than ontology. In *Geschlecht*, not a "what" or "who" as a kind or category is given but as the very gesture of handing over responsibility to the succeeding generations. For this reason *Geschlecht* is polyvocative, which is to say, overburdened with meanings that cannot be disentangled from their having been given to oneself by others, meanings that exceed being rendered unambiguously in one's own voice. When one speaks, one speaks the voices of one's forebearers as well. And yet one bears uniquely the burden of this pluralism. In being so oriented, the asymmetry of this handing over—one cannot hand back the responsibility, one cannot disown the gesture of being burdened by one's forebearers—keeps the term *Geschlecht* from becoming either a "we" of self-justification or a reduction of the human to a particular kind or category. The orientation of *Geschlecht*, of a birthing and of a being-birthed of the next generation, is like the Levinasian orientation of ethics— one lives in the accusative, one is already obligated and involved. If any "we" is to be articulated, it can only come about through a recognition of the weight of this accusation. One's "kind" only comes in the aftermath of one's generation, of one's being-birthed, of one's *Geschlecht*.

23. *Aeon*, which comes from the Greek *aiōn*, is often construed to mean eternity, or a world age. This meaning is particularly true of Platonic texts. But in Homer it meant one's "lifetime" or "life" and in Aeschylus an "age" or "generation." The original meaning of *aiōn* was evidently *not* eternity but "a period of existence" (*An Intermediate Greek-English Lexicon*, ed. Lidell and Scott [Oxford: Oxford University Press, 1975]). This meaning is what is at the root of *aenocide* as it corresponds to Auschwitz, the murdering of ethical time through the annihilation of all the following generations. One finds this very theme treated in Greek mythology in the struggle between Zeus and his father Cronos. As each generation arises, Cronos eats his own children until

Zeus, by means of a subterfuge, grows to maturity, overthrows his father, castrates him, and casts him down into the earth. Zeus, in turn awaits his own overthrow by a figure known only to Prometheus. In these struggles are figured the extreme insecurity that comes from living in a time that is *not* eternal in terms of duration but rather in terms of one's differentiation from the other. Eternity is time articulated as an infinite difference between oneself and the other, as well as between one's generation and the succeeding one. In this sense of eternity, human beings are the equals of the Greek gods who also had their generations.

24. To describe, as is being done in this section, the attempt to colonize time should not be taken to suggest that such a project could be actually achieved, or that its achievement would then signify the collapse of any sort of metaphysical resistance to its will. In reality, the notion that everything is possible is a delusion. As the analysis in the next chapter makes clear, one cannot undermine the alterity of an address that has commanded one before one was free to decide whether one should listen to it. One will already have been addressed by the generations whether one will hear them or not. But this does not mean that Hitler's delusion that he could by a *force majeure* wipe out the generations was without an effect. For empirically, future generations were wiped out, even if the address of those generations persists in spite of their nonexistence. The *Shoah* teaches us that the delusions of the evil-doer can have enduring, irremediable effects even as they utterly fail to accomplish what they *secretly* intend.

25. Consider, for example, Arendt's discussion of the centrality of the leader to totalitarian society, as well as its indifference to ideological constraint. What Hitler demanded was not belief in certain facts or truths but utter obedience to his will. National Socialism was held accountable to nothing other than what it chose to accomplish. Arendt points out that no less a figure than Himmler argued that within the SS the ideology of racial cleansing served only as a temporary "focal point" whose ultimate purpose was the building up of "the revolutionary idea of the *Führer*" (See *OT*, 386).

26. William Shirer (*The Rise and Fall of the Third Reich: A History of Nazi Germany* [New York: Simon & Schuster, 1960], p. 1104) records this account of Hitler's conversation with Speer in the last days of the Third Reich: "But Hitler, his own personal fate sealed, was not interested in the continued existence of the German people, for whom he had always professed such boundless love. He told Speer: 'If the war is lost, the nation will also perish. This fate is inevitable. There is no necessity to take into consideration the basis which the people will need to continue a most primitive existence. On the contrary, it

will be better to destroy these things ourselves because this nation will have proved to be the weaker one and the future will belong solely to the stronger eastern nation [Russia]. Besides, those who will remain after the battle are only the inferior ones, for the good ones have been killed.'" See: "Hitler's destruction order of 19 March 1945," as well as the commentary upon it, in Jeremy Noakes and Geoffrey Pridham, eds., *Documents on Nazism, 1919–1945* (New York: Viking Press, 1975), p. 676.

27. As was made clear in the first chapter, to say these descendants would be responsible is not to claim that they would be guilty.

28. To situate aenocide as the historical background for an event is radically paradoxical. Here one singles out an event that is itself the very undermining of the event, the withdrawal of history into the irreparable. Insofar as aenocide succeeds, there will have been no history. But the very attempt to implode history is itself a historical event, although one that also transcends historical dimensions.

29. See Terrence Des Pres' discussion of a transport, as well as his citation of a witness's description of one, in *The Survivor: An Anatomy of Life in the Death Camps* (New York: Oxford University Press, 1976), pp. 170–71. As Des Pres' discussion makes clear, the transport car was but one of a series of confining spaces into which *Häftlinge* were crammed to the point of precipitating dehumanization.

This is not to suggest that every "transport" was organized under such inhumane conditions. In fact some transports were organized as a "*Sonderfahrt*," chartered trains whose participants traveled in relative luxury, unaware that they were being shipped to their deaths (see Claude Lanzmann's *Shoah: An Oral History of the Holocaust* [New York: Pantheon Books, 1985], p. 40). The Nazis had many methods of luring populations into the gas chambers, one of the most effective being to play to the Jewish illusion that human nature was simply incapable of such radical evil as the wholesale slaughter of an entire race.

The point that is to be made, however, is that the basic principle of the death camps at some point took over—this principle was one of radical dehumanization.

30. The "memory" being discussed here is not simply that of one's recollection of another's face or the chronicle of his or her life. It includes as well the language one speaks, the habits by which one responds to others, those bodily gestures bearing the world's moods that are acquired from another. Ultimately, religion, culture, society, and self emerge into being only through the memories of others and the achievements those memories pass on to their

inheritors. See Edward Casey's discussion of this point in *Remembering: A Phenomenological Study* (Bloomington: Indiana University Press, 1987), p. 216ff., as well as my discussion in "Impossible Mourning: Transcendent Loss and the Memory of Disaster" (Doctoral dissertation, State University of New York, 1990), ch. 4, and "Impossible Mourning: Two Attempts to Remember Annihilation," in *The Centennial Review* 35.3 (Fall 1991): 445–59.

31. See Terrence Des Pres, *The Survivor: An Anatomy of Life in the Death Camps* (New York: Pocket Books, 1976), especially ch. 2.

32. Elie Wiesel, "Why I Write," in *Confronting the Holocaust: The Impact of Elie Wiesel*, ed. Alvin Rosenfeld and Irving Greenberg (Bloomington: Indiana University Press, 1978), p. 79 (henceforth, WW).

33. This point is taken up in some detail in chapter 6.

34. Gabriel Marcel, *The Philosophy of Existentialism*, trans. Manya Harari (Secaucus, N.J.: Citadel Press, 1984), p. 93.

35. See the remarks on this issue in connection with Alan Udoff's "On Poetic Dwelling" in chapter 1.

36. To argue that memory is a necessary condition for ethical responsibility does not mean it is the sufficient condition. One's submission to the address of the other emerges in the ongoing discussion of the following chapters as the "sufficient" condition, although one that does not act as a condition or cause but as a commandment preceding the determination of a cause. As the analysis of Derrida and Levinas both indicate, one's relation to the other involves one in the very breach of memory by an address that is immemorial, that was registered before awareness of its being registered could ever have been made possible. But this situation does not change the necessity of an empirical memory of other persons, if one is to actually be the guarantor of their address within history.

37. Yet the very vulnerability of ethical life to a will-to-death provides a resistance to evil unanticipated by its *force majeure*.

38. Immanuel Kant, *Religion within the Limits of Reason Alone*, trans. Theodore Greene and Hoyt Hudson (New York: Harper, 1960), p. 32.

3. The Transcendence of the Face

1. Levinas argues that the violence of war is held not so much in "injuring and annihilating persons as in interrupting their continuity, making them play roles in which they no longer recognize themselves, making them betray not only commitments but their own substance, making them carry

out actions that will destroy every possibility for action" (*TI*, 21). Based on the discussion of aenocide in the last chapter, I would argue that insofar as annihilation comes to mean the collapse of not only one's future but also the futures of all the others coming after one, that this form of annihilation coupled with the crushing of the *Häftling*'s autonomy fits what Levinas means when he speaks of carrying out actions that will destroy every possibility for action. What needs to be emphasized is how this corruption of activity, of substance, attacks not only the other but oneself as well. Once war is unleashed, all beings become expendable, one's weapons can also be turned against oneself. Not only the other's alterity is ignored but also one's own.

2. These terms—translatable from German or Yiddish as "shit," "rags," "puppets," and "items,"—were used in the death camps to refer to the corpses of the *Häftling*. Levinas comments: "but the flesh . . . of the murdered people transported on the lorries . . . it was referred to in neutral terms—*die Scheiß*—they weren't human bodies. That was what was exceptional. It was murder carried out in contempt, more than in hatred" (RM, 21). The other terms come from testimony given by survivors and governmental documents in Lanzmann's *Shoah* (pp. 13, 103).

3. See his "Introduction," in Emmanuel Levinas, *Basic Philosophical Writings*, ed. Adriaan Peperzak, Simony Critchley, and Robert Bernasconi (Bloomington: Indiana University Press, 1996), p. 9.

4. Levinas's own words in regard to the development of his thought between *Totality and Infinity* and *Otherwise than Being* are instructive here: "The ontological language which *Totality and Infinity* still uses in order to exclude the purely psychological significance of the proposed analysis is henceforth avoided. And the analyses themselves refer not to the *experience* in which a subject always thematizes what he equals, but to the *transcendence* in which he answers for that which his intentions have not encompassed" (*DF*, 295).

5. Emmanuel Levinas, "The Paradox of Morality: An Interview with Emmanuel Levinas," trans. Andrew Benjamin and Tamara Wright, in *The Provocation of Levinas*, ed. David Wood and Robert Bernasconi (London: Routledge, 1988), p. 176.

6. Insofar as *logos* comes to be interpreted merely in terms of a pattern or arrangement of the real, then it fails to be addressed by how *logos* is itself an address and how reality is in the first instance the revelation of proximity and responsibility. One could think in this regard of how in *Bereshit* or Genesis the very act of creation is an addressing of beings into their being—G-d speaks to the light and only in its response to that address does it become real. A creative *logos* speaks prior to its being organized into a content, a calcula-

tion, a paradigm. In Susan Handelman's words: "The critical point is that for Levinas . . . saying as 'revelation' . . . is the 'meaning of meaning' as the awakening of the listener to the proximity of the other . . . (*OB*, 147)." (Susan Handelman, *Fragments of Redemption* [Bloomington: Indiana University Press, 1991], p. 279). This notion of a creative discourse in turn leads Handelman to speak of "another kind of reason" in Levinas (p. 239), one that is not in the first instance preoccupied with the Socratic search for first principles and definitions but with the prophetic submission to a responsibility that had always already left one in accusation before one could have been justified in one's reason. This structure of an obligation that precedes its justification has driven the phenomenological analysis of Levi's Prologue in chapter 1.

7. Emmanuel Levinas, "Philosophy and the Idea of Infinity," in *CP*, p. 55. The french, *Je ne peux plus pouvoir*, is translated by Lingis as "I am no longer able to have power." In *TI* Levinas writes, "The expression the face introduces into the world does not defy the feebleness of my power, but my ability for power [*mon pouvoir de pouvoir*]" (*TI*, 198).

8. "Assignation" in this context refers to its meaning as "a summons to appear in court" (*The Compact Edition of the Oxford English Dictionary*, 1979). In this sense it reflects its French cognate which is used by Levinas as a technical term for defining the subjectivity of the one who is responsible: one is an assignation, a for-the-other. The term is defined in French as "an order to present oneself for the purpose of being arraigned or giving testimony before a judge" (*Le Petit Larousse*, 1979 [translation mine]). While this meaning is related in its concept to the more common notion of assignation in English as a lover's tryst (in that both senses of the word involve being summoned to a particular time and place), the term does not carry the latter connotation in its use by Levinas.

9. For a detailed discussion of Arendt's reading of Eichmann's guilt, as well as a Levinasian response to that reading, see my "The Sincerity of Apology: Levinas's Resistance to the Judgment of History," in *Phenomenology, Interpretation and Community*, ed. Lenore Langsdorf, Stephen Watson, and Marya Bower (Albany: State University of New York Press, 1996).

10. Herbert Kelman, "Violence without Moral Restraint," in *Varieties of Psychohistory* (New York: Springer, 1976), p. 290.

11. Wolfgang Sofsky (in *The Order of Terror: The Concentration Camp* [Princeton: Princeton University Press, 1993], p. 234, henceforth *OT*) reports: "It is true that aggression might be intensified if the victim whined in agony, begging for mercy. Moaning and pleading sometimes triggered an outbreak of rage on the part of the perpetrator, who then stopped at nothing."

12. Antje Kapust of the University of Bochum, in a paper delivered at the 1997 conference of the Society for Phenomenological and Existential Philosophy, argues in a similar vein: "The misrepresentation and obliteration of the other would not take place, if the anti-Semite would not have practiced that disastrous form of *sundering* that Todorov described in the catchword '*fragmentation*,' in which the perpetrator . . . splits off from the victim. By sundering is meant that the perpetrator, as well as those 'impartial observers' who are complicit in their silence, break off even the most minimal touching of and contact with the victim." While Kapust's further development of this point is dependent on the philosophy of Merleau-Ponty, I am heavily indebted to her thought for my own formulation of a notion of surreptitious denial of the other. My thoughts on this particular issue receive greater amplification in a paper delivered at the Fifth International Philosophical Symposium held in 1996 in Alto Adige, Italy, titled "Resisting Xenophobia: The Question of Ethical Singularity in Kristeva and Levinas." This paper is eventually to be published in a book of proceedings from the conference.

13. Wolfgang Sofsky argues that of the various strategies used in the camps to encourage a climate of violence, the distancing of the victimizer from the victim was especially important. In making his point Sofsky assumes that rage against the victim on the part of the perpetrator might be effectively distinguished from this indifference. But if the analysis above is correct, rage was simply another form of indifference, another manner of establishing that "the victim is no longer perceived as a feeling, thinking, acting human being" (*OT*, 234). In the perpetrator's rage the victim became nothing more than an obstacle in one's way, an irritating problem to be disposed of. But one also needs to keep in mind that the cultivation of this rage, as well as other modes of indifference, was itself a symptom of a prior nonindifference.

14. Emmanuel Levinas, *Autrement que savoir*, ed. unknown (Paris: Editions Osiris, 1988), p. 61.

15. Citation taken from Karl Heinz Schmeer, *Die Regie des öffentlichen Lebens in Dritten Reich* (Munich: Paul, 1956), p. 20.

16. See Joachim Fest's discussion of similar statements made by Rudolf Höss and what they indicated about his character: "The constant repetition of the personal pronoun reveals his intolerable self-centeredness; the victims emerge only remotely as a burdensome and fundamentally annoying source of personal disquiet" (*The Face of the Third Reich*, trans. Michael Bullock [New York: Pantheon Books, 1970], p. 285).

17. See Philip Hallie, "The Evil that Men Think—and Do," in *Vice and Virtue in Everyday Life*, ed. Christina and Fred Sommers (New York: Harcourt Brace Jovanovich, 1989).

18. See Hannah Arendt, *Eichmann in Jerusalem: A Report on the Banality of Evil* (New York: Penguin, 1977), chapters 2 and 15. On page 245, Arendt summarizes Eichmann's last statement: "The court did not understand him: he had never been a Jew-hater, and he had never willed the murder of human beings. His guilt came from his obedience, and obedience is praised as a virtue. His virtue had been abused by the Nazi leaders." In his own words: "I am not the monster I am made out to be, I am the victim of a fallacy" (p. 246). My own account of Eichmann diverges from that of Arendt's insofar as she argues the banality of Eichmann's evil-doing, that he was incapable of seeing a difference between good and evil because he was not sufficiently self-aware. From my perspective, the insensitivity of Eichmann's conscience is a pose of innocence, a ruse.

19. Göbbels at one point spoke of cultivating "a delirium of unconsciousness" in the German masses (Karl Heinz Schmeer, *Die Regie des öffentlichen Lebens*, p. 20). For some relevant reflections concerning National Socialism's emotional impact upon its citizens, see Richard Grunberger (*The Twelve Year Reich: A Social History of Nazi Germany* [New York: Holt, Rinehart and Winston, 1971], pp. 75–76), who describes what he terms "a permanent emotional mobilization" in the German populace: "If the first casualty of war is usually truth, then the very first casualty of the Third Reich was calm and equanimity. . . . The regime's immense thrust stemmed from its capacity to make increasing numbers of Germans regard themselves as anonymous combatants with leave-passes revocable at a moment's notice, rather than as individuals rooted in their civilian existence. . . . All complex social organisms involve their members in diverse but simultaneous roles—within the family, the work situation, the local community, etc.; the Third Reich, in contrast, conditioned its subjects to act out on command a single role to the exclusion of all others."

20. For example, see *OB*, p. 56: "The uniqueness of the chosen or required one [i.e., of the one elected to responsibility by the face of the other], who is not a chooser, is a passivity not being converted into spontaneity. This uniqueness not assumed, but subsumed, is *traumatic*; it is an election in persecution. Chosen without assuming the choice!" [italics mine]

21. Joachim Fest reports how Himmler orders a "model execution" of a hundred prisoners: "At the first salvo, however, he almost fainted, and he screamed when the execution squad failed to kill two women outright. In significant contrast to his abstract readiness to commit murder was the heartfelt

emotion, described elsewhere, which overcame him at the sight of blond children, and his positively hysterical opposition to hunting" (*FT*, 121).

However, it should also be pointed out that during both of his inspections of a death camp, Himmler showed no compassion for either the prisoners or the camp administrators (Roger Manvel and Heinrich Fraenkel's *Himmler* [New York: G. P. Putnam's Sons, 1965], pp. 72–73, 147–48). Manvel and Fraenkel discuss how Kersten, Himmler's own physician, testified to Himmler's many physical ailments, including nausea and stomach-convulsions, and concluded they were "the expression of a psychic division which extended over his whole life" (187). I would argue that not a psychic division but the delusion that one could act *as if* the other's address were irrelevant to one's own animation, undermined Himmler's health. In the author's own words: "Like many men, he learned how to strengthen the weakness of his nature by fostering obsessions on which he could constantly lean for protection against his conscience and reason" (185). Only in his illness, which signaled the breakdown of these consciously cultivated obsessions, did Kersten come "into contact with the human side of Himmler's character" (187).

22. See Robert Jay Lifton ("Medicalized Killing in Auschwitz," *The Future of Immortality and Other Essays for a Nuclear Age* [New York: Basic Books, 1988], p. 92) in regard to the specific case of doctors involved in the running of Auschwitz: "Heavy drinking—virtually every night and for some during the day—contributed importantly to the numbing. Discomfort felt by newcomers was often expressed, and vaguely put aside, at these drinking sessions, as were questions about Auschwitz in general. This was part of the transition period for newcomers. Their psychic numbing was encouraged—one may say demanded—by virtually everything around them."

23. For this insight, as well as the inspiration for many of the ideas developed in this and the preceding section, I am indebted to Sandor Goodhart's "The Witness of Trauma: A Review Essay" (*Modern Judaism* 12.2 (1992): 203–17). In his comments on Shoshana Felman and Dori Laub's *Testimony*, Goodhart argues against the view that witness has become impossible after the *Shoah*. "Rather than a 'crisis of witnessing' or a 'collapse of witnessing' . . . it seems to me we must speak of the proliferation of witness everywhere, of the collapse of the limitation of witness to the cognitive dimension. We cannot now *but* bear witness—unconsciously, repetitively, as a version of acting out—to what we cannot (consciously) bear to witness" (p. 213). But I must add that although one cannot help to bear witness, what one bears witness too is aenocide, to a vulnerability of history to ontological collapse. Also, the issue of how torture destroys the autonomy of a human being, how one's mourning in the wake of that torture is not

"restorative" (see Frieda Aaron's comments in the last section of this chapter) must be addressed. One must at some point make a distinction between witnessing the nonvictim and the victim, let alone the victimizer and the victim.

24. Psalm 14:4.

25. Emil Fackenheim (in *God's Presence in History* [New York: Harper Books, 1972], p. 70) argues: "Even actual cases of genocide, however, still differ from the Nazi holocaust. . . . Whole peoples have been killed for 'rational' (however horrifying) ends such as power, territory, wealth, and in any case supposed or actual self-interest. No such end was served by the Nazi murder of the Jewish people. Fantastic efforts were often made to hunt down even a single Jew; Adolf Eichmann would not stop the murder trains even when the war was as good as lost, and when less 'sincere' Nazis thought of stopping them in an effort to appease the victorious Allies."

26. For instance, see where Levinas describes the outcome of one's obsession by the face of the other *OB*, p. 92: "It is always to be *coram*, disturbed in oneself to the point of no longer having any intention." Or again, *OB*, p. 143: "proximity [to the other] is not confusion with another but incessant signification, a restlessness for the other, without any 'taking up of attitudes.' This responsibility is like a cellular irritability."

27. On the other hand, it is not scandalous for Levinas to find that he is already called to a piety without reward.

28. This statement, although true, needs an important qualification. In Levinas's own words: "I have said . . . that I am responsible for the persecution that I undergo. But only me! My 'close relations' or 'my people' are already the others and, for them, I demand justice" (*EI*, 99). Even when one is victimized, one still is called upon to be responsible for the other. But one cannot preach to the other victims that they should do likewise!

29. Michael Morgan, "Jewish Ethics after the Holocaust," in *Contemporary Jewish Morality*, ed. Elliot Dorf and Louis Newman (Oxford: Oxford University Press, 1995), pp. 110–11.

30. Frieda Aaron, "Epilogue," in her *Bearing the Unbearable* (Albany: State University of New York Press, 1991), p. 198. Henceforth cited as E.

4. Testimony and History

1. See *TI*, part C: "The Ethical Relation and Time."

2. For example, the Christian citation of the Torah as the Pentateuch within the Old Testament presents an appropriation of Jewish writings that

from the Jewish perspective can be interpreted as a profound alienation of their original intention. Of course, the Jewish interpretation of Torah runs the same risk, although one that the practice of talmudic reading seems more capable of appreciating. The issue of the Christian rereading of Jewish writing receives an extended discussion in relation to the poetry of Paul Celan in chapter 6.

3. As this sentence suggests, two modes of sincerity are at stake here. At one level, one must be sincere about the manner in which one's own presuppositions both color and limit what one can say about the other's situation. One might call this hermeneutical sincerity. At this level, one is called upon to an open-ended critical discourse about the unintended effects of one's own biases. But at another level, one must also be sincere about the utter impossibility of representing the other *as other*. No matter how aware one might ultimately become of one's presuppositions, the other transcends the whole manner in which one makes sense of her or him within a description about his or her situation. These two aspects of sincerity will be developed later in this chapter in regard to prophetic witness (treating the latter mode of sincerity) and deliberative witness (treating the former mode of sincerity).

4. This point is treated extensively below on pp. 000–000.

5. In *The Centennial Review* 35.3 (Fall 1991) can be found Morris Grossman's lengthy and rather polemical review of Lang's *Act and Idea in the Nazi Genocide*, titled "The Holocaust, or Once More with Feeling," to which Lang gives a brief reply. In this review one can find a spirited defense of what Morris calls "anarchic deconstruction" (p. 652) and its alleged historical relativism (see especially his discussion of "Poetry and Truth," pp. 628–32). My own response, while in sympathy with Grossman's insistence upon the hermeneutical instability of truth, finds that beyond this instability is a responsibility to determine, *as best as one can*, the reality of the victim's plight. That this plight transcends any final determination does not mean we are relieved from making a judgment about its reality. The other's suffering is not simply the opportunity for a deconstructive play or slippage of meaning. The "laterality" of the historical text is already oriented in terms of the other who suffers.

But this very laterality is the inflection of multiple voices. History is not about facts in the first instance but about the persons to whom those facts occur and for whom those facts have significance.

6. As Friedlander points out, Hillgruber's use of this term allows him "a point of identification with his subject," namely, "the fighting units of the *Wehrmacht* and the suffering German populations of the east," that moves him "from neutrality to empathy" (*MHE*, 78). Unfortunately his "empathy" with

German suffering allows him to marginalize how the very process of *Resistenz* led to the continuation of Jewish suffering in the concentration camps located behind German lines. In being subjected to the claims of particular parties who suffer, Hillgruber must remain responsible to all the other others who suffer as well! For this reason, Levinas argues that one's being claimed by another's suffering should not be characterized in terms of empathy but sincerity, an exposure of one's exposure before the other. From the initial stance of sincerity before the particular other one progresses to a questioning of what is a just response to *this* other given all the other others.

The danger of empathy is that it expresses a partiality that is not an exposure of exposure but a yielding to one's desire to remain enclosed within one's own domain. One reaches out to the other only to return into a community of the same. This community forgets or represses the other that does not fit comfortably within it, as in the case of Hillgruber's use of *Resistenz* to forget the urgency of Jewish suffering. In the next section a notion of deliberative witness is developed in which one must continually pose the question of one's sincerity as one elaborates a discourse that must compare incomparables, that must speak of the other's suffering to all the other others.

7. See especially Levinas's remarks in *TI*, p. 203, where he contrasts poetic writing with the discourse that is called for before the face of the other: "To poetic activity—where influences arise unbeknown to us out of this nonetheless conscious activity, to envelop it and beguile it as a rhythm, and where action is borne along by the very work it has given rise to, where in a dionysian mode the artist (according to Nietzsche's expression) becomes a work of art—is opposed the language that at each instant dispels the charm of rhythm and prevents the initiative from becoming a role. Discourse is rupture and commencement, breaking of rhythm which enraptures and transports the interlocutors—prose."

8. Emmanuel Levinas, "Reality and its Shadow," in *CP*, p. 9. Henceforth, RS.

9. See Emmanuel Levinas, *Proper Names*, ed. Michael Smith (Stanford: Stanford University Press, 1996), p. 46. Henceforth, *PN*.

10. See Sara Horowitz, *Voicing the Void: Muteness and Memory in Holocaust Fiction* (Albany: State University of New York Press, 1997) (henceforth, *VV*) for a newly published, extended, and excellent response to Lang's criticisms of literary writing about the *Shoah*.

11. This turn to the biblical prophetic tradition in developing the implications of Levinas's thought is hardly fortuitous. See Adriaan Peperzak, *To the Other: An Introduction to the Philosophy of Emmanuel Levinas* (West Lafayette,

Ind.: Purdue University Press, 1993), pp. 105 and 127–28, for how the prophetic functions for Levinas as a tradition providing an irenic alternative to Greek notions of rationality in which *polemos* or conflict is at the basis of one's discourse. Levinas's turn to asymmetrical relation, in which a conflict between equals is interrupted by a prior responsibility for the other, is directly attributed by Levinas to the prophetic tradition, a tradition that Peperzak points out is "at least as ancient as the presocratic philosophers" (p. 105n43).

See also Susan Handelman's *Fragments of Redemption* (Bloomington: Indiana University Press, 1991), chapter 8 (henceforth, *FR*) for an extended discussion of the prophetic in Levinas's thought.

12. In his own philosophic prose, Levinas often makes use of figurative language in a manner that is reminiscent of the poetic aspects of prophetic writing. For instance, consider the pivotal figures of "cellular irritability" and "restlessness for the other" in his description of the situation of being called into responsibility (*OB*, 143). Or his characterization of the witness as being "torn up from the secrecy of Gyges, 'taken by the hair'" (*OB*, 149). That this last figure comes directly from Ezekiel (as Levinas himself makes clear in a footnote) serves as a reminder of how many biblical citations are scattered throughout the body of his writing. There is a subtext of biblical metaphors and rhythms redolent of the creation story, of Abraham's ceaseless wandering, of Isaiah's call to prophecy. Consider as well the manner in which Levinas will write sentences that pile up figure upon figure, leading to metonymy: "It is sincerity, effusion of oneself, 'extraditing' of the self to the neighbor" (*OB*, 149). This prosaic rhythm has much about it that is poetic.

13. See Yosef Yerushalmi, *Zakhor: Jewish History and Jewish Memory* (Seattle: University of Washington Press, 1982), p. 15.

14. John Sawyer, *Prophecy and the Biblical Prophets* (Oxford: Oxford University Press, 1993), p. 26 (henceforth, *PB*).

15. Abraham Heschel, *The Prophets*, vol. 2 (New York: Harper Colophon, 1975), p. 147.

16. André Neher, *Ezekiel* 30, 30–33: "un paroxysme du psychodrame prophétique," in *Textes pour Emmanuel Lévinas*, ed. Jean Michel Place (Paris: Collection surfaces, 1980): 71–76. Henceforth, E. Sara Horowitz points out in *VV* (p. 17) that like Lang, Neher criticizes literary writing about the Holocaust as "an artificial construct" that encourages an interpretive response that undermines historical accuracy (see André Neher, *The Exile of the Word: From the Silence of the Bible to the Silence of Auschwitz*, trans. David Maisel [New York: Jewish Publication Society, 1981]). Yet Neher also argues for the necessity of a figurative, poetic space (at least in the essay on *Ezekiel* cited above) within

the limits of prophetic discourse. The analysis that follows takes Neher's remarks in a limited way to suggest that a certain genre of historical writing,
that which gives a prophetic witness in regard to the victim and the perpetrator, not only can but must express itself in a certain mode of figurative discourse that will be termed metatropic. Whether one can argue that this
insight also applies in terms of writing about the *Shoah* will be taken up more
directly in the succeeding chapters' discussion of Paul Celan.

17. Emmanuel Levinas, "Jewish Thought Today," in *Difficult Liberty*,
trans. Sean Hand (Baltimore: John Hopkins University Press, 1990), p. 159.

18. Levinas's notion of transcendence requires that it be thought otherwise than in terms of ontology. G-d's transcendence does not require a revelation in terms of a being or even the Being of beings but in terms of "an
enigma" in which the very revelation of transcendence "owes it to itself to interrupt its own demonstration and monstration, its phenomenality." G-d
comes near by withdrawing so that "the pure one-for-the-other" is signified
(Emmanuel Levinas, "G-d and Philosophy," in *CP*, 173). In G-d's *illeity*, as
Levinas terms it, G-d's "obliqueness . . . goes higher than straightforwardness." By remaining a third person in the epiphany of the other's face, G-d remains discrete and confronts one with an order of goodness that "does not fill
me up with goods, but compels me to goodness, which is better than goods received" (*CP*, 165).

At least two traditional religious concepts provide a background for Levinas's characterization of the withdrawal of G-d for the sake of the other: In
tsimtsum, a notion derived from the kabalistic tradition, G-d contracts, withdraws from G-d's self into G-d's self, so that the nothingness can be given from
out of which created beings can then be called into being. (See Philip Birnbaum, *A Book of Jewish Concepts* [New York: Hebrew Publishing Company,
1964], p. 533.) Without G-d's *tsimtsum* there would be no room for a created
order. Susan Handelman refers to the abyss coming in the wake of G-d's *tsimtsum* as a "non-human emptiness" (*FR*, 95). Gershom Scholem speaks of the
highest emanation (*sefira*) of G-d in the Kabalah, the *En Sof*, as already holding
"as it were the eternal yet sudden movement into creation that makes a Nothing from out of the Infinite, an infinite abyss of G-d in G-d, that is signified by
the biblical word for the 'depth of the abyss' in Genesis 1:2: *tehom*" (Gershom
Scholem, *Über einige Grundbegriffe des Jüdentums* [Frankfurt am Main: Suhrkamp, 1970], pp. 76–77).

Levinas also makes reference to the Greco-Christian conception of *kenosis*, the emptying out of G-d's identity into the human, of G-d's willingness
to "bend down to look at human misery or *inhabit* that misery" ("Judaism

and Kenosis," in *TN*, 114). But Levinas would argue that not incarnation but an obsession for the suffering of the other is the necessary outcome of this kenosis. Levinas quotes the treatise Megilla *31a*, where Rabbi Yohanan turns to among others the prophets to speak of G-d's humility in terms of a concern for the human other: "It is said again in the *Prophets*: 'For thus said the Holy: I dwell in the high and holy place, but also with him that is of contrite and humble spirit, to revive the spirit of the afflicted' (Isaiah *57:15*)" (*TN*, 115). In G-d's *kenosis*, "elevation becomes descent" (*TN*, 116) and vice-versa. In unfolding a Jewish interpretation of *kenosis*, Levinas turns in particular to *Nefesh haChaim* (*The Soul of Life*) by the Chaim of Volozhin whom Levinas paraphrases as arguing the following: "G-d associates with or withdraws from the worlds, depending upon human behavior. Man is answerable for the universe! Man is answerable for others. His faithfulness or unfaithfulness to the Torah is not just a way of winning or losing his salvation: the being, elevation and light of the worlds are dependent upon it" (*TN*, 125). Implied here is an ethical articulation of *tsimtsum*, a withdrawal of G-d that leaves humans uniquely responsible for others. This responsibility is itself the revelation of G-d's *chabod* or glory, a term that Levinas uses to express the articulation of justice in *Otherwise than Being*. One should keep in mind that, in spite of Levinas's separation of his writings into a philosophic and religious canon, much of the terminology in his philosophic writings and in particular in *Otherwise than Being* are translations and indirect derivations from Judaic intellectual and religious traditions.

Emil Fackenheim in his *To Mend the World* (Emil Fackenheim, *To Mend the World* [New York: Schocken Books, 1989]) also turns to the notion of *tsimtsum* in order to evoke the dependency of G-d upon the human in order to engage in *tikkun*, the mending of the world. As in Levinas's notion of an extermination without justice, Fackenheim speaks of the Holocaust as "a total rupture" (250) that exceeds the rational unfolding of an historical dialectic and that demands "human power must aid the divine" (253).

19. See Abraham Heschel, *The Prophets: An Introduction* (New York: Harper & Row, 1962), p. 192, for a discussion of hardness of heart in the prophetic tradition and the part it plays in the articulation of *teshuvah*, of a return to repentance and ethical sincerity.

20. Levinas characterizes the poetry of Paul Celan as being particularly sensitive to this gesture of prophetic witness, of that *hineni* sounding in one's mouth before the face of the other. One finds the following comment in Levinas's response to Celan's poetry: "a chant rises in the giving, the one-for-the-other, the signifying of signification. A signification older than ontology and

the thought of being and that is presupposed by knowledge and desire, philosophy and libido" (*PN*, 46). These remarks make clear how Levinas hears Celan's poetry as particularly sensitive to the prophetic voice, that "signification older than ontology" upon which Levinas's own turning of philosophy from an ontological to an ethical emphasis is dependent. The relationship between Celan and the prophetic voice is considered in greater depth at the beginning of the next chapter.

21. Notice that this formulation differs from a Heideggerian "being-for-the-other." In *Otherwise than Being*, Levinas often uses the notion of signification, of one-standing-for-another as a decisive figure in his turning around of the ontological presuppositions embedded into the Western tradition of thought and language.

22. See Martin Heidegger, *Being and Time*, trans. John Macquarrie and Edward Robinson (New York: Harper & Row, 1962), paragraph 38. Henceforth, *BT*.

23. See in particular Heidegger's discussion of *Schuld* and conscience in *BT*, paragraphs 54–60.

24. This argument is given in BC, 39.

25. See PM, 177–78: "justice is always a justice which desires a better justice. This is the way I characterize the liberal state . . . it continues to preach that within its justice there are always improvements to be made in human rights. Human rights are the reminder that there is no justice yet."

26. See Susan Handelman, *The Slayers of Moses: The Emergence of Rabbinic Interpretation in Modern Literary Theory* (Albany: State University of New York Press, 1982) for an extended discussion of the forms of textual instability cultivated in talmudic discourse.

In his essay, "Revelation in the Jewish Tradition," Levinas goes so far as to characterize revelation as "exegesis": "scribes and doctors known as slaves to the letter, would try to extort from the letters all the meanings they can carry or can bring to our attention" (*LR*, 194).

27. As Levinas puts it in his "Revelation in the Jewish Tradition": "I do not mean that truth is anonymously produced within History, where it finds its own 'supporters'! On the contrary, I am suggesting that the totality of truth is made out of the contributions of a multiplicity of people: *the uniqueness of each act of listening carries the secret of the text* " (*LR*, 195, italics mine).

28. This term comes from Krzysztof Ziarek, *Inflected Language: Toward a Hermeneutics of Nearness* (Albany: State University of New York Press, 1994). Henceforth, *IL*.

29. See Ziarek's *Inflected Language*, particularly the chapter titled "Semantics of Proximity: Levinas on Non-Indifference."

30. Victor Klemperer's recently published diaries ("The Klemperer Diaries," in *The New Yorker*, trans. Martin Chalmers [April 27 & May 4, 1998]: 120–35), written as a witness to the "everyday life of tyranny" during the Hitlerian era, provide many instances of how powerfully tone—whether it be carried in words or in a look—expresses the struggle to be sincere or to hide one's insincerity. Nazi "sociality," through a variety of techniques and policies including the incessant baiting of Jews, managed to utterly disrupt and pervert the tone of even the most innocuous encounters.

For reflections of Klemperer on Hitler's particular tone of address, see chapter 5.

31. This suffering for the other involves taking the other's place in her or his suffering. One *substitutes* one's own susceptibility to violence for the susceptibility of the other. One takes the bread out of one's mouth, one sacrifices one's own advantages for the good of the other. In the act of substitution, Levinas does not mean to suggest that one actually feels the other's suffering. It is important to note that Levinas's discussion of this issue in his essay, "Useless Suffering," which was referred to in the last chapter, does not make clear how one comports oneself in those situations where one finds it impossible to replace the other's suffering by means of one's own. In the aftermath of the other's death, for example, one cannot mourn that death in the place of the other's child. This other other is also claimed uniquely—no one can stand in for her or him either. To act as if one could stand in for him or her is to discount the other's responsibility to all the other others. In this situation, one must honor the inviolability of the other other's suffering and its inevitability as well.

32. This acuity of effacement and the resulting ongoing critique of one's own self-interest in what one writes is what Friedlander judges is lacking in revisionist histories of contemporary German scholarship. This critique takes its form in part of how affect is rendered: one writes in a manner that makes dreary or boring what should be disturbing and compelling.

33. In doing so, he cites Micah 1:3–4.

34. See *CP*, 163n5, where Levinas speaks of the prophetic voice as announcing in nonintentional affect a "structure . . . which is, so to speak, destructure itself."

35. See *OB*, p. 158: "The relationship with the third party is an incessant correction of the asymmetry of proximity in which the face is looked at.

There is weighing, thought, objectification, and thus a decree in which my anarchic relationship with illeity is *betrayed*" (Italics mine).

36. See *OB*, p. 157: "The third party introduces a contradiction in the saying whose signification before the other until then went in one direction." The contradiction is literally a contra-diction, a "saying-against" that does not indicate a struggle for the control of discourse but the inevitability of a plurality of voices articulating discourse.

37. But in articulating the proximity of two singularities (the other who accuses myself), this address should not be thought of as symmetrical. Each figure (the other and myself) are singular but in an entirely different manner. The other is singularly vulnerable to my violence and I am singularly responsible for her or his vulnerability.

38. From an interview with Lanzmann filmed at the Fortunoff Video Archive for Holocaust Testimonies on May 5, 1986. Quoted in *T*, p. 223.

5. Witnessing Trauma

1. Robert Bernasconi, "'Only the Persecuted . . .': Language of the Oppressor, Language of the Oppressed," in *Ethics as First Philosophy*, ed. Adriaan Peperzak (New York: Routledge, 1995), p. 80. Henceforth, OP.

2. In submitting to this priority, the articulation of the scene is not merely lateral but lateral in favor of the other. The mania of signification that ensues in one's submission to the other's address is not without the orientation of its tone, its vulnerability to the other's vulnerability.

3. Is not this empirical witness here also undergirded by another notion of witness, such as that of Levinas, in which one suffers the other's suffering as a wounding? For example, Mary's witness of Jesus is a wounding of Mary as well—her seven sorrows, as it is commemorated in Catholicism.

4. Paul Celan, trans. Amy Colin, in *HD*, 117–20. I am heavily indebted to Amy Colin's interpretation of this poem for my own remarks about it.

5. For example, see John Felstiner, *Paul Celan: Poet, Survivor, Jew* (New Haven: Yale University Press, 1995), pp. 70–71, where Felstiner reports how some reviewers are fascinated by what they term Celan's "surrealism," or "*poésie pure*," and speak of his poems as existing "wholly on metaphor." Felstiner himself observes: "Imagine Paul Celan at a newsstand in Paris, seeing 'the words he spoke so as to live' (Celan on Éluard applied to himself) labeled 'finger exercises.'"

6. See *PC*, pp. 72, 154–55. Amy Colin's account of this same controversy in *HD*, 127, is more emphatic concerning the libelous nature of Claire Goll's attack and the negative consequences it carried for Celan's reputation and the reception of his poetry.

7. The complexity of Celan's personal (as opposed to poetic) reaction to these charges, which is in part colored by a growing instability in his mental life, will receive a more direct consideration below. As Felstiner insightfully points out, the very fact that Celan's own memory of his parent's death was deeply traumatic, that he "could barely bring home to himself" (*CP*, 154) the actuality of their murder, could only mean that Claire Goll's insinuation of its being fictive was doubly disturbing to Celan.

8. Katja Garloff of the University of Chicago, in remarks addressed to me on August 2, 1994, mentions that in the early sixties Celan read Neher's *L'Essence du prophetisme* with intensity. She also points out that several of Celan's earlier versions of his poems carried more explicit Jewish names—for example, "*Dein Hinübersein*" was originally titled "*Schechina*." Thus, Celan's use of the prophetic figure in "Huhediblu" deserves careful consideration. One needs to question in what manner Celan consciously writes in a prophetic rather than simply poetic voice and how that voice relates to the traditional voice of the Jewish prophet.

9. John Sawyer, *Prophecy and the Biblical Prophets* (Oxford: Oxford University Press, 1993), p. 27.

10. This citation is taken from a major speech given to the Reichstag on January 30, 1939. Found in Noakes and Pridham, *Documents on Nazism*, pp. 485–86.

11. Citation taken from *The Klemperer Diaries*. The first is written on March 10, 1933 (p. 120); the second on September 6, 1933 (p. 122).

12. See Sara Horowitz, *Voicing the Void*, ch. 7 ("The Night Side of Speech") for an extended analysis of how National Socialism used language as a weapon against its victims.

13. The verb "*episteln*" mixes allusions to the New Testament Epistles with letters of denunciation, as well as the correspondence occurring in a conspiracy.

14. See Celan's poem, *WELCHEN DER STEINE DU HEBST*, in *Paul Celan Gedichte I* (Frankfurt am Main: Suhrkamp Verlag, 1986), p. 129. See a further discussion of the exact meaning of *Verderben* in chapter 6.

15. It should be noted that at the end of *King Lear* precisely this mode of pity is denied to Edmund, Goneril, and Regan, who have functioned within the play as persecutors. Given the report of their deaths, Albany states (*King

Lear, V.iii.323–33): "This judgment of the heavens, which makes us tremble / Touches us not with pity." Levinas's analysis of persecution puts the certainty of this claim into question.

16. The translation here of *WELCHEN DER STEINE DU HEBST* is by John Felstiner and can be found in *PC*, 71.

17. These claims should not be taken as a dismissal of the possibility of healing. But healing itself cannot occur until one ceases to deny the irremediableness of the suffering that has been undergone.

6. Blaspheming G-d

1. "*The Nameless*" has been used from the beginning as a supplemental term to the "*Häftling*." Either term has its strengths and shortcomings in witnessing that singular, suffering other to whom this text again and again finds itself turning. The use of these two terms, each of which searches out a *certain* singular other who transcends all naming, will occur in this chapter according to a distinction made roughly between the figured and the nonfigured. When referring to the more empirical conditions of a particular person within the death camps, the term *Häftling* will be used. When referring to the manner in which the other always transcends its particular figure, *the Nameless* will be employed. But it should be kept in mind that *the Nameless* is also a figure. Its naming does not resolve the issue of how *the Nameless* might be given as a theme. It should also be kept in mind that figures here proliferate: the "persecuted," the "tormented," the "annihilated" are yet other figures used in connection with the two mentioned above.

2. Elisabeth Weber (see her "Persecution in Levinas's *Otherwise than Being*," in *Ethics as First Philosophy*, ed. Adriaan Peperzak [New York: Routledge, 1995], p. 75) refers to William Niederland's work with survivors traumatized by Nazi persecution in order to point out that the survivor often is involved in the "deep guilt of having survived." In this guilt Niederland finds the situation in which "not the perpetrators and executioners of Nazi crimes but rather their victims seem to suffer the guilt of having survived" to be a "macabre irony" (William G. Niederland, *Folgen der Verfolgung: Das Überlebenden-Syndrom Seelenmord* [Frankfurt am Main: Suhrkamp, 1980], p. 231). Yet, as Weber's own essay suggests, this very irony is itself the revelation of another sort of involvement in the other's succumbing, one in which one is already responsible for the other regardless of one's guilt. What appears to be a mere

lapse of one's mental stability becomes the sign of one's suffering of the other's address, a suffering for which no other can take one's place. This other interpretation of "survivor's syndrome" does not justify its undermining of the survivor's animation but it does indicate how that very animation is already inspired by the other in a manner that cannot be dismissed. As Levinas points out in *Otherwise than Being*: "The psyche signifies the claiming of the same by the other, or inspiration" (*OB*, 141).

3. The opened hand proffered to another, as well as the hand grasping what it would honor, are also figures appearing in several of Celan's letters to Nelly Sachs written around the time of *Die Niemandsrose*: (a) "I am sending you here something to help against the small uncertainties . . . a bit of bark from a plane tree. One grasps it between the thumb and the index finger, holds it firmly and thinks of something good" (July 28, 1960); (b) "there are so many friendly heart and hands around us, Nelly!" (August 9, 1960); (c) "You have your hands, you have the hands of your poems, the hands of Gudrun—please take ours as well" (August 19, 1960) (Werner Hammacher and Winfried Menninghaus, eds., *Paul Celan* [Frankfurt am Main: Suhrkamp, 1988], p. 16ff., translation mine).

One remarks in reading these letters how thoroughly they are permeated by Celan's address of Sachs. Particularly in German, in which *Du*, *Dir*, and *Dich* are capitalized and so stand out all the more, the letters seem to be composed of a series of invocations directed to Nelly Sachs and connected together by various thoughts about the importance of those invocations. The letters give the impression that for Celan address itself would be his offering of help to Sachs during her crisis. For Celan the hand becomes that healing gesture that holds the reassurance of the immediate and undeniable goodness of one's address to the world and the world's address to oneself, of Celan's address to Sachs and of her address to those around her. In this way, one would fend off "the evil that haunts you—that haunts me too" (July 28, 1960). See Felstiner's discussion of the letter of July 28th in *PC*, 160.

4. Claude Lanzmann, like Celan, resists a merely indexical witness. For instance, Lanzmann refuses to use in his *Shoah* the sort of documentary footage of corpses and emaciated bodies that are so crucial in Resnais's *Night and Fog*. Such footage, in some cases from Nazi archives, only memorializes the cruelty of the victimizer's gaze. (For this insight I am thankful to Sandor Goodheart, as well as the other members of the panel on Witnessing the Holocaust, which occurred at the 1988 meeting of the International Association for Literature and Philosophy, held at the University of Notre Dame, South Bend, Indiana.)

In the corpus of both Celan and Lanzmann resides an ongoing suspicion of and aversion to how indexical witness can further subject the other to persecution—one points to the distress of the other, *as if* it were merely a piece of evidence before an impartial observer. But the involvement of the persecuted not only in their own persecution but also in the persecution of others provides a witness beyond the indexical, a witness of exposure to the point of wounds. For this reason, Lanzmann would bring a former *Häftling* back to the location of her or his persecution and then hear in her or his words what transpired at that location. This method of "indexing" the other's wounds does so by letting the address of the witness by the persecuted, in which the witness is submitted to the other's (i.e., the persecuted's) suffering and the other's (i.e., the persecutor's) cruelty, become the measure of the impact of those wounds.

5. The following is the line as it stands in Verlaine's poem: "*Ah, quand refleuriront les roses de septembre!*" (Paul Verlaine, *Selected Poems*, ed. R. C. D. Perman (Oxford: Oxford University Press, 1965, p. 97). Henceforth, *V*.

6. This brief history is taken from notes written by Perman in *V*, p. 8ff.

7. Jacques Derrida, "Shibboleth for Paul Celan," in *Word Traces*, ed. Aris Fioretos (Baltimore: John Hopkins University Press, 1994), p. 27. Henceforth S.

8. "*On tue*" is French for "one kills." Not only the scene and the date are decentered in Celan's poetic praxis but also language itself. Celan's poems are filled with puns and citations incorporating other languages within his German text. Further, note that the citation in French is made in the impersonal voice—not "I" or "he" or "she" or even "you" kill but "one" kills. This voice articulates the impersonality of "*Nimmermenschtags.*"

9. Colin speaks of how Celan does not integrate the multiplicity of traditions and languages he cites but "*dissolves* them" [italics mine]. In doing so, she argues, Celan creates "a poetic space in which traditions incessantly assert and annihilate themselves" (*HD*, 131). While Colin's observations are apt, should one not also add that beyond either this assertion or annihilation of a tradition lies the burden of the other's address and the other's suffering on that tradition? This burden in turn leaves any tradition in an ambivalent saying caught up in multiple times and multiple addresses. The mania or instability of signification in this saying in turn signifies in its own right the infinity of the other's address before that tradition. Traditions are not simply lexical entities but are ultimately made up of speakers who are addressed by others. In the aftermath of this address not the stability or instability of the tradition becomes the overriding issue but the tradition's responsibility to those who address it. The point of textual instability is not to provide the poet with a

weapon that would strike out against a tradition but with an address of that tradition that is disarming and that incessantly brings one to the burdening by and exposure to the other that is entailed in any language whatsoever.

On the other hand, Colin's suggestion that what is at stake in Celan's poetry is not an "amount of knowledge but rather its use" (a point that she in turn cites from Szondi [*HD*, 132]), fits well with the interpretation given above. What one must keep in mind is that the use of knowledge is always in relation to the other whose address already burdens one's own saying.

10. In responding to this tradition, Celan often identifies the poet Mallarmé as his chief interlocutor. See Pöggler's discussion of Celan's reception of Mallarmé in *Spur des Worts* (Freiburg: Karl Alber, 1986), p. 113f. Also see Dorothee Kohler-Luginbühl, *Poetik im Lichte der Utopie* (Frankfurt am Main: Peter Lang, 1986), pp. 154–56. Pöggler argues that while Celan wishes to preserve Mallarmé's reticence in speaking of the mundane world, this occurs in order that the tone of lament permeating the Celanian poem not become sentimental or trivial. But Pöggler also argues that unlike Mallarmé's hermetic voice, Celan's lament would mark out in history "the difference between good and evil, the murdered and their murderers."

On the other hand, Shoshana Felman argues that Mallarmé's preoccupation with the development of arrhythmic free verse stems from his claim that revolutions fail because they change governments but not their notion of prosody (see Shoshana Felman and Dori Laub, *Testimony* [New York: Routledge, 1992], pp. 19–24). In this sense, Mallarmé's preoccupation with the formal aspects of his poetry does not signal a decadent obsession with poetic effect but the setting in motion of a political and historical revolution in which the poem teaches oneself and one's fellow citizens to "reach out for what cannot be anticipated" (p. 19), for that which in Mallarmé's words "explodes or splits" (p. 21). Thus, the poem becomes an attack upon all those ways of speaking about the world that deny or cover over its transcendence of one's own experience. Certainly Celan is deeply influenced by this aspect of the Mallarméan project but resists the narrowness of a gesture that would focus upon the disruption of the poem's form in order to effect a historical revolution. For Celan, not the form of the poem but the trajectory of its address is the central issue. The poet seeks out that particular other who lives a historical existence and for whom the poet is responsible.

11. Paul Celan, "Der Meridian," in *Celan's Gesamte Werke*, ed. Bela Alleman and Stefan Reichert (Frankfurt am Main: Suhrkamp, 1983), p. 189 (translation mine). The corresponding passage in Rosemarie Waldorp's translation is found in *CPr*, p. 40.

12. See *V*, p. 97.

13. See *V*, p. 181 (note 72) where Perman works out the Christian interpretation of the poem.

14. Paul Verlaine, *Selected Poems*, p. 97 (translation mine).

15. See in particular the following passages: Apocalypse 1:8, 22:13. The "axle-note" that becomes "the Oh-note, ah / the Alpha and Omega" in "Huhediblu" is a citation of Apocalypse 11:15–19, when the seventh trumpet and last trumpet sounds out the mastery of "the lord and his anointed" over the world. Another passage from Apocalypse important to the reading of Celan's poetry is 20:1–6, which describes the thousand-year rule of Christ on earth.

16. The discussion of typology in this paragraph is dependent upon Erich Auerbach's essay, "Figura," in *Gesammelte Aufsätze zur Romanischen Philologie* (Berlin: A. Francke, AG, 1967), esp. pp. 66–78, and *Typologische Motive in der mittelalterlichen Literatur* (Krefeld: Scherpe Verlag, 1953), pp. 11–16.

17. Arthus A. Cohen, *The Tremendum: A Theological Interpretation of the Holocaust* (New York: Crossroads, 1988), pp. 65–66.

18. One should keep in mind that much has occurred since the end of World War II to resist this condescending and ultimately annihilative tone of address toward Judaism on the part of Christianity. But the issue of the rhetorical relationship between the "faiths" of the "New" and "Old" Testaments, as well as the Christian interpretation and use of the passion narratives from the Gospels, will not be easily resolved issues. Yves Dubois points out: "the twisting of Scriptural texts to make them mean that G-d has made Judaism . . . redundant" is deeply troubling, since it implies G-d was both untruthful and unfaithful to the Jewish people in the initiation of the Covenant with Abraham. Dubois calls for a culling out of all liturgical passages in which the notion that Judaism is to be superseded by Christianity remains at play. (Yves Dubois, "An Orthodox Perspective," in *Christian Jewish Dialogue: A Reader*, ed. Helen Fry [Exeter: University of Exeter Press, 1996], pp. 34–35). For further reflections on this issue see n. 35.

19. This prayer occurred, until removed by Pope John XXIII, in the Catholic services for Holy Week.

20. See the discussion above in chapter 5, pp. 145–47.

21. See *TI*, p. 228ff.: "Fate does not precede history; it follows it. Fate is the history of the historiographers, accounts of the survivors, who interpret, that is, utilize the works of the dead. . . . Historiography recounts the way the survivors appropriate the works of dead wills to themselves; it rests on the usurpation carried out by the conquerors, that is, by the survivors; it recounts enslavement, forgetting the life that struggles against slavery."

22. This reversal goes so far as to effect the line Celan cites from Verlaine. Verlaine's "Ah" becomes "Oh" in Celan's rendition of it in "Huhediblu"!

23. Consider Walter Benjamin's breaking open of a similar structure in his "Theses on the Philosophy of History," in *Illuminations* (New York: Harcourt Brace & World, 1968), p. 259. There he characterizes the relation of those living to the history that has preceded them in terms of an angel whose face is turned toward the past: "Where we perceive a chain of events, he sees one single catastrophe which keeps piling wreckage upon wreckage and hurls it in front of his feet. . . . But a storm is blowing from Paradise; it has got caught in his wings with such violence that the angel can no longer close them. This storm irresistibly propels him into the future to which his back is turned, while the pile of debris before him skyward grows. This storm is what we call progress." In this typology of history, those who inherit the suffering of others are without a means of appropriating it into their own vision of what is to come. One suffers the past without being able to consume it—reading history becomes "a process of empathy whose origin is the indolence of the heart, *acedia*, which despairs of grasping and holding the genuine historical image as it flares up briefly" (258).

24. The reader should keep in mind the distinction between being commanded by the other's saying, as opposed to what is said in that saying. This distinction will become crucial in making sense of Celan's response to Christianity, as well as to any other tradition of language.

25. Alvin Rosenfeld, *A Double Dying: Reflections on Holocaust Literature* (Bloomington: Indiana University Press, 1988), 30. Henceforth *DD*.

26. Götz Wienold, "Paul Celan's Hölderlin Widderruf," *Poetica* 2 (1968): 216–28.

27. "Sacrifice" means here the surrender of the illusion of a certain notion of autonomy, in which one presumes one could speak for oneself without that speaking already having been claimed by the suffering of the other. What is not implied in this notion of sacrifice is an immolation of a victim for the ends of propitiation or homage. What is implied is the placing of oneself and one's speaking under accusation for the sake of those who have been victimized. The ethical obligation to substitute oneself for the other's suffering, to place oneself on the side of the victim, interrupts any contemplation of the victim that might elevate the victim as a saving substitute for one's own shortcomings. As Levinas puts it in *Otherwise than Being*, sacrifice involves "the approach of him for [whom] one is responsible" and for whom "a fine risk [is] to be run" (*OB*, 120). In speaking in such a manner that one's words are under the burden of the victim, one learns to acknowledge how violence has been institutionalized in one's own language.

In its submission to the victim's address, *Widerruf* runs counter to what might "traditionally" be considered the manner in which a metaphorics of sacrifice would be applied to the *Häftling*: The *Häftling* is not to be considered a sacrificial victim whose suffering in innocence discloses a compensatory elevation of the meaning of that victimization but rather as the other who claims the sacrifice (in the Levinasian notion of sacrifice) of those witnessing her or his victimization.

In a similar vein, Sandor Goodhart (in his *Sacrificing Commentary* [Baltimore: Johns Hopkins University Press, 1996]) takes up with Girard's rereading of sacrifice to argue against a notion of it that would expel violence by means of a "sacrificial substitution." Goodheart criticizes "the collective transfer of a generalized reciprocal violence against a unique member of the community who is perceived in the wake of his removal as different from others but who has been in fact a humble double, an enemy twin, a surrogate victim" (p. 182). In place of this notion of sacrifice, Goodhart argues for a prophetic revealing of "where our violence is going in order that we might give it up" (p. 183).

28. One student, after having watched Resnais' *Night and Fog* for the first time, went to her dormitory room and reported to her roommate in the best words she could find what she had just witnessed, as well as its effect upon her own thoughts and feelings. Her roommate, upon hearing the student's description, expressed a desire to see the film for herself, stating something along the lines of the following: "This is something I would want to experience for myself." The student responded in the following manner: "This film is something I would never want anyone to see. It's not about what you can experience. You watch this film and you wish the whole time you had never had to watch it. Watching this film is a duty not an experience. I can't recommend it but it is absolutely necessary to see it."

29. See Werner Hammacher, "The Second of Inversion," in *Word Traces*, ed. Aris Fioretos, p. 220. Henceforth SI.

30. Precisely this possibility of poetry to effect what was termed an "ontological silence" was treated and criticized in the opening chapter.

31. See G. W. F. Hegel, *Phänomenologie des Geistes*, ed. Johannes Hoffmeister (Berlin: Ullsteing, 1973), p. 29; preface, paragraph 32. Translated by Hammacher.

32. T. W. Adorno, *Aesthetic Theory*, trans. C. Lenhardt (London: Routledge and Kegan Paul, 1984), p. 400. I am also indebted to Alan Udoff for his thoughts on how Celan's poetry is especially responsive to the shamefulness

of the Holocaust (see "On Poetic Dwelling: Situating Celan and the Holocaust, " in *Argumentum e Silentio*, p. 335).

33. As Levinas puts it in regard to Celan: "The ineluctable: the interruption in the playful order of the beautiful and the play of concepts, and the *play of the world*" (PN, 46).

34. Quoted with permission from John Felstiner's translation of these lines in *Paul Celan: Poet, Survivor, Jew*, p. 74. The German version of the poem (*VOR EINER KERZE*) is found in *Paul Celan Gedichte*, vol. I, pp. 110–11.

35. Speaking about a Christian alliance with the perpetrators of the *Shoah* need not and does not imply that the National Socialists and Christians were in league with one another. But tones of address cultivated by Christianity in regard to Jews and Judaism were not without their effect on the disposition of many Europeans to embrace National Socialism. Infamous in this regard is Martin Luther's own words in which he recommended Jews "be treated with a sharp mercy, their synagogues be set on fire with sulphur and pitch thrown in, their houses be destroyed" and that they "be herded together in stables like gypsies" (quoted by Barclay Newman in *Explorations: Rethinking Relationships Among Protestants, Catholics and Jews* 12.1 [1998]: 1). The World Council of Churches, undoubtedly thinking of such moments of scorn, argues: "Teaching of contempt for Jews and Judaism in certain Christian traditions proved a spawning ground for the evil of the Nazi Holocaust. The Church must learn so to preach and teach the Gospel as to make sure that it cannot be used towards contempt for Judaism and against the Jewish people" (Cited in *Christian-Jewish Dialogue: A Reader*, ed. Helen Fry [Exeter: University of Exeter Press, 1996], p. 37). The issue here is not simply one of doctrine but also of the face-to-face relationship, of being addressed by the other's vulnerability, the other's claim to my responsibility.

But contemptuous address is not simply a matter of whether one chooses at this moment to speak abusively. Underlying that address are doctrinal elements within Christianity that cultivate an imbalance between Jews and Christian *in favor of the Christian*. For instance, Helen Fry points out how the soteriological position that all human beings can be saved only through the Christian Church inevitably leads Christians to address the Jew in a tone of denigration no matter what other intentions may be involved in that address. Also see Howard Clark Kee and Irvin Borowsky, eds., *Removing the Anti-Judaism from the New Testament* (Philadelphia: American Interfaith Institute/World Alliance, 1998).

36. This term is borrowed from Rosenfeld (*DD*, 32).

37. A more extensive discussion of the various sources for this figure and the remainder of the poem can be found in my doctoral dissertation, "Impossible Mourning: Transcendent Loss and the Memory of Disaster" (Doctoral dissertation, State University of New York at Stony Brook, 1989), ch. 7.

38. Elisabeth Weber, "Persecution in Levinas's *Otherwise than Being*," p. 79. Nevertheless, I am worried by the implicit collapse of a betrayal that is entirely unnecessary (the Nazi's utter disregard for the address of her or his victims) into Levinas's notion of the so-called "necessary betrayal" of the other's address (which occurs because the address of the other *as* other already transcends one's capability to render it in one's own words). In the same vein, I am disconcerted by the confusion of a mourning that mourns its incapability to mourn with the mourning described in chapter 2 in which one palpably inherits a particular address of responsibility across the diachronic gap in time of a generation. Certainly witnessing the other's suffering must delineate between a suffering that occurs due to the very mortality of any subject and that which is imposed upon another by a persecutor who willfully ignores the other's address and annihilates the other's body. That second suffering is not necessary and it demands a mourning of an entirely different dimension than does the first.

39. Celan coins this term in a poem found in *Zeitgehöft* titled "*Die Pole.*" See *PPC*, pp. 344–45.

40. This is a particularly complex figure that alludes both to a woman's vagina and to the *sefirot*, the emanations of G-d, as established in kabbalistic traditions. The color blue, according to Amanda Walker (in a diagram for reproduction copyrighted in 1992), is associated in the Briatic tradition with *chesed*, loving-kindness, as well as with authority (as opposed to power) and the creation of form. In his poem Mandorla (*CP*, 188–89), also found in *Die Niemandsrose*, Celan uses the color blue to allude to kingship: *Königsblau*. Further, to speak of G-d in terms of a "chasm" suggests Scholem's discussion of the *En Sof*, of G-d as transcending any emanation or type, in "terms" of *tehom*, the "depth of the abyss" (ch. 4, fn. 18).

In assessing the kabbalistic implications of this figure in regard to the argument being advanced in the text above, Shira Wolosky (in her article "Mystical Language and Mystical Silence in Paul Celan's "Dein Hinübersein," in *Argumentum e Silentio*, ed. Amy Colin, pp. 370–71) provides some illuminating comments concerning the kabbalistic doctrine of *tsimtsum*, the contraction of G-d in the creation of the world (along with the doctrines of "the breaking of the vessels" and *tikkun* [see also ch. 4, n. 18]), in which Celan's blasphemy of G-d can also be interpreted as indicating a *kenosis* of G-d.

41. This image also reverberates in a troubling manner within the Christian tradition of the Incarnation.

42. See Irene Kummer's discussion of the paradoxical nature of this blasphemous inversion in *Unlesbarkeit dieser Welt* (Frankfort: Athenäum Press, 1987), pp. 127–31.

43. See Martin Buber's discussion of "heart" as it is used in this Psalm in his *Good and Evil*, trans. Ronald Gregor Smith (New York: Charles Scribner's Sons, 1952–53), p. 31ff.

44. See the ending sections of chapter 4.

45. See Alan Mintz's discussion in *Ḥurban: Responses to Catastrophe in Hebrew Literature* (New York: Columbia University Press, 1984), part 1.

46. See Richard Cohen, *Elevations: The Height of the Good in Rosenzweig and Levinas* (Chicago: University of Chicago Press, 1994). Cohen argues that for Levinas "atheism *conditions* a veritable relationship with a true G-d" but that this claim does not mean one is without G-d in one's atheism (p. 182). In atheism one becomes a being capable of acting out of one's own capacities rather than being utterly overwhelmed by G-d's infinity. Nevertheless, one is still called into relation with G-d precisely by means of this "necessary atheism," but a relationship articulated in the height or transcendence of the other's face, rather than in the epiphany of G-d as a particular entity. Cohen concludes: "*G-d imposes Himself on humankind, commands humans, by way of and exclusively by way of inter-human relationships*" (p. 187). In Levinas's own words, the "divinity of G-d" is "manifested" only in the ethical response of one human to another, "as if one reads the commandment of G-d in the face of the other man" (Emmanuel Levinas, "La mémoire d'un passé non révolu: Entretien avec Foulek Ringelheim," in *Les Juifs entre la mémoire et l'oubli*, ed. Paul Bertelson *et al.* [Brussels: Ministère de la Communauté française de Belgique, 1987], p. 12, translation mine).

In a paper titled "What Good is the Holocaust?" (Presented at the 1996 conference, "Ethics after the Holocaust," held at the University of Oregon), Cohen argues that Levinas's denucleation of the figure of G-d imposes an end to "religious infantilism." Cohen argues for a mature religious consciousness in which the just person suffers for a justice *that will not triumph*.

See also the discussion above of *illeity* and *kenosis* in ch. 4, n. 18.

47. Avivah Gottlieb Zornberg, *The Beginnings of Desire: Reflections on Genesis* (New York: Doubleday, 1995), p. 86. Henceforth *BD*. Zornberg is citing Bereshit Rabbah 39:2.

48. Paul Celan, "Ansprache Anlässlich der Entgegennahme des Literaturpreises des Freien Hansestadt Bremen," in *Celan Gesammelte Werke III*, pp. 185–86. Also see *CPr*, 34.

49. Marlies Janz, *Vom Engagement absoluter Poesie: Zur Lyric und Ästhetik Celans* (Frankfort: Athenäum Press, 1976), p. 162. Henceforth, ZL.

50. Janz speaks of Celan's poetic project as the elaboration of a "speech, which realizes (*vergegenwärtigt*) all the historical forms of human oppression." Such a speech would remain unheard in a world still enamored with the "show-horses of history" (ZL, 162).

51. See Felman and Laub's discussion of trauma and history in *Testimony: Crises of Witnessing in Literature, Psychoanalysis and History* (New York: Routledge, 1992). Also, "Psychoanalysis, Culture and Trauma" *American Imago* 48.2, and 4 (Spring and Winter 1991); "Literature and the Ethical Question," *Yale French Studies* 79 (1991).

Bibliography

Aaron, Frieda. *Bearing the Unbearable*. Albany: State University of New York Press, 1990.

Adorno, Theodore. *Aesthetic Theory*. Trans. C. Lenhardt. London: Routledge and Kegan Paul, 1984.

Alighieri, Dante. *The Divine Comedy*. Trans. John Ciardi. New York: W. W. Norton, 1977.

Améry, Jean. *At the Mind's Limits: Contemplations by a Survivor on Auschwitz and Its Realities*. Trans. Rosenfeld. Bloomington: Indiana University Press, 1980.

Antelme, Robert. *L'espèce humaine*. Paris: Gallimard, 1957.

Arendt, Hannah. *Eichmann in Jerusalem*. New York: Penguin, 1977.

———. *The Origins of Totalitarianism*. New York: Harcourt, Brace and Javanovich, 1973.

Auerbach, Erich. "Figura." In *Gesammelte Aufsätze zur Romanischen Philologie*. Berlin: A. Francke AG, 1967.

———. *Typologische Motive in der mittelalterlichen Literatur*. Krefeld: Scherpe, 1953.

Baumann, Gerhart. *Erinnerungen an Paul Celan*. Frankfurt am Main: Suhrkamp, 1986.

Bauman, Zygmut. *Modernity and the Holocaust*. Ithaca: Cornell University Press, 1989.

Benjamin, Walter. "Theses on the Philosophy of History." In *Illuminations*. Trans. Harry Zohn. New York: Harcourt Brace and World, 1968.

Berkovits, Eliezer. *Faith after the Holocaust*. New York: KTAV Publishing House, 1973.

Bernasconi, Robert. "'Only the Persecuted . . .': Language of the Oppressor, Language of the Oppressed." In *Ethics as First Philosophy*. Ed. Adriaan Peperzak. New York: Routledge, 1995.

Bernstein, Joseph, ed. *Baudelaire, Rimbaud, Verlaine: Selected Verse and Prose Poems*. New York: The Citadel Press, 1947.

Bernstein, Michael. *Foregone Conclusion: Against Apocalyptic History*. Berkeley: University of California Press, 1994.

Bettelheim, Bruno. *Surviving and Other Essays*. New York: Random House, 1980.

Birnbaum, Philip. *A Book of Jewish Concepts*. New York: Hebrew Publishing Company, 1964.

Blanchot, Maurice. *The Writing of Disaster*. Trans. Ann Smock. Lincoln: University of Nebraska Press, 1986.

Borowski, Tadeusz. *This Way for the Gas, Ladies and Gentleman*. Trans. Barbara Vedder. New York: Penguin, 1976.

Bosmajian, Hamida. *Metaphors of Evil*. Iowa City: University of Iowa Press, 1979.

Brierly, David. *Der Meridian: Ein Versuch zur Poetik und Dichtung Paul Celans*. Frankfurt am Main: Peter Lang, 1984.

Broda, Martine, ed. *Contre jour: Études sur Paul Celan*. Paris: Cerf, 1986.

———. *Dans la main de personne: Essai sur Paul Celan*. Paris: Cerf, 1986.

Buber, Martin. *Das Dialogische Prinzipp*. Heidelberg: Lambert Schneider, 1984.

———. *Good and Evil*. New York: Charles Scribner's Sons, 1953.

Caruth, Cathy. *Unclaimed Experience: Trauma, Narrative, and History*. Baltimore: Johns Hopkins University Press, 1996.

———, ed. *Trauma: Explorations in Memory*. Baltimore: Johns Hopkins University Press, 1995.

Casey, Edward. *Remembering: A Phenomenological Study*. Bloomington: Indiana University Press, 1987.

Celan, Paul. *Celans Gesamte Werke*. Ed. Bela Alleman and Stefan Reichert. Frankfurt am Main: Suhrkamp, 1983.

———. *Collected Prose*. Trans. Rosmarie Waldrop. Riverdale-on-Hudson, N.Y., Sheep Meadow Press, 1986.

———. *Gedichte*, Vols. I & II. Frankfurt am Main: Suhrkamp, 1985.

———. *Last Poems*. Trans. Katherine Washburn and Margaret Guillemin. San Francisco: North Point Press, 1986.

———. *Paul Celan: Poems*. Trans. Michael Hamburger. New York: Persea Books, 1980.

Cohen, Arthur. *The Tremendum: A Theological Interpretation of the Holocaust*. New York: Crossroads, 1988.

Cohen, Richard. *Elevations: The Height of the Good in Rosenzweig and Levinas*. Chicago: University of Chicago Press, 1994.

————, *Face to Face with Levinas*. Albany: State University of New York Press, 1986.

————. "What Good is the Holocaust?" Paper delivered at the "Ethics after the Holocaust" Conference. 1996. Eugene, Oregon. Sponsored by the University of Oregon.

Colin, Amy, ed. *Argumentum e silentio: International Paul Celan Symposium*. New York: de Gruyter, 1987.

————. *Paul Celan: Holograms of Darkness*. Bloomington: Indiana University Press, 1991.

Dawidowicz, Lucy. *The War Against the Jews: 1933–1945*. New York: Bantam Books, 1986.

Derrida, Jacques. "Geschlecht II." In *Deconstruction and Philosophy*. Ed. John Sallis. Chicago: University of Chicago Press, 1987.

————. "Schibboleth for Paul Celan." In *Word Traces*. Ed. Aris Fioretos. Baltimore: John Hopkins University Press, 1994.

————. *Schibboleth: Pour Paul Celan*. Paris: Galilee, 1986.

Des Pres, Terrence. "The Dreaming Back." *Centerpoint: The Holocaust* 4.1 (Fall 1980).

————. *The Survivor: An Anatomy of Life in the Death Camps*. New York: Pocket Books, 1976.

Ezrahi, Sidra DeKoven. *By Words Alone: The Holocaust in Literature*. Chicago: University of Chicago Press, 1980.

Fackenheim, Emil. "Authentic Responses to the Holocaust." *Holocaust and Genocide Studies* 1.1, 1986.

————. *God's Presence in History*. New York: Harper & Row, 1972.

————. "Hegel and Judaism: A Flaw in the Hegelian Meditation," In *The Legacy of Hegel: Proceedings of the Marquette Hegel Symposium, 1970*. Ed. O'Malley, Kainz, and Rice. The Hague: Martinus Nijhoff, 1973.

————. *The Jewish Return into History*. New York: Schocken Books, 1978.

————. "Kant and Radical Evil." *University of Toronto Quarterly* 23.4 (1954).

————. *Metaphysics and Historicity*. Milwaukee: Marquette University Press, 1961.

————. *The Religious Dimension in Hegel's Thought*. Bloomington: Indiana University Press, 1967.

———. *To Mend the World: Foundations of Post-Holocaust Thought.* New York: Schocken Books, 1989.

Felman, Shoshana and Dori Laub. *Testimony: Crises of Witnessing in Literature, Psychoanalysis and History.* New York: Routledge, 1992.

Felstiner, John. *Paul Celan: Poet, Survivor, Jew.* New Haven: Yale University Press, 1995.

Fest, Joachim. *The Face of the Third Reich.* Trans. Michael Bullock. New York: Harcourt Brace Jovanovich, 1989.

———. *Hitler.* Trans. Richard and Clara Winston. New York: Harcourt Brace Jovanovich, 1974.

Fisher, Eugene, ed. *Interwoven Destinies: Jews and Christians Through the Ages.* New York: Paulist Press, 1993.

———, ed. *Visions of the Other: Jews and Christians Assess the Dialogue.* New York: Paulist Press, 1994.

Fisher, Eugene, Joseph Kelly, and Leon Klenicki, eds. *The Rochester Agreement: An Agreement between the Rochester Board of Rabbis, the Jewish Community Federation of Rochester and the Roman Catholic Diocese of Rochester, May 8, 1996.* New York: Anti-Defamation League, 1996.

Foti, Veronique. "The (Dis)place of the Other in the Poetics of Paul Celan." In *Ethics/Aesthetics: Postmodern Positions.* Washington D.C.: Maisonneuve Press, 1987.

———. *Heidegger and the Poets.* Atlantic Highlands, N.J.: Humanities Press, 1992.

———. "Paul Celan's Challenge to Heidegger's Poetics." Unpublished paper presented to the Heidegger Circle in 1987.

Friedlander, Albert. *Out of the Whirlwind: A Holocaust Anthology.* New York: Schocken Books, 1976.

Friedlander, Saul. Keynote Address for International Scholars Conference, "Remembering the Future." Oxford, England. July 10–13, 1989.

———. *Memory, History and the Extermination of the Jews of Europe.* Bloomington: Indiana University Press, 1993.

Gadamer, Hans-Georg. *Wer bin Ich und wer bist Du? Kommentar zu Celans "Atemkristall."* Frankfurt am Main: Suhrkamp, 1977.

Goodhart, Sandor. *Sacrificing Commentary.* Baltimore: Johns Hopkins University Press, 1996.

———. "The Witness of Trauma: A Review Essay." *Modern Judaism* 12.2 (May, 1992): 203–17.

Grossman, Morris. "The Holocaust, or Once More with Feeling." *The Centennial Review* 35.3 (Fall 1991): 628–32.

Grunberger, Richard. *The Twelve Year Reich: A Social History of Nazi Germany*. New York: Holt Rinehart and Winston, 1971.

Hamaoui, Lea. "Historical Horror and the Shape of Night." In *Elie Wiesel: Between Memory and Hope*. Ed. Carol Rittner. New York: New York University Press, 1989.

Hammacher, Werner. "The Second of Inversion." In *Word Traces*. Ed. Aris Fioretos. Baltimore: John Hopkins University Press, 1994.

Hammacher, Werner and Winfried Menninghaus, eds. *Paul Celan*. Frankfurt am Main: Suhrkamp, 1988.

Handelman, Susan. *Fragments of Redemption*. Bloomington: Indiana University Press, 1991.

———. *The Slayers of Moses: The Emergence of Rabbinic Interpretation in Modern Literary Theory*. Albany: State University of New York Press, 1985.

Hartman, Geoffrey, ed. *Bitburg in Moral and Political Perspective*. Bloomington: Indiana University Press, 1986.

Hatley, James. "Celan's Poetics of Address: How the Dead Resist their History." In *Signs of Change*. Ed. Stephen Barker. Albany: State University of New York Press, 1996.

———. "*Grund* and *Abgrund*: Questioning Poetic Foundations in Heidegger and Celan." In *Continental Philosophy V: Questioning Foundations*. Ed. Hugh Silverman. New York: Routledge, 1993.

———. "Impossible Mourning: Two Attempts to Remember Annihilation." *Centennial Review*. Discourses of Mourning, Survival and Commemoration: Discourses of Mourning 35.3 (Fall 1991): 445–59.

———. "*Impossible Mourning: Transcendent Loss and the Memory of Disaster*." Doctoral dissertation, State University of New York, Stony Brook, 1990.

———. "Resisting Xenophobia: The Question of Ethical Singularity in Kristeva and Levinas." To be published in a book of proceedings from the Fifth International Philosophical Symposium. 1996. Alto Adige, Italy.

———. "The Sincerity of Apology: Levinas's Resistance to the Judgment of History." In *Phenomenology, Interpretation and Community*. Ed. Lenore Langsdorf, Stephen Watson, and Marya Bower. Albany: State University of New York Press, 1996.

Hegel, Georg Wilhelm Friedrich. *Lectures on the Philosophy of World History: Reason in History*. Trans. Nisbet. London: Cambridge University Press, 1975.

Heidegger, Martin. *Basic Writings*. Ed. David Krell. New York: Harper & Row, 1977.

———. *Being and Time*. Trans. John Macquarrie and Edward Robinson. New York: Harper & Row, 1962.

Heschel, Abraham. *The Prophets: An Introduction*. New York: Harper and Row, 1962.

Hilberg, Raul. *The Destruction of the European Jews*. New York: Holmes & Meier, 1985.

———. *Perpetrators, Victims, Bystanders*. New York: Harper, 1992.

Horowitz, Sara. *Voicing the Void: Muteness and Memory in Holocaust Fiction*. Albany: State University of New York Press, 1997.

Janz, Marlies. *Vom Engagement absoluter Poesie: Zur Lyrik und Ästhetik Paul Celans*. Frankfurt am Main: Athenäum, 1976.

Jonas, Hans. *Der Gottesbegriff nach Auschwitz*. Frankfurt am Main: Suhrkamp, 1987.

———. *The Imperative of Responsibility*. Trans. Hans Jonas and David Herr. Chicago: University of Chicago Press, 1984.

———. *Zwischen Nichts und Ewigkeit*. Göttingen: Vandenhoeck und Ruprecht, 1987.

Kant, Immanuel. *Critique of Practical Reason*. Trans. Lewis White Beck. New York: Macmillan, 1989.

———. *Ethical Philosophy*. Trans. James Ellington. Indianapolis: Hackett, 1983.

———. *Religion within the Limits of Reason Alone*. Trans. Theodore Greene and Hoyt Hudson. New York: Harper, 1960.

Kapust, Antje. "The Ethical Eminence of the Flesh: Toward Being 'with a Plurality of Faces.'" Paper presented at the Annual Conference of the Society for Phenomenological and Existential Philosophy, Lexington, Ky., 1997.

Kearney, Richard and Joseph O'Leary, eds. *Heidegger et la Question de Dieu*. Paris: Bernard Grasset, 1980.

Kelman, Herbert. "Violence without Moral Restraint: Reflections on the Dehumanization of Victims and Victimizers." In *Varieties of Psycho-History*. Ed. George Kren and Leon Rappaport. New York: Springer Publishing, 1976.

Kee, Howard and Irvin Borowsky, eds. *Removing the Anti-Judaism from the New Testament*. Philadelphia: American Interfaith Institute/World Alliance of Interfaith Organizations, 1998.

Klemperer, Victor. *I Will Bear Witness*. Trans. Martin Chalmers. New York: Random House, 1998.

————. "The Klemperer Diaries." Trans. Martin Chalmers. *The New Yorker.* April 27 and May 4, 1998: 120–35.

Kofman, Sarah. *Paroles suffoquées.* Paris: Galilée, 1987.

Kohler-Luginbühl, Dorothee. *Poetik im Lichte der Utopie.* Frankfurt am Main: Peter Lang, 1986.

Kummer, Irène. *Unlesbarkeit dieser Welt: Spannungs-felder moderner Lyrik und ihr Ausdruck im Werk von Paul Celan.* Frankfurt am Main: Athenäum, 1987.

Kunz, George. *The Paradox of Power and Weakness.* Albany: State University of New York Press, 1998.

Lang, Berel. *Act and Idea in the Nazi Genocide.* Chicago: University of Chicago Press, 1990.

Lang, Berel, ed. *Writing and the Holocaust.* New York: Holmes and Meier, 1988.

Langer, Lawrence. *The Holocaust and the Literary Imagination.* New Haven:, Yale University Press, 1975.

————. *Holocaust Testimonies: The Ruins of Memory.* New Haven: Yale University Press, 1991.

Lanzman, Claude. *Shoah: An Oral History of the Holocaust.* New York: Pantheon Books, 1985.

Lesch, Walter. "Die Schriftspur des Anderen—Emmanuel Levinas als Leser von Paul Celan." *Freiburger Zeitschrift für Philosphie und Theologie* 35.3 (1988).

Levi, Primo. *Survival in Auschwitz.* Trans. Stuart Woolf. New York: Macmillan, 1961.

————. *Moments of Reprieve.* Trans. Ruth Feldman. New York: Summit Books, 1986.

————. *The Drowned and the Saved.* Trans. Raymond Rosenthal. New York: Vintage International, 1989.

————. *The Mirror Maker.* Trans. Raymond Rosenthal. New York: Shocken Books, 1989.

Levinas, Emmanuel. *Autrement que Savoir.* Ed. Unknown. Paris: Editions Osiris, 1988.

————. "Bad Conscience and the Inexorable." In *Face to Face with Levinas.* Ed. Richard Cohen. Albany: State University of New York Press, 1986.

————. "Celan." In *Noms Propres.* Paris: Fata Morgana, 1976.

————. "Useless Suffering." In *The Provocation of Levinas.* Ed. Robert Bernasconi and David Wood. London: Routledge, 1988.

————. *Collected Philosophical Papers*. Trans. Alphonso Lingis. Dordrecht: Martinus Nijhoff, 1987.

————. *Difficult Freedom*. Trans. Sean Hand. Baltimore: John Hopkins University Press, 1990.

————. *Emmanuel Levinas: Collected Philosophical Papers*. Trans. Alphonso Lingis. The Hague: Martinus Nijhoff, 1987.

————. *En découvrant l'existence avec Husserl et Heidegger*. Paris: Librairie Philosophique, 1982.

————. *Ethics and Infinity: Conversations with Philippe Nemo*. Trans. Richard Cohen. Pittsburgh: Duquesne University Press, 1985.

————. *In the Time of Nations*. Trans. Michael Smith. Bloomington: Indiana University Press, 1994.

————. *L'au-delà du Verset: Lectures et discours talmudiques*. Paris: Minuit, 1982.

————. *The Levinas Reader*. Ed. Seán Hand. Oxford: Basil Blackwell, 1989.

————. *Le temps et l'autre*. Paris: Quadrige/PUF, 1979.

————. *Nine Talmudic Readings*. Trans. Annette Aronowicz. Bloomington: Indiana University Press, 1990.

————. *Otherwise than Being and Beyond Essence*. Trans. Alphonso Lingis. The Hague: Martinus Nijhoff, 1981.

————. *Outside the Subject*. Trans. Michael Smith. Stanford: Stanford University Press, 1994.

————. *Proper Names*. Trans. Michael Smith. Stanford: Stanford University Press, 1996.

————. *Totalité et infini*. The Hague: Martinus Nijhoff, 1984.

————. *Totality and Infinity*. Trans. Alphonso Lingis. Pittsburgh: Duquesne University Press, 1969.

Lewinska, Pelagia. *Twenty Months at Auschwitz*. Trans. A. Teichner. New York: Lyle Stuart, 1968.

Lifton, Robert Jay. *The Broken Connection*. New York: Basic Books, 1983.

————. *The Future of Immortality and Other Essays for a Nuclear Age*. New York: Basic Books, 1988.

Lyotard, Jean-François. *The Differend: Phrases in Dispute*. Trans. Georges van den Abbeele. Minneapolis: University of Minnesota Press, 1988.

Mandelstamm, Osip. *Selected Poems*. Trans. Clarence Brown and W. S. Merwin. New York: Atheneum, 1973.

Manvel, Robert and Heinrich Fraenkel. *Himmler*. New York: G. P. Putnam's Sons, 1965.

Marcel, Gabriel. *The Philosophy of Existentialism*. Trans. Manya Harari. Secaucus, N.J.: Citadel Press, 1984.

Meinecke, Dietlind. *Wort und Name bei Paul Celan: Zur Widerruflichkeit des Gedichts*. Berlin: Verlag Gehlen, 1970.

Menninghaus, Winfried. *Paul Celan: Magie der Form*. Frankfurt am Main: Suhrkamp, 1980.

Mintz, Alan. *Ḥurban: Responses to Catastrophe in Hebrew Literature*. New York: Columbia University Press, 1984.

Morgan, Michael. "Jewish Ethics after the Holocaust." In *Contemporary Jewish Morality*. Ed. Elliot Dorf and Louis Newman. Oxford: Oxford University Press, 1995.

Mortley, Raoul, ed. *French Philosophers in Conversation*. New York: Routledge, 1991.

Neher, André. "Ezekiel 30, 30–33: Un paroxysme du psychodrame prophétique." In *Textes pour Emmanuel Lévinas*. Ed. Jean Michel Place. Paris: Collection surfaces, 1980: 71–76.

———. *The Exile of the Word: From the Silence of the Bible to the Silence of Auschwitz*. Trans. David Maisel. New York: Jewish Publication Society, 1981.

Nemo, Philippe. *Job et l'excès du mal*. Paris: Bernard Grasset, 1978.

Newman, Barclay. "Removing the Anti-Judaism from the New Testament." *Explorations* 12.1 (1998): 1.

Niederland, William. *Folgen der Verfolgung: Das Überlebenden-Syndrom Seelenmord*. Frankfurt am Main: Suhrkamp, 1980.

Noakes, Jeremy and Geoffrey Pridham, eds. *Documents on Nazism, 1919–1945*. New York: The Viking Press, 1974.

Nouvet, Claire, ed. *Yale French Studies 79: Literature and the Ethical Question*. New Haven: Yale University Press, 1991.

Patruno, Nicholas. *Understanding Primo Levi*. Columbia, S.C.: University of South Carolina Press, 1995.

Peperzak, Adriaan, ed. *Ethics as First Philosophy*. New York: Routledge, 1995.

———. *To the Other: An Introduction fo the Philosophy of Emmanuel Levinas*. West Lafayette, Ind.: Purdue University Press, 1993.

Pöggeler, Otto. *Spur des Wort: Zur Lyrik Paul Celans*. Freiburg: Karl Alber, 1986.

Rapaport, Herman. *Heidegger and Derrida*. Lincoln: University of Nebraska Press, 1989.

Rosenfeld, Alvin. *A Double Dying: Reflections on Holocaust Literature*. Bloomington: Indiana University Press, 1980.

Rosenfeld, Alvin and Irving Greenberg, eds. *Confronting the Holocaust: The Impact of Elie Wiesel*. Bloomington: Indiana University Press, 1978.

Roskies, David. *Against the Apocalypse: Responses to Catastrophe in Modern Jewish Culture*. Cambridge, Mass.: Harvard University Press, 1984.

Rubenstein, Richard. *After Auschwitz: Radical Theology and Contemporary Judaism*. New York: Macmillan, 1966.

———. *The Cunning of History: The Holocaust and the American Future*. New York: Harper & Row, 1975.

Sawyer, John. *Prophecy and the Biblical Prophets*. Oxford: Oxford University Press, 1993.

Scarry, Elaine. *The Body of Pain: The Making and Unmaking of the World*. Oxford: Oxford University Press, 1985.

Schell, Jonathan. *The Fate of the Earth*. New York: Alfred Knopf, 1982.

Schmeer, Karl Heinz. *Die Regie des öffentlichen Lebens in Dritten Reich*. Munich: Paul, 1956.

Scholem, Gershom. *Von der mystischen Gestalt der Gottheit*. Frankfurt am Main: Suhrkamp, 1977.

———. *Zur Kabbala und ihrer Symbolik*. Frankfurt am Main: Suhrkamp, 1973.

Shapiro, Susan. "For Thy Breach Is Great Like the Sea: Who Can Heal Thee." *Religious Studies Review* 13.3 (July 1987).

Shirer, William. *The Rise and Fall of the Third Reich: A History of Nazi Germany*. New York: Simon & Schuster, 1960.

Sofsky, Wolfgang. *The Order of Terror: The Concentration Camp*. Princeton: Princeton University Press, 1997.

Steiner, George. *In Bluebeard's Castle: Some Notes toward the Redefinition of Culture*. New Haven: Yale University Press, 1971.

Strelka, Joseph, ed. *Psalm und Hawdalah: Zum Werk Paul Celans*. Frankfurt am Main: Peter Lang, 1985.

Szondi, Peter. *Celan Studien*. Frankfurt am Main: Suhrkamp, 1972.

Udoff, Alan. "On Poetic Dwelling: Situating Celan and the Holocaust." In *Argumentum et Silentio*. Ed. Amy Colin. New York: de Gruyter, 1987.

Verlaine, Paul. *Selected Poems*. Ed. R. C. D. Perman. Oxford: Oxford University Press, 1965.

von Westernhagen, Dörte. *Die Kinder der Täter*. Munich: Kösel-Verlag, 1988.

Weber, Elisabeth. "Persecution in Levinas's *Otherwise than Being*." In *Ethics as First Philosophy*. Ed. Adriaan Peperzak. New York: Routledge, 1995.

Wienold, Götz. "Paul Celan's Hölderlin Widderruf." *Poetica* 2 (1968): 216–28.

Wiesel, Elie. *Night*. New York: Bantam Books, 1982.

Wiesenthal, Simon. *The Sunflower: On the Possibilities and Limits of Forgiveness*. Ed. Harry Cargas and Bonny Fetterman. New York: Schocken Books, 1997.

Wyschogrod, Edith. *Emmanuel Levinas: The Problem of Ethical Metaphysics*. The Hague: Martinus Nijhoff, 1974.

———. *Spirit in Ashes: Hegel, Heidegger and Man-Made Mass Death*. New Haven: Yale University Press, 1985.

Yerushalmi, Yosef Hayim. *Zakhor: Jewish History and Jewish Memory*. Seattle: University of Washington Press, 1982

Ziarek, Krzysztof. *Inflected Language: Toward a Hermeneutics of Nearness*. Albany: State University of New York Press, 1994.

Zornberg, Avivah Gottlieb. *The Beginnings of Desire: Reflections on Genesis*. New York: Doubleday, 1995.

Index